COMING TO PUBLIC JUDGMENT

The Frank W. Abrams Lectures

COMING TO
PUBLIC
JUDGMENT

Making Democracy Work
in a Complex World

DANIEL YANKELOVICH

 SYRACUSE UNIVERSITY PRESS

First Edition 1991

        91 92 93 94 95 96 97 98 99   6   5   4   3   2   1

The paper used in this publication meets the minimum requirements of American National Standard for Information Sciences—Permanence of Paper for Printed Library Materials, ANSI Z39.48-1984. ∞™

Library of Congress Cataloging-in-Publication Data

Yankelovich, Daniel.
        Coming to public judgment : making democracy work in a complex
    world / by Daniel Yankelovich.
            p.   cm. — (The Frank W. Abrams lectures)
        Includes bibliographical references and index.
        ISBN 0-8156-2515-4 (cloth). — ISBN 0-8156-0254-5 (paper)
        1. Public opinion—United States.   2. Public opinion.
    3. Democracy.   I. Title.   II. Series.
    HN90.P8Y36   1991
    303.3′8 — dc20   90-19667
                                                         CIP

Manufactured in the United States of America

I enthusiastically dedicate this book to those friends and colleagues with whom I have worked side by side for more than thirty years. It is the people in the following organizations who have helped to shape the theory of public opinion I describe on the pages that follow:

Yankelovich, Skelly & White, Inc.
The Public Agenda Foundation
DYG, Inc.
The Charles F. Kettering Foundation
WSY Consulting Group, Inc./S.A.G.E.
Brown University's Center for Foreign Policy Development

DANIEL YANKELOVICH, educated at Harvard University and The Sorbonne, pioneered many research techniques that have become standard in the field, assessing the impact of social values on public policy and consumer behavior. He is Chair of DYG, Inc., as well as President and cofounder of The Public Agenda Foundation and WSY Consulting, Inc., a nonpartisan, not-for-profit organization dedicated to improving the quality of public debate on important policy issues. His previous books include the best-selling *New Rules, Putting the Work Ethic to Work*, and *Ego and Instinct*.

CONTENTS

Part Three: UNRAVELING THE MYSTERY

ILLUSTRATIONS

PREFACE

The concepts elaborated in this book evolved over a number of years. They grew out of my experience in conducting thousands of studies of public opinion, involving millions of interviews with cross sections of the American public.

What impresses me most in these years of studying people's feelings is how difficult it is to understand public opinion in all of its shadings and complexity. I have never conducted a public opinion survey that did not surprise me in one way or another. If public opinion were as simple and one-dimensional as it is usually represented in newspaper headlines, (e.g., "51 percent of the public support protective tariffs"), then one would think that after more than thirty years it would be fairly predictable and surprise free. But instead, American public opinion reveals itself as rich and subtle and endowed with a depth of thought and feeling that must win the respect of all who study it seriously.

In studying it seriously, I have found myself forced to modify the concepts I inherited from the pioneering work of others. The new concepts have a life of their own, forcing themselves on me whatever my reluctance to accept them. In writing this book, I realize how far they have carried me away from my initial starting point, and how strange—and perhaps implausible or even outrageous—they will first seem to those accustomed to existing paradigms.

The conclusions I have reached, elaborated later in this book, include the following:

1. Paradoxically, in this Age of Information, the importance of information in shaping responsible public opinion is vastly exaggerated.
2. As a nation, we have learned a great deal about how to measure public opinion (and how to manipulate it), but almost nothing

about how to improve it. An appalling lack of know-how exists on how to create the kind of national consensus needed to cope with the nation's problems. Furthermore, even though the nation's elites complain about the public's "apathy" and "ignorance," they resist most efforts to enhance the quality of public opinion.

3. Most public opinion polls are misleading because they fail to distinguish between people's top-of-the-mind, offhand views (mass opinion) and their thoughtful, considered judgments (public judgment).

4. Public judgment, the most advanced form of public opinion, is a genuine form of knowledge that on certain aspects of issues deserves to carry more weight than that of scientific experts. (You *can* argue with Einstein.)

5. There are "laws" that describe the evolution of public opinion from mass opinion to public judgment through three invariant stages of development. And there are discoverable principles for overcoming the obstacles that retard the movement of public opinion through these stages. The knowledge of these laws and principles provides the basis for a new theory of public opinion—and the key to creating national consensus on the great issues of our times.

Taken together, these conclusions have carried me further from the mainstream of thinking in the field of public opinion than I had intended to go. And yet, I suspect that they will win readier acceptance among my fellow professionals than among journalists, business and community leaders, and public policy experts who take public opinion into account in their work without studying it directly. Experienced practitioners of public opinion research will recognize the source of these conclusions in their own work and will find resemblances to concepts that they have evolved to fit their own studies. To many others, however, these concepts may initially seem strange and implausible because they rub against the grain of current trends in American life.

Part of the interest for me in writing this book has been the three very different sources on which I have been obliged to draw in forming the theory of public opinion presented here. The first is the field of public opinion research reflected in the early parts of the book. The second draws on my experience as a corporate director and trustee of a number of organizations, both business and not-for-profit. This experience has indelibly impressed on me the difference between "managing" and "governing," which, I believe, applies in a stunning way to the relationship of our leaders (to whom we, the public, delegate the task of managing our democracy) to the general public whose responsibilities for governance are being usurped by creeping expertism. The third source is the discipline of philosophy, my first intellectual love and a continuing interest throughout my life. I am pleased to be able to weave these diverse interests into a common framework.

In writing this book I received invaluable help from a number of people, above all from my assistant and friend, Mary Komarnicki. Mary helped to shape the Abrams Lectures I gave at Syracuse University that anticipated the book. For both the lectures and the book she matched my theoretical concepts with appropriate case histories of public opinion. Her case histories give the new theory of public opinion a concreteness and vividness it would not otherwise have. In addition, she prepared the tables, charts, and bibliography; made sure the endnotes were proper; and in general made herself indispensable.

Jean Johnson of the Public Agenda Foundation contributed some telling examples of the public struggling to come to public judgment. Other colleagues at the Public Agenda — Debra Wadsworth, Keith Melville, and John Doble — read the manuscript and contributed valuable editorial insight.

Professor John Immerwahr helped me struggle with the organization of the book. As always, his lucid intelligence cut through the murkiness and complexity and clarified essential points. Professor Richard Smoke helped me to avoid some subtle pitfalls.

David Mathews and Robert Kingston of the Kettering Foundation read the full text and gave me the benefit of their own rich experience. The creative work of the Kettering Foundation in recent years, under David Mathews's leadership, has contributed immeasurably to the development of public judgment in America and to the theory delineated in these pages.

Dr. Leo Bogart, a leading figure in the field of public opinion, read the book and offered many valuable suggestions, which I gratefully accepted.

Among my friends and other associates who read the full text and offered helpful suggestions, I would single out Page and Ted Ashley, Florence Skelly, Arthur White, and Ruth Clark for their help, their insights, and their support.

I would like also to thank the Roper Center at the University of Connecticut, under Everett Ladd's leadership, for their invaluable data base POLL. It has turned research into public opinion archives from a nightmare into a rewarding experience. I want to thank Dean Guthrie S. Birkhead, Chancellor Melvin A. Eggers, and James Gies of Syracuse University for their warm hospitality in inviting me to give the Abrams Lectures, which provided the inspiration for this book. I am also grateful to the staff of Syracuse University Press.

My secretary and friend, Sona Beshar, showed monumental patience and skill in preparing the various drafts of this manuscript, for which acts of grace I am deeply grateful.

DANIEL YANKELOVICH

New York City
July 1990

COMING TO PUBLIC JUDGMENT

INTRODUCTION

Crowding out the Public

Because democracy has flourished in the United States for more than two hundred years, Americans watch with a certain complacency as countries in other parts of the world — Eastern Europe, Latin America, Asia — grope and stumble to learn how it works. The complacency, however, is unwarranted. Even with America's long experience with democracy, important lessons still elude us (this book explores one of them). Moreover, as the 1990s unfold, our own democratic practices are being tested in harsh new ways.

Americans today are not as worried about their political freedom as their material well-being because they take their freedom *almost* for granted. The qualification is important. The precious gift of freedom is never far from people's minds, and Americans explicitly count it among their chief blessings.

Most of the time Americans think about freedom negatively — as freedom *from* — from tyranny, from censorship, from having their movements restricted, from the 2:00 A.M. knock on the door of the secret police. This form of freedom gives people what they want most in life — the liberty to pursue their private happiness.

But the soul of the American Dream also harbors a conception, however vague, of positive freedom — freedom *to* take part in shaping the common destiny. Throughout our history, one of the most persistent themes in American political thought has been how to create a community in which all Americans participate fully as citizens. This is the Dream of Self-governance — of free people shaping their destiny together as equals. "You may be richer and smarter than I am but my vote counts as much as yours." This article of faith is as important to Americans as the chance to better

1

themselves materially. The dream is that of having a say on the fundamental issues that shape people's lives: war and peace, taxes, justice, freedom from crime and violence, fairness, caring for the family, social stability, preserving the environment, ensuring that America plays a special role in the world, living together in a neighborly way with one's fellow Americans.

This expression of the American Dream, the Dream of Self-governance, is also threatened. Assuredly, the threat is not to the kind of freedom Americans care about most. Our political liberty is not endangered. No dictator looms on the horizon. No military coup is in the offing. Whatever danger communism may have posed to our political freedom in the past, that threat has now waned. Americans will be as free in the future as in the past to vote for the candidate of their choice, to speak their minds, and to enjoy the advantages of a free press.

The danger, rather, lies in the eroding ability of the American public to participate in the political decisions that affect their lives. The fateful decisions are made in Washington, in corporate boardrooms, on Wall Street, in state legislatures, and in city halls. They are shaped by economic experts, military experts, scientific experts, trade experts, PR experts, media experts. Less and less are they shaped by the public.

On the surface, citizen participation seems to have improved. Much new legislation requires citizen review; the political parties are no longer dominated by decisions made behind the scenes in those infamous "smoke-filled rooms"; there are more referendums and polls than ever before. In recent years, the public has gained greater influence in foreign policy, once the exclusive preserve of an elite. And yet, paradoxically, the more "democratic" the formal side of American political life has become, the less real voice the American public has in shaping national policies. The more formal power "we, the people" acquire, the less actual influence we seem to have.

Talk to members of Congress and they will tell you that they spend most of their time being responsive to their constituents. But if you ask them who these constituents are, they turn out to be lobbyists and special interests, not individual citizens — or at least not those with average incomes. In their speeches they may refer to the "folks," but it is not the folks who finance their campaigns.

Talk to high-level policy makers and they will tell you how much input they get from economists and scientific advisers and legislative experts. But if you ask about input from the public, invariably they will misunderstand the question. When formulating important national policies, it would never even occur to most policy makers to consult average citizens.

The long-standing decline in voter participation is one symptom of the problem. It is common knowledge — and a much lamented fact — that voter participation in presidential elections has been steadily declining, from 63 percent of those eligible to vote in 1960 to 50 percent in 1988. In congressional elections the drop is even more dramatic—from 59 percent in 1960 to 33 percent in 1986![1]

The conventional explanation is voter apathy: the view that Americans do not get involved because they do not care. Decades of public opinion poll data, however, show that this charge of voter apathy is a bum rap. Average Americans, including those who do not vote, hold deep and passionate convictions on many issues of public concern; for example, concern about the growth of homelessness in America, the government's use of tax dollars, the threat to the environment, the suspicion that greed and self-seeking pervade our public life, the rise of crime and drug abuse, the workings of the criminal justice system, the savings and loan rip-off, and so forth. If apathy means not caring, it is simply untrue that the electorate is apathetic. The chief reason so many Americans do not vote is because they do not think their votes will make a difference.

The woman's movement has an apt image for an obstacle encountered by women in corporate life. In many corporations women reach a certain level and then are blocked. There is no visible barrier to their advancement. All of the rhetoric and overt policies of the corporation would suggest that the way is clear to advancement. And yet, it is not; some invisible barrier seems to stop them at the level just below top management. To describe this barrier, women refer to the "glass ceiling" that blocks that final step to the top. They can see the top, but they cannot break through that glass ceiling.

Some such barrier seems to block the public. Beneath the surface of formal arrangements to ensure citizen participation, the political reality is that an intangible something separates the general public from the thin layer of elites—officials, experts, and leaders who hold the real power and make the important decisions.

In recent years my work has made me conscious of the enormity of the gap that separates the public from the experts. As an interpreter of public opinion, I serve as a go-between for the two worlds of public opinion and expert policy making. Each year the distance between the two worlds grows greater. It is sometimes difficult to believe that the public and policy-making experts in the United States share the same language and culture. History tells us about the distance separating the aristocracies of prerevolutionary France and Russia from the average people in their countries. The distance between America's elites and its average citizens is, I sometimes feel, equally great or even greater—not so much in the form of social snobbery (there is less of this in the United States than in Western

Europe or, oddly, in the Communist countries) but in the form of intellectual snobbery.

When there are problems to address, elites discuss them exclusively with other elites. Political leaders talk among themselves or with business leaders, with educators, with lawyers, with economists, with lobbyists. It is against the American credo to stratify people by social class, but one of the most rigid barriers in today's America is the barrier that separates the men and women who "serve" the public from the public itself.

An adversarial struggle exists between experts and the public on who will govern America. On one side are the experts — smaller in number and weaker than the public in formal power but holding an indispensable piece of the solution. As a group, these experts respect the institution of democracy and would be chagrined if their good faith were challenged. At the same time, however, their view of the general public is that it is ill informed and ill equipped to deal with the problems to which they, the experts, have devoted their lives. Few experts attempt deliberately to mislead the public. Unwittingly and automatically, they use technical jargon that excludes the public. They dismiss the views of citizens who do not command their factual mastery of the subject. Often without realizing it, they impose their personal values on the country because they fail to distinguish their own value judgments from their technical expertise (see chap. 14).

The other contender is the public. In theory, it has the last word. To offset creeping expertism the public must be able to stand its ground against the experts better than it is now doing. Unfortunately, however, most average citizens are ill-prepared to exercise their responsibilities for self-governance, even though they have a deep-seated desire to have more of a say in decisions. People want their opinions heeded — not every whim and impulse that may be registered in an opinion poll, but their thoughtful, considered judgments. But in present-day America, few institutions are devoted to helping the public to form considered judgments, and the public is discouraged from doing the necessary hard work because there is little incentive to do so. In principle, the people are sovereign. In practice, the experts and technocrats have spilled over their legitimate boundaries and are encroaching on the public's territory.

Although this struggle between experts and public has become adversarial, there can be no such thing as the "victory" of one side over the other. If the experts overreach themselves and further usurp the public's legitimate role, we will have the formal trappings of democracy without the substance, and everyone will suffer. If the public dominates and pushes the experts out of the picture altogether, we will have demagoguery or disaster or both. A better balance of power and influence is needed, with each side performing its function in sympathy and support of the other.

The issue, it should be stressed, is not one of naked power. If the experts grow too bold, the electorate will express itself in populist fury and launch another episode of native know-nothingness. (Anti-intellectualism runs like a thread through American history.) In political life, abuse breeds abuse, and if the problem is permitted to fester, the backlash is likely to prove worse than the disease. The erosion of self-governance in America is not an overt power-grab but a relationship between experts and public that has grown adversarial rather than mutually supportive, resulting in decline in the quality of public participation.

To resolve the expert-public gap, two things must happen. The first is that the public's freedom to contribute to self-governance must be strengthened and built up. Second, expert resistance to having this happen must be reduced. To understand the first task, I will present a concept I call public judgment. To understand the second, I will need to describe the sources of resistance that are rooted in a phenomenon I call the Culture of Technical Control.

PUBLIC JUDGMENT

The strategy I propose in this book is to strengthen a special form of public opinion I define as public judgment. Enhancing the quality of public judgment can, potentially, counter the threat of creeping expertism that is undermining self-governance.

The subject of how to enhance the quality of public judgment will be covered in detail in chapters 1 through 13. Throughout the book I will use the term "public judgment" to mean a particular form of public opinion that exhibits (1) more thoughtfulness, more weighing of alternatives, more genuine engagement with the issue, more taking into account a wide variety of factors than ordinary public opinion as measured in opinion polls, and (2) more emphasis on the normative, valuing, ethical side of questions than on the factual, informational side.

Most expressions of public opinion, as measured in opinion polls, do not reflect public judgment. For example, opinion polls report that Americans believe the threat of global warming to be of the utmost gravity, so much so that people say the nation should not wait for scientific proof to take far-reaching remedial action. And yet, these same studies also show that Americans are unwilling to consider even modest sacrifices or changes in life-style (e.g., a tax on gasoline or paying more for exhaust emission controls).[2] This specimen of public opinion is *not* public judgment. Rather, it is merely a snapshot of public opinion at a moment in time caught in the turmoil of grappling with an abstract threat that is not yet real and that Americans have not yet genuinely engaged. Two years from now, or five, or twenty years from now, events may force the public to confront the issue more fully, struggle with the pain of hard choices, and make a fateful decision to accept the changes needed to counter the threat. Then we will have true public judgment.

Public judgment does not always take decades to form or to wait upon catastrophic events. Studies of public opinion on immigration policy, for example, show that people's first impulse is strikingly different from their considered judgments. The public's first impulse is to close the door on refugees and immigrants coming to America because "we have to take care of our own first." But then, after reflecting on the moral meaning of what this country stands for, many people shift their views toward supporting more open and generous immigration policies. This is an expression of public judgment.[3]

As I use the term in this book, "public judgment" is the state of highly developed public opinion that exists once people have engaged an issue, considered it from all sides, understood the choices it leads to, and accepted the full consequences of the choices they make (see chap. 1 for a fuller definition).

Judgment, in this sense, is an old-fashioned word, much valued in the American tradition before the current age of expertise and information. Today, the term "public judgment" has an odd and unfamiliar ring to it. But the downgrading of judgment in favor of expertise is relatively new in American history. Historian Paul Gagnon gives a good description of the importance assigned to judgment in the America of a century ago.

Gagnon describes an 1892 commission report (the so-called Committee of Ten) that recommends four years of history for all college students on the grounds that the study of history promotes "the invaluable mental power we call judgment." As Gagnon describes it, judgment is the indispensable quality citizens in a democracy must possess to raise the level of public debate. It implies the ability

> to question stereotypes . . . to discern the difference between fact and conjecture . . . to distrust the simple answer and the dismissive explanation . . . to realize that all problems do not have solutions . . . to be pre-

pared for the irrational, the accidental in human affairs . . . to grasp the power of ideas and character in history . . . to accept the burden of living with tentative answers, with unfinished and often dangerous business . . . to accept costs and compromises, to honor the interests of others while pursuing their own . . . to respect the needs of future generations, to speak the truth and do the right things when falsehood and the wrong thing would be more profitable, and generally to restrain appetites and expectation — all this while working to inform themselves on the multiple problems and choices their elected officials confront.[4]

Gagnon's characterization of judgment, though considerably broader and more sweeping than my own, identifies the essential elements of judgment. He recognizes the complexity and variety of judgments citizens must make. Unambiguously, he includes the ethical dimension of opinion as well as the cognitive one. Most importantly for our purposes, he implicitly distinguishes between judgment and information. After citing the multiple facets of judgment, Gagnon adds that citizens must also — *in addition to* exercising judgment — "inform themselves on multiple problems and choices."[5]

In this book, I will return again and again to this distinction between judging and being well informed because in our own era we are plagued by a fatal confusion between the two — as if information were a satisfactory substitute for judgment. In our era of proliferating public opinion polls and endless lamentation about how poorly informed public opinion is, an astonishing amount of confusion exists about the relationship of information to judgment in policy making.

Though my definition of judgment is narrower than Gagnon's, both point to the same phenomenon — to the thoughtful side of the public's outlook, the side that belongs with the world of values, ethics, politics, and life philosophies rather than with the world of information and technical expertise.

THE CULTURE OF TECHNICAL CONTROL

At the end of V. O. Key's classic work, *Public Opinion and American Democracy*, he admits to a puzzle that has eluded his long 558-page analysis. Throughout his work he had concentrated unflaggingly on the question of how public opinion affects the day-to-day functioning of our democratic system. His analysis had led him inexorably to the conclusion that our system succeeds or fails on the strength of the relationship between the general public and the nation's elites. (He defines elites as "that thin stratum of persons referred to variously as political elites, the political activists, the leadership echelons, or the influentials.")[6] Key is thinking broadly of leadership in the nation's civil society as well as in its formal government structures. And he confesses that "the missing piece of our puzzle is this elite element of the opinion system."[7] He admits that he does not know how the leadership piece of the democratic system fits with the public opinion piece, but he does know that this is the heart of the matter.

My own inquiries have led me to share Key's conclusion: when the proper balance exists between the public and the nation's elites, our democracy works beautifully. When that balance is badly skewed, as in the present era, the system malfunctions. The chief symptom of imbalance is the nation's inability to arrive at consensus on how to cope with its nation's most urgent problems.

What would recreate the right balance between the public and leadership? It would take serious and systematic efforts to cultivate higher levels of public judgment. The reality is, however, that in today's America, such efforts are almost nonexistent. Their absence is not owing to practical constraints. There *are* practical difficulties. But if the political will existed, these difficulties could be surmounted or reduced (see chap. 13).

Why is our political will growing weaker? The answer lies deep in our contemporary culture. The sad fact is that cultural trends have been moving in the wrong direction. We are moving toward more creeping expertism, not less. The dominant mind-set of the culture stresses information, not judgment. The gap between the public and elites grows larger by the day.

I have come to think of this trend as an imperative of our Culture of Technical Control. As this name implies, our culture is busy exercising technical control over as many aspects of the human environment as it can — the economy, the physical environment, provisions for food and shelter, threats to health and longevity, national security, and conquering space. The method our culture has chosen for exercising such control is the application of expert thinking in science, technology, economic enterprises, government, the policy sciences, and large organizational structures.

All of the advanced industrial democracies today, especially the United States, are firmly committed to the control way of life and to using expert-driven technology to achieve it — whatever the cost. This cultural imperative generates very little controversy. The only controversy lies in calibrating its human costs. Its devotees minimize the costs or shrug them off as the price one pays for progress. Its critics complain about its dehumanizing tendencies, but except for a brief period in the 1960s, no one pays them much heed. Little thought has been given to strategies for preserving the benefits of the Culture of Technical Control while at the same time curbing its excesses. (In pt. 3, I elaborate this concept of the Culture of Technical Control and discuss how contemporary philosophers believe it can be made less destructive.)

My thesis in this book is that the Culture of Technical Control is undermining the country's ability to reach agreement between the public and experts on the serious problems that beset the society. We have lost this capability because the Culture of Technical Control has developed a series of assumptions that work against bringing the public into constructive engagement with these problems.

The Culture of Technical Control assumes:

- that policy decisions depend essentially on a high degree of specialized knowledge and skills;
- that only experts possess this knowledge;
- that the American people lack the relevant knowledge, are concerned largely with their own pocketbook interests, and are likely to be apathetic to issues not directly related to these interests;
- that where the public does have a view it is accurately reflected in public opinion polls;
- that America's elected officials know what the views of the electorate are and, by and large, represent them well;
- that on issues where public understanding and support are mandatory, they can be achieved through "public education" where experts who are knowledgeable share some of their information with the voters;
- that the media, through vigorous consciousness raising, impart to the American public the information and understanding it needs to develop responsible judgments on the key issues facing the nation.

In this book I take issue with the accuracy of every one of these assumptions. In my view, they range from half-truths to fraudulent falsehoods. Most of them rationalize the role of experts and specialists in our political life. Their combined effect is to erode democratic self-governance.

If a balance between experts and public is to be restored (or built anew) there are tasks the country's leaders and experts must undertake and tasks for the public.

In this book, I focus almost exclusively on the public rather than on the expert side of the balance. The reason is not that the public side is more important—it is equally important to the expert side. My reasons for concentrating on it are (1) I know it better, (2) it has proven more elusive and is burdened with more misunderstandings than the expert side, and (3) a wholly personal reason: over the past three decades, the organizations with which I have been affiliated have acquired a working knowledge of how to improve the quality of public judgment that I believe ought to be shared with others.

To show how public judgment can be enhanced, three tasks need to be undertaken on the public side. Each one corresponds to one of the three parts of the book.

The first task is to define *quality* as it applies to public opinion. How does ordinary public opinion evolve into public judgment? What is sound opinion and what is unsound opinion? When does public opinion deserve to be heeded, and when does it not? How does public judgment differ from expert judgment? (These questions are addressed in pt. 1, chaps. 1 through 4.)

The second task is to show how the quality of public opinion improves as it moves along the bumpy road from mass opinion to public judgment. Part of the task here is to identify the obstacles public opinion must overcome to evolve into public judgment. (This task is undertaken in pt. 2, chaps. 5 through 13, culminating in the ten rules summarized in chap. 13 for converting mass opinion to public judgment.)

The third task is to give intellectual respectability to the concept of public judgment by bulwarking its claim to represent a genuine form of knowledge (different, to be sure, from scientific knowledge). This is probably the most controversial proposition advanced in this book, but the ground has been well prepared for it in the evolution and history of twentieth-century philosophy.

The dominant philosophy underlying the Culture of Technical Control is that of empiricism or "objectivism," as some philosophers call it. In part 3, chapters 14 through 18, I will show that in its eagerness to exalt the truths of science, empiricism has, crudely and blindly, undermined other modes of knowing, including public judgment. It is this distorted perspective that leads to what is perhaps the epochal fallacy of our times. In this Age of Information, American culture grossly overvalues the importance of information as a form of knowledge and undervalues the importance of cultivating good judgment. It assumes, falsely, that good information automatically leads to good judgment: we demand of our experts primarily that they be well informed. This fallacy, which is all-pervasive in our society, is difficult to examine rationally and dispassionately because it is so deeply rooted in the Culture of Technical Control.

The history of twentieth-century philosophy can, in general terms, be told as the seduction of philosophy (especially Anglo-American academic philosophy) by empiricism, followed by self-doubt, followed by a searching and sometimes profound analysis into the nature of knowledge and various modes of knowing. What I have done is to abstract some of the painful lessons learned by twentieth-century philosophy and apply them to the concept of public judgment.

A final chapter (chap. 19) discusses what actions the nation can take to reduce the resistance to democratic self-governance bred by the Culture of Technical Control, and to strengthen the ability of the media, the education system, and political leadership to enhance public judgment.

SUMMARY

The thesis of this book can be stated as follows:

The key to successful self-governance in our Age of Information is to create a new balance between public and experts. Today that relationship is badly skewed toward experts at the expense of the public. This out-of-balance condition is not the result of a power struggle (though this is not wholly absent) but of a deep-rooted cultural trend that elevates the specialized knowledge of the expert to a place of high honor while denigrating the value of the public's potentially most important contribution — a high level of thoughtful and responsible public judgment. This prejudice is rooted in the dominant Culture of Technical Control, which on its positive side has made science, the benefits of modern technology, political freedom, and democracy possible. Yet, even with these impressive accomplishments, a serious difficulty exists. The Culture of Technical Control saps the national will to confront the obstacles standing in the way of strengthening the quality of public judgment indispensable to self-governance and consensus building. For democracy to flourish, it is not enough to get out the vote. We need better public judgment, and we need to know how to cultivate it. The public is not magically endowed with good judgment. Good judgment is something that must be worked at all the time and with great skill and effort. It does not exist automatically; it must be created. Creating more and better public judgment is what this book is about.

Part One

SEARCHING FOR QUALITY IN PUBLIC OPINION

A MISSING CONCEPT

There is a missing concept in American democracy, with a mystery attached to it. The mystery is not what the concept is — that is easy to state — but rather, why it is missing. For almost thirty years this question has puzzled me, and I am writing this book partly to see if I can figure it out.

The missing concept is a set of terms to describe the *quality* of public opinion and to distinguish "good" public opinion from "bad." Quality judgments are commonplace in our culture. Standards of excellence exist for automobiles, movies, plumbers, surgeons, CEOs, chefs. We know what we mean when we say, "She is a good friend; he is a good neighbor; they are good parents." There are tests and standards, formal and informal, for quality for tangible products and intangible ideas. Its resale value is a good pragmatic test of a car's worth. If the doctor's patient dies, the operation is *not* a success. Good friends are those who stand by you in times of trouble and need. Winning an Oscar for a movie, winning a Pulitzer Prize for a book, winning a Nobel Prize for a scientific achievement — these are society's methods for designating quality and excellence. But when it comes to public opinion, there are no standards for quality.

Students of public opinion have learned that Americans are a highly opinionated people; Americans hold an opinion on almost every subject, whether they know anything about it or not, whether they feel passionately or are indifferent to it. Sometimes the seriousness and generosity of the public's judgments are startling. At other times the public seems mindless and irresponsible. Surely, the reader of public opinion polls must sometimes wonder, "Is this really the public's opinion? How can people be so blind, so foolish, so easily manipulated?" Americans hold strong views on drug abuse, abortion, capital punishment, nuclear power, sex education in the schools, the Strategic Defense Initiative (SDI), protectionism, ethics in government, rising health care costs, acid rain, affirmative action, censorship, and so forth. On some of these issues, the quality of public opinion is amazingly good—on others, abysmally bad.

How does one distinguish "good" from "bad" in a reasonably objective manner? Is public opinion "good" when it agrees with my personal point of view or happens to coincide with the experts' well-informed conclusions or forms part of a coherent political philosophy and "bad" when it fails to meet such criteria? Various influential groups in the society adhere to one or another of these standards of quality, but all are severely flawed.

To begin our search for a viable standard of quality for public opinion, let us briefly glance at how the experts who analyze, measure, and report on public opinion deal with the quality issue.

MEDIA AND PUBLIC POLICY EXPERTS

Many of the most influential observers and analysts of public opinion come from the worlds of journalism and public policy. By inference, they do distinguish good public opinion from bad. Good public opinion is being "well informed"; being poorly informed is synonymous with bad quality.

Journalists, above all others, equate being well informed with high quality. The media are fascinated with opinion polls that show how ignorant the public is. Conduct a poll that reveals that the majority of Americans cannot name a single justice of the Supreme Court, or cannot locate Siberia on a map, and it is sure to get wide TV and newspaper coverage. Journalists hold as an article of faith the traditional belief that a well-informed citizenry is indispensable to the proper functioning of democracy.

It would be perverse to deny that information is relevant to the quality of public opinion. But in a professional lifetime devoted to its study, I have come to the conclusion that equating quality opinion with being well informed is a serious mistake. Obviously, information plays some role in shaping public opinion. But often it is a minor role. To assume that public opinion is invariably improved by inundating people with information grossly distorts the role of information. A society operating on this assumption misconstrues the nature and purpose of public opinion in a democracy.

Admittedly, some experts do harbor misgivings about the relevance of information. Daniel Boorstin, the noted historian, writes, "It is a cliché of our time that what this nation needs is an 'informed citizenry.' By which we mean a citizenry that is up on the latest information, that has not failed to read this week's newsmagazine, today's newspapers, or to watch the seven o'clock news (perhaps also the news at ten o'clock!) — always for more information, always to be better informed." Boorstin adds, "I wonder if that is what we need."[1]

Most experts do not, however, share Boorstin's reservations. They assume that public opinion is of good quality when it agrees with their own views and of poor quality when it does not. The logic is this: they, the experts, are well informed; the public is poorly informed. Give the public more information, and it will agree with them.

But what if even after being better informed, the public still does not agree? Rarely do the experts conclude that the public has a different point of view equally worthy of consideration. They conclude instead that the public is still not sufficiently informed. I have participated in many "public education" campaigns with officials and experts who were chagrined that the public, after being more fully informed, did not come to the "right" conclusion; for example: U.S.–Soviet relations, prison overcrowding, welfare reform, the spread of AIDS among intravenous drug users, the decline of quality of education in the public schools, and so forth. I will elaborate these examples in later chapters.

POLITICAL SCIENTISTS

Political scientists have at various times proposed other criteria for judging quality of opinion. There is no need to review their work in detail, but several of their main currents of thought are relevant to our search for a viable definition of quality.

In the 1960s and 1970s, one of the nation's most influential groups of political scientists was associated with the University of Michigan's Survey Research Center. Based on surveys conducted among voters in congressional and presidential elections, they arrived at a severe judgment of the quality of American public opinion. Analyzing the 1956 presidential election, Angus Campbell and his coauthors concluded in their classic work, *The American Voter*, that quality opinion depends on inner coherence — how well a person holding an opinion has developed what coauthor Philip E. Converse called a "political ideology."[2]

By political ideology, the Michigan political scientists meant something different than the customary usage that links ideologies to deeply felt emotional commitments. Their emphasis was wholly cognitive: by ideology they meant a set of broad political principles, carefully thought through and internally consistent, from which one derives one's opinions on particular issues. An ideology, in this sense, is a rationalistic political philosophy that leads to thinking about politics in abstract terms.

The authors of *The American Voter* failed to find many such "ideological" thinkers among the mass of American voters. Even when they stretched the criteria of ideological thinking, they could find only 2.5 percent of the American electorate who could be considered to hold a coherent political ideology. Stretching still further, they added an additional 9 percent whom they categorized as "near Ideologues"—persons who bring some shred of conceptual sophistication to their views.

In an often-quoted article published in 1964, Converse amplified this line of thought.[3] People with well-structured political ideologies should, he maintained, hold predictable views on various issues. If their ideology is liberal and you know their views on one issue, you should be able to predict their position on all the other liberal issues. Similarly, conservative ideologists should also hold readily predictable opinions of a conservative persuasion. Converse reconfirmed the earlier conclusion of the Michigan analysts that average voters do not have well-structured political ideologies: knowing their views on any one issue does not help to predict their views on other issues.

The judgment in *The American Voter* is brutally clear: "Our failure to locate more than a trace of 'ideological' thinking in the protocols of our surveys emphasizes the *general impoverishment of political thought* in a large proportion of the electorate" (emphasis added). Owing to its inadequate level of knowledge about particular policies, "the mass electorate is not able to appraise either its goals or the appropriateness of the means chosen to serve these goals."[4] So much for the ability of Americans to govern themselves!

In subsequent years, other political scientists would seek to soften the harshness of this judgment. In *The Changing American Voter* (1976), Harvard's Sidney Verba, representing another group of political scientists, commented on the earlier studies: "No one expected the average American to be a political philosopher. Yet the gap between the way in which the average citizen thought about political matters and the way in which those matters were conceived by the more politically sophisticated was larger than expected."[5] Reanalyzing the Michigan 1956 and 1958 congressional elections and the presidential elections of 1960, 1964, 1968, and 1972, the new analysis discovered ground for optimism. The authors found the American voter much improved. They concluded that "The proportion of citizens who think in ideologically structured ways about parties and candidates . . . has grown substantially."[6] Using modified measures of ideological sophistication, they arrived at an estimate of 22 percent of voters who bring to bear a modicum of ideological thinking. The authors hastened to add this caveat: "Our category of ideologues is not populated by citizen-philosophers, each with an elaborate and well considered political world view."[7]

The political scientists from Michigan, Harvard, and the other university centers who were engaged in this analysis are scholars of stature: Angus Campbell, Warren Miller, Philip Converse, Sidney Verba, and the others have all done pioneering work in their field. Their empirical analysis shows the average American voter to be minimally involved in politics, inattentive to the issues, poorly informed, pragmatic, inconsistent, and focused on concrete concerns rather than on general principles. Mountains of subsequent opinion research studies validate this picture: average American voters are *not* intellectuals or ideologists. They are *not* abstract thinkers. They do *not* approach issues or candidates conceptually.

These conclusions have led some social scientists to place their hopes for democracy on a subset of the electorate, usually referred to as the "attentive public." Though the majority may be ill-informed and lack coherence in their thinking, there is an elite minority of the public that is more "with it." They read the *New York Times*, the national news magazines, watch the "MacNeil-Lehrer News Hour" and otherwise fit into the approved model of informed citizen favored by political scientists. Some studies analyze opinions by contrasting the views of this "attentive public"—usually a minority ranging from 5 percent to 25 percent of the population—with those of the "inattentive majority."[8]

In principle, the distinction between an attentive and an inattentive public is a useful one; on most issues only a minority of the public is truly involved and it can be revealing to contrast the views of those paying attention with those who are inattentive. In practice, however, the concept of the attentive public is essentially elitist. Elites define quality by their own standards of ideological coherence and being well informed. The concept of the attentive public presupposes this elite definition and seeks to find among the public that minority of people whose thought processes mirror this model most closely. But the public is neither ideological nor well informed. It is pragmatic and usually poorly informed. Does this mean that public opinion is inherently inferior to well-informed expert opinion?

A DIFFERENT PERSPECTIVE

Not all political scientists believe that the quality of the public's thought must be inferior to that of experts because the public does not think conceptually and is not well informed. Professor Everett Ladd who heads the

Roper Center for Public Opinion Research at Storrs, Connecticut, and is, in his own right, a distinguished political scientist, takes direct issue with the Converse thesis. In a recent textbook on American politics, Ladd discusses it at length. He readily acknowledges that voters are not well informed: "On first review, research seems to raise serious doubts about whether Americans know enough about the various questions of public affairs to play the part democratic theory assigns them. A cursory examination of poll data reveals an extraordinary lack of interest and unawareness, even on basic facts of political life."[9]

He aptly summarizes the canonical thesis:

> An influential study by political scientist Philip E. Converse addressed this subject. Converse concluded that the amount of political information people have goes far toward determining the structure, constraint, and stability of their beliefs. Without much factual information, the beliefs of large segments of the populace bounce around wildly over time. Between 1956 and 1960, the Institute for Social Research at the University of Michigan posed the same questions to the same people on three separate occasions, asking their views on issues such as school desegregation, federal aid to education, foreign aid, and federal housing. Many respondents moved from one side to the other on these questions in successive interviews. After closely examining this pattern, Converse concluded that most of the movement was not true opinion change but rather the result of respondents answering in essentially a random fashion. Only a distinct minority had something close to hard core opinions.[10]

Ladd, however, goes on to cite another body of research that shows the public in a more positive light: "Another type of public opinion research yields conclusions very different from Converse's or even those of his critics. It focuses on the overall patterns of responses Americans give. These turn out to be remarkably stable and predictable."[11]

Ladd is referring here to Gallup poll data, accumulated month by month since the mid-1930s. Ladd finds no inherent contradiction between the Converse image of a poorly informed and unpredictable public and the stable and persisting public suggested by the Gallup data. The two pictures reflect different aspects of the same public: Converse is looking at the coherence with which people hold information; Gallup is reflecting people's underlying values and attitudes. Ladd sums it up cogently:

> Opinion research in the U.S. does reveal a public strikingly inattentive to the details of even the most consequential and controversial policies. This suggests a potential for manipulation. But the research also indi-

cates great stability and coherence in the public's underlying attitudes and values. Americans show themselves perfectly capable of making the distinctions needed to determine what Harwood Childs called "the basic ends of public policy," and of pursuing these logically and clearly. There is a persisting structure to American opinion that belies the picture of a populace helpless before the "engineers of consent."[12]

The two positions lead to radically different conclusions; they concern nothing less than the ability of Americans to govern themselves in keeping with the principles of democracy.

THE POLLING PROFESSION

When we turn to the professionals who do most of the public opinion polling in America we find yet another set of concerns. Practitioners of public opinion have long been aware of the difficulty of distinguishing good from poor quality. As early as 1947, George Gallup called for a method in opinion research to distinguish between people's "snap judgments" and opinions that have been carefully thought through—an unmistakable dimension of quality.[13]

The technical literature on public opinion surveys from the 1950s to the present shows some modest follow-up on Gallup's proposals, but by and large it moves in other directions. The nation has now had more than one-half century of experience with public opinion polling—from the 1936 presidential election to the present. This experience reveals a mixed picture. On the one hand, opinion polling techniques have proven a cost-effective way to elicit the views of cross sections of the American public. But on the other hand, they have also proven fallible, easy to misinterpret, and subject to abuse. The profession has been preoccupied with improving polling techniques to make them less fallible.

In her presidential address to the American Association of Public Opinion Research (AAPOR) in May 1988, Eleanor Singer inventoried the difficulties that beset the modern public opinion survey, as reflected in the questions raised by scholars and practitioners in the field.[14] The list includes:

- the lack of truthful responses to survey questions;
- the failure to do justice to the richness of people's experience;
- the failure of people to understand certain types of questions that depend on memory or insight into their own feelings;

- the tendency of survey researchers to impose their own framework on the public;
- the fact that certain words in questions mean different things to different people;
- the tendency of people to give an opinion even when they do not have a real point of view on the subject, and,
- the tendency of people to modify their answers to questions when the context shifts or question wording changes.

This is an imposing list. Some of these difficulties are exaggerated; few reflect inherent limitations of the opinion survey method. Most, however, as Singer points out, are solvable through a combination of care, time, and money. In other words, they are practical problems, not conceptual, theoretical, or technical. At the end of her address, Singer quotes Howard Schuman, a past president of AAPOR, who, like herself, has concluded that opinion surveys are beset with difficulties — not so much because of technical or theoretical flaws, but "because human responses are inherently both subtle and complex."[15]

These judgments — that survey methods are potentially capable of giving an accurate picture of public opinion but that to do so they need to be as subtle and complex as public opinion itself — certainly reflect my own experience in conducting public opinion polls. But the conclusion that the difficulties of the polling profession are largely practical does not mean that they are being resolved. Unhappily, the trend is moving in the opposite direction. For subtle and complex human responses, one needs subtle and complex opinion surveys. These demand time, money, and skill. Today, the trend is toward oversimplified, cheap, crude public opinion polls, not subtle and complex ones. This is not because the profession wants it that way: opinion research professionals have never been more alert to the dangers of superficial polls. The villains are the mass media who increasingly commission, pay for, and themselves conduct public opinion polls. The "quickie" opinion polls that make newspaper headlines ("Public Disagrees with High Court on Abortion") or 30-second sound-bites based on simplistic questions are a menace that has grown all too familiar.

Many of these opinion polls are worthless because they ignore every trap and pitfall the profession has uncovered, at great pains and cost, in its more than half century of analyzing poll results. As public opinion polls have grown in popularity and as magazines, newspapers and TV stations have come to believe they must have their own proprietary opinion polls, corners are cut, polls grow shorter and cheaper, and being the first to publish an instant poll is regarded by the press as a desirable coup. Ironically, the more the polling professionals have come to appreciate the subtlety and complexity of human responses, the more the media have worked to oversimplify and falsify that complexity. There are honorable exceptions, like the CBS News/*New York Times* poll and the polls sponsored by the *Los Angeles Times.* But, in general, Gresham's law has prevailed: the bad opinion polls are driving out the good ones.

SUMMARY

The media and policy world equate good public opinion with being well informed; political scientists equate it with holding a sophisticated political philosophy; the professionals who conduct opinion polls focus their attention on improving the instruments for measuring public opinion rather than on improving the quality of the opinion being measured. There exists today no commonly accepted and tenable standard of what constitutes good-quality public opinion.

2

WHAT IS QUALITY IN PUBLIC OPINION?

I f being well informed is not the defining characteristic of quality opinion, and if the model admired by an older generation of political scientists — adherence to an ideology — is not, then what is? A definition of quality suitable to judge the thinking of political philosophers, technical experts, or scientists does not fit the public. In the American social system the public performs a different function than these elites do. Our society requires a definition of quality that relates to the roles the public is expected to perform. We do not judge the quality of a musician's work by how good a parent he or she may be. It is how well the music is performed that counts. We need to know what quality means when the public performs its various roles as voters, consumers, employees, participants in the society, and members of the community — including the national and world community.

Fortunately, there is a conception of quality that applies to all of these roles. It realistically reflects the strengths and weaknesses of public opinion as it actually exists, neither idealizing it nor selling it short. *I propose that the quality of public opinion be considered good when the public accepts responsibility for the consequences of its views and poor when the public, for whatever reason, is unprepared to do so.* When the public offhandedly rejects the need for tax increases to reduce the federal budget deficit on the unrealistic grounds that correcting "waste, fraud, and abuse" would cause the problem to disappear — this is poor quality. There may be sound grounds for opposing tax increases, but the ritualistic incantation about "waste, fraud, and abuse" serves merely as a rationalization that people seize upon because it permits them to avoid the issue.

When Iran's Ayatollah Khomeini took Americans hostage in 1979, the public's impulsive first reaction was violent. Some people wanted to send the marines to rescue the hostages. Others growled, "Nuke 'em. Drop

some nuclear bombs on Tehran!" Anger, wounded pride, hatred, fear—
these were the emotions Americans were feeling and expressing. Yet, within
a few days most Americans began to have second thoughts. As they confronted the realities of the problem, the majority came to support a policy
that called for more patience and forbearance. They began to take responsibility for the consequences of their views. The initially poor quality of
public opinion showed marked improvement in a brief period.

Some years ago when the Intermediate Nuclear Forces (INF) treaty
eliminating all intermediate-range American and Soviet missiles based in
Europe was being negotiated with the Soviet Union, a CBS News/*New
York Times* survey reported that a 56 percent majority of the public approved it. But when the same people were asked if they would continue
to support the treaty even if it meant that afterwards the Soviets and their
allies would have a bigger military force in Europe than the United States
and its allies, the 56 percent majority shrank swiftly to a 21 percent minority! The original majority view was poor in quality because people were
not mindful of the consequences of their views.[1]

Similarly, when people were asked in an NBC News/Associated
Press poll about their opinion of a constitutional amendment to require
the Federal government to balance its budget, a 63 percent majority said
they approved. Yet, as soon as people learned that such an amendment
might result in higher taxes, the 63 percent majority, as if by magic, shrank
to a 39 percent minority.[2]

The opinion survey literature abounds in similar examples in which
people express opinions without being mindful of their consequences, and
as soon as these consequences are raised their opinions change. A series
of Roper polls shows that for many years a large majority of the public
said they favored protectionist legislation against foreign imports in the
interests of protecting American jobs.[3] An NBC News/*Wall Street Journal*
poll shows a similar pattern: a 51 percent majority favor "greater limits
on goods imported into the United States."[4] But when the same people
were told that such limits might restrict the variety and choice of products
available to them, the 51 percent dropped to 41 percent; when they were
told they might have to pay more for products, support for protectionism dropped to 36 percent. And, when the public was confronted with the
possibility that with protectionism they might have to sacrifice quality in
products, the 51 percent majority became a meager 19 percent minority.
Obviously, people had not given the possible consequences of protectionism a moment's thought. (In 1988, presidential aspirant Richard Gephardt
was misled by public opinion polls on protectionism. He learned the hard
way how fragile and volatile the public's views were on this issue.) When

people's views flip-flop the moment the possible consequences of their opinions are raised, this is a sure sign of poor quality.

Does public opinion on all issues show this extreme fickleness as soon as consequences are mentioned? If so, public opinion would be just what its critics claim: undependable, erratic, thoughtless, and manipulatable by demagogues and image makers. But, in fact, it does not. On many issues the public shows solid, unshakable, thoughtful opinions.

The contrast between those issues about which the public has not confronted the consequences of its views and those issues about which it has is striking. On the latter group of issues, the public's views, though stable and responsible, are not always in accord with elite views; often they are opposed. This is one reason why some experts are reluctant to accept as good quality opinions with which they disagree and may even hold in contempt. But agreement or disagreement with expert views is emphatically *not* the criterion of quality advanced here.

A good example of public opinion in which people accept the consequences of their views (and in which the public's views conflict with the views of many elites) is capital punishment. Before the 1970s, the majority of Americans were not in favor of the death penalty for murder and other serious crimes. Majority support for the death penalty built slowly over the next two decades, reaching an average of 73 percent in the 1980s (see chart 2.1). Interviews with people who hold this position show that most have struggled with the argument that imposing the death penalty means that some innocent people will die. Supporters of the death penalty realize and accept this implication, but they do not change their views even when contemplating these consequences.

Many experts disagree with the public's judgment on the death penalty, and I am not claiming that the public is correct either morally or factually. I *am* emphasizing the important fact that unlike public opinion on issues such as protectionism and constitutional amendments to balance the federal budget, the public is conscious here of the consequences of its views and is prepared to accept them.

The public also discriminates very clearly in their views. In a 1989 poll in which 75 percent of the public stated they favored the death penalty for serious crimes, support for it dropped to 57 percent when the crimes were committed by sixteen- or seventeen-year-old youths and to only 27 percent when the mentally retarded committed the crimes.[5] The majority of Americans oppose the death penalty under these circumstances.

A similar pattern emerges with even greater clarity on the issue of abortion. Men and women both hold strong views on this issue. After years of agonized thought, they have made up their minds about where they

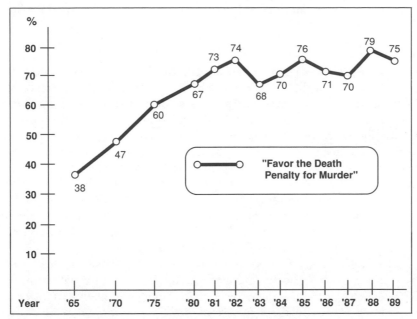

SOURCES: 1965, 1970, and 1983 — Harris; 1975, 1980, 1982, and 1984 through 1987 — National Opinion Research Center; 1981 — ABC News; 1988 — Gallup; and 1989 — Yankelovich Clancy Shulman for *Time*/CNN.

CHART 2.1. Attitude change toward the death penalty.

stand. They have resolved their inner conflicts and ambivalences, though they continue to be troubled by them. They are aware of the consequences of their views and are prepared to accept them. And, because they have resolved their positions, they discriminate sharply and clearly about the conditions under which abortion is or is not acceptable to them.

On the surface, the abortion issue may appear to be confused in the public's mind. A 1989 poll suggests that the public is sharply divided (49 percent believe abortion should be legal, 39 percent add critical qualifications, and 9 percent believe abortion should not be permitted under any circumstances).[6] A closer analysis of survey findings on abortion over a number of years reveals that most people are not confused. Survey data over a fifteen-year period show that opinions on abortion are remarkably stable. Results have not changed significantly either for the general question ("Do you favor or oppose the legalization of abortion?") or for questions focusing on specific circumstances (e.g., abortion in the case of rape, or not being able to afford the child, or pregnancies that threaten the life of the mother).[7]

People's views on abortion reflect a number of distinctions and nuances. For example, support for abortion when the pregnancy threatens the mother's life has remained steady for years at about the 85 percent level, and at about the 75–80 percent level "if there is a strong chance of a serious defect in the baby" or in the case of pregnancy resulting from rape.[8] The public is more closely divided over the right to abortion when "the family has a very low income and cannot afford any more children" (41 percent in favor, 56 percent opposed) or when "the woman is not married and does not want to marry the man" (38 percent in favor, 58 percent opposed), or when "a married woman does not want to have any more children" (39 percent in favor, 58 percent opposed).[9] And opposition to abortion reached majority status (about 60 percent) in response to questions probing views on abortion for women who seem to lack a concrete or compelling reason for ending their pregnancy.[10]

In recent years, new medical and scientific knowledge about the first stages of life has been heavily publicized. Has this new information made a difference to the public's views on abortion? Evidence shows that the new information matters to about 20 percent of the public and, taking this new information into account, there has been a five percent shift overall toward a more conservative position. But the new information has not affected the position of most Americans on abortion.[11] People themselves acknowledge this reality. When survey questions ask people about the firmness of their stands on abortion, about 80 percent say their views are unlikely to change.[12]

Sex education in the schools provides another example of people accepting the consequences of their views. For many years, opinion polls have asked cross sections of the American public whether they favor sex education in the schools. For over fifteen years, year after year, the vast majority of Americans (about 80 percent), have firmly endorsed the practice.[13] Even when arguments are urged against it (e.g., it might encourage teenage sexual activity and pregnancy), poll results show that Americans have made up their minds about the stands they wish to take.[14] The only circumstances that elicit a variation in response concern the age of the child and content of the subject to be taught. Fewer Americans favor teaching sex education in elementary schools, and certain aspects of sex education, such as abortion, homosexuality, and premarital sex (when discussed with young children), make some Americans uncomfortable.[15] This pattern of response is firmly established. Americans have thought through and come to judgment on how they feel about this touchy subject.

Other examples of issues—less heated, perhaps—wherein the public has come to appreciate and fully accept the consequences of their opinions would include: a firm rejection of government censorship of news and acceptance of the role of the press as a critic rather than as an instrument of government; a consensus that a nuclear arms race with the Soviet Union is the wrong way to enhance national security, and an increasingly firm opinion that women should receive equal pay for work equal to that of men.

REASONS FOR NOT ACCEPTING CONSEQUENCES

The reasons why people accept the consequences of their opinions on some issues and not on others are implicit in the examples cited above. The reason easiest to detect and to measure is simple lack of awareness. On some issues, people are unaware of the consequences of their opinions, and once these are brought to their attention, they begin to take them into account. This process is one of the ways information *is* relevant to the quality of public opinion. But note that the information is of a special kind: it is information explaining the consequences of specific policy choices. This is not the "names and faces in the news" sort of information that journalists usually associate with being well informed.

The role of information in shaping the quality of public opinion is often subtle. The type of information that is always relevant assists people in grasping the trade-offs that their opinions entail, thereby giving them the opportunity to confront whatever ambivalence they may feel. But the information by itself does not resolve the ambivalence or lead to resolution.

Consider the following example from the debate in the mid-1980s about funding for the Nicaraguan Contras. In the conventional meaning of being well informed, some Americans were very well informed about U.S. policy toward Nicaragua. They knew where Nicaragua is (most Americans did not). They knew who the Contras were and that it had been U.S. policy to support them. And they knew a great deal about Nicaraguan politics, Daniel Ortega, and the Sandinistas. But they were in conflict about the desirability of the United States intervening in Nicaraguan internal affairs. Despite being well informed, their ambivalence remained unresolved; they did not have a clear position; they did not accept the consequences of their own views one way or the other.[16]

On the other hand, the majority of Americans were poorly informed about Nicaragua—they not only did not know where it is, but did not even know which side the United States supported. Nonetheless, they held very firm opinions and fully accepted their consequences. They felt they knew what they needed to know: that Nicaragua is a small country with a complex set of problems that was somehow involved in the U.S.–Soviet struggle, just as Vietnam was. They were convinced that if we sent U.S. troops there, for whatever reason and in support of whatever side, we would get bogged down in a Vietnam-like quagmire (or a Soviet–Afghanistan-like quagmire), and they emphatically rejected this strategy. It violated their values and their commonsense convictions. They judged intervention in Nicaraguan affairs by a single, simple standard: "no more Vietnams." Sophisticated elites may hold this view in contempt as simpleminded and ill informed. But it is not fickle. It has endured for a long time under varying conditions. Making these Americans "better informed" about Nicaragua would have been an irrelevant exercise.

People also may not confront the consequences of their opinions simply because they have not had time to do so. For most people, it takes an irreducible amount of time to digest important events and sort out feelings. The public's first responses to virtually all far-reaching events are likely to be misleading. For example, experienced opinion pollers know that the public's first response to any presidential foreign policy action will be positive, however misbegotten it may be and however negative people's considered judgments may grow to be in the weeks and months that follow. According to a Gallup poll, in the first few days after Jack Kennedy's disastrous Bay of Pigs invasion of Cuba, his approval rating actually rose from 72 percent to 83 percent![17]

The single most important reason people have for failing to accept the consequences of their opinions is their difficulty in resolving their own conflicting values and ambivalences. The ability to resolve internal conflicts of values is the foundation of good-quality public opinion. On issues like capital punishment, abortion, and sex education, people have done so. But this is true only of a minority of issues. Resolving conflicts of values takes time; it is painful work, and people avoid it as much and as long as they can. (Discovering how to expedite this process is one of the major objectives of this work.)

Often people's first line of defense against facing consequences is wishful thinking ("Tackle waste, fraud, and abuse in the government and the budget deficit will go away") and simple avoidance and procrastination. In their personal lives people may not be able to procrastinate indefinitely, but it is easy to do so on public issues.

The essence of the quality issue in public opinion resides in the struggle to resolve the conflicting values raised by many of today's complex issues. It is only when we begin to grasp how subtle and deep this struggle is that we realize how truly fatuous are journalistic attempts to squeeze public opinion on a complex subject into a single poll question in an instant poll.

OTHER ASPECTS OF QUALITY

Two other characteristics should be included in the definition of quality. One is the degree of firmness or volatility with which an opinion is held, and the other is the extent to which the opinion contradicts other views the person holds. These formal properties of opinion — volatility and consistency — are, logically speaking, not stand-alone factors. They are related to the basic criterion of whether or not people are taking the consequences of their opinions into account. As we have seen, people's views jump around erratically as they become aware of the consequences of their opinions and begin to confront the implications. (There are other reasons for volatility, but none are as important.)

Similarly, there are several reasons why people do not always hold self-consistent views. We are not a nation of logicians. Most of the time, most people's opinions remain unexamined and suffer some inconsistency. In the present context I am less concerned with *logical* consistency as a dimension of quality, as with a tendency toward "compartmentalized thinking."[18]

Among the many devices people have for avoiding coming to grips with reality, the most common is to keep related aspects of an issue mentally separated, failing to make the proper connections between them. By compartmentalizing their thinking, people can maintain contradictory and conflicting opinions without being mentally discomforted. When people think about preserving American jobs, they endorse protectionism. When they think about consumer values — lower prices, better quality, and more choice — they oppose protectionism. As long as their thinking is compartmentalized, they are unable to take a firm and unwavering stand on the issue.

The tendency to compartmentalize thinking is common to many issues and often results in blatant contradictions. For example, in a survey discussing whether U.S. policy should seek military superiority over the Soviets, 62 percent of the voters agreed that "We should do everything in our power to achieve military superiority — nuclear and nonnuclear — over the Soviet Union." But later in the same survey, when the question about seeking a balance of military strength with the Soviets was brought up, a 74 percent majority agreed that "there is no practical way to achieve military superiority over the Soviet Union; we should seek a balance of military strength with them."[19]

It is contradictions such as these that cause the experts to throw up their hands in disgust and pronounce the public incapable of dealing with complex problems, or else they denounce opinion polls as unreliable and worse than useless. To the experienced survey researcher who knows that the public is capable of holding firm, consistent, and highly discriminating views on complex subjects, a whopper of a contradiction such as this is a signal not that the public is incapable of holding consistent views but that the researcher is tackling an issue about which people have compartmentalized their thinking.

Frequently, compartmentalized thinking is linked to certain words or phrases that have become politically tainted — code words to which the public responds in ways that do not reflect their true feelings. Thus, people automatically oppose government spending in the abstract but simultaneously endorse programs that involve government spending for causes they support, such as the war on drugs. Politicians shy away from the term *detente* because it is linked in people's minds with a failed policy. But the same people who reject the word detente endorse a policy of reduced tensions with the Soviets (in other words, detente).[20] One of the most tainted words in the political vocabulary is *welfare*. Americans dislike the word and the concept. But, in practice, they support the content of welfare programs — as long as the word is not used. Polling data reported in *Public Opinion* magazine show just how compartmentalized the public's thinking is on welfare. When Americans are asked whether the country is now spending "too little" or "too much" or "the right amount" on "assistance to the poor," by a ten to one margin (68 percent to 7 percent), Americans think we are spending too little. But when people are asked the same question about welfare spending, by two to one (42 percent to 23 percent), they say we are spending too much![21]

In 1988, the editors of *Public Opinion* used this and other examples to make an important point about the state of our knowledge of public opinion and the responsibility of opinion surveys. "Looking back on the surveys reviewed for this magazine, we are most struck by how they have enlarged and sharpened our understanding of the properties of public opinion. Ambivalence is one of these essential properties. We have come to see that the public's being pulled this way and that by conflicting or competing values isn't simply an occasional occurrence but instead a fundamental, recurring characteristic of opinion on a wide range of policy questions."[22] After giving various examples of ambivalence, the editors draw the clear lesson that when people struggle with conflicts in values, their views cannot be represented accurately without revealing all sides of their ambivalence. As an indicator of good-quality public opinion, consistency means that people have succeeded in breaking down their compartmentalized thinking and have made the proper connections in confronting — and accepting — the consequences of their own opinions.

The firmness or volatility of an opinion is closely related to consistency but exhibits itself in a different form. Compartmentalized thinking shows up in the form of contradictions. Volatility shows up when people change their answers to questions asked at different times or when question wording is varied slightly. For example, in studies conducted in 1988, public attitudes about the desirability of building SDI changed depending on how the question was worded. A majority (56 percent) said the country should not give up SDI in order to negotiate deep nuclear arms cuts.[23] Yet, when the question wording was changed to evoke the highly desirable goal of cooperating with the Soviets, public response flip-flopped, with 59 percent vs. 36 percent saying the country *should* give up SDI "to work with the Soviets to solve problems facing both countries."[24]

In a study on combating the spread of communism in the Third World, attitudes also changed with question wording. In response to one question, 40 percent said they opposed "recognizing and establishing trade relations with Cuba."[25] But in a follow-up question that suggested that recognition might strengthen the Communist regime, opposition jumped to 54 percent.[26] In another series of questions, almost two-thirds of respondents (64 percent) wanted the United States to aid anti-Communist groups in the Third World,[27] but support fell to 39 percent when the fact that sometimes this meant supporting dictators was mentioned.[28]

Volatility and consistency — as these examples suggest — indicate a failure to grasp, confront, and accept the consequences of one's opinions. Of the two, volatility is the more frequent phenomenon. People try to avoid blatant contradictions in their thinking and will often qualify their opinions to avoid the appearance of inconsistency. But, by and large, they are more casual about giving stable answers to questions. If they have not resolved their ambivalences, they may change their views from week to week or day to day or even in the same hour-long interview. Above all other properties of public opinion, it is this fickleness of opinion that confirms elites in their conviction that public opinion cannot be taken seriously on its merits but must be managed almost in an adversarial fashion.

THE "MUSHINESS" INDEX

People's views are most volatile when an issue is new or when it is so rife with conflict that they avoid coming to grips with it. Every time the issue is presented in a slightly different light or when a new bit of information is revealed about it, people shift their views.

When this type of instability crops up in public opinion surveys, it is cited as a criticism of survey methodology. ("How can you believe the results when one poll tells you one thing and another poll with a slightly different question tells you something else?") But methodology is not the culprit. The public gives stable answers to questions on many issues about which they have made up their minds, even though the question wording may vary considerably from survey to survey. Volatility does not stem from changes in question wording; it pops up when people have not yet made up their minds.

In the early 1980s, *Time* magazine agreed with my former firm (Yankelovich, Skelly & White, Inc.) to undertake a research program designed to investigate the problem of volatility in public opinion polling. At that time, volatility was particularly severe on foreign policy issues, and *Time* agreed that it would be a service to readers to distinguish between public views that were firm and stable (on which foreign policy decisions could be securely grounded) and views that were unstable and mushy. *Time* also agreed that the results of the project would be contributed to the public domain — a contribution toward enhancing the quality of public opinion polling used in journalism.[29]

The project involved more than two years of work, including an extensive literature search, a series of small-scale laboratory experiments, and a specially designed national survey. The purpose of the project was practical rather than theoretical. Recognizing that journalistic resources are limited and that no media would be willing to devote either the money or time or space needed to do full justice to people's complex and ambivalent views, we agreed on a minimum objective: to design a practical, low-cost method of flagging volatile opinions. With such a method in hand, editors could use a symbol or other visual device to indicate whether public opinion on an issue could be relied upon to mean what it said, or whether it should be taken with a grain of salt because people's views on that particular issue had not yet jelled and the opinion was mushy. (The index we developed came to be known formally as the volatility index and informally as the "mushiness index" — the expression *Time*'s then editor-in-chief, Henry Grunwald, used to refer to it.)

To develop the mushiness index the project analysts examined a total of twenty-five issues, a mix of domestic and foreign. It found multiple sources of volatility: how deeply an individual is personally involved with an issue (on issues in which people are not personally involved, volatility is much greater than on issues that engage them); how knowledgeable people *feel* about an issue; whether or not respected authority figures have taken a firm stand on the issue; how firm the positions are of one's friends, neighbors and co-workers; whether or not the issue fits neatly into an already established belief system, and, most importantly, whether or not individuals have "worked through" their own ambivalences about the issue.

Further, it found that opinions on foreign policy were far more volatile than on domestic issues. After comparing current public attitudes on foreign policy with those of the pre-Vietnam period, the project analysts concluded that the country was undergoing a period of unusual volatility on these issues. In the immediate post–World War II period, the country stood solidly behind the policies of containment and the concepts of security that dominated the cold war era. The war in Southeast Asia destroyed that stability. The war undermined the credibility of the dominant foreign policy without replacing it with new policies the electorate could wholeheartedly support. A new stability and the beginnings of a new national consensus began to emerge at the close of the Reagan administration as the Gorbachev initiatives opened the way for new choices. But in the early 1980s when our project was underway, public volatility was at a peak.

The project met its primary objective. Researchers identified a number of "mushy" foreign policy issues, such as establishing diplomatic relations with Cuba, giving military support to anticommunist allies who were major violators of human rights, cutting back on U.S. military aid to Israel if it continued to oppose Palestinian rights, and so forth. These were issues about which more than 50 percent of the public held views that changed with the slightest provocation (e.g., changing the wording of a question, giving the individual a new tidbit of information, or presenting an argument for the opposite point of view). These issues contrasted with domestic issues, such as equal pay for equal work, about which majorities held firm, unshakable opinions. Analysts found that by asking people a few simple additional questions on any issue, such as how personally involved they were with it, how much they had thought about it and discussed it with others, and how likely they were to change their minds, that one could determine which opinions were volatile and which were firm. These questions were shaped into an index that was then checked for validity and reliability.

Pleased with the success of the project, our firm held a press conference to publicly announce the results and turn over all of its findings and raw materials to anyone who wanted them, especially other colleagues and competitors in the public opinion polling profession. The profession is small, people know each other, and the climate is collegial. Virtually all involved in the profession share the common goal of improving the accuracy and utility of public opinion polling.

The reader may be curious to find out what happened as a result of this considerable effort. The answer, sad to say, is that nothing happened. To my knowledge, the volatility index has never been used, not even by *Time* magazine, whose support and stated interest in improving the reporting of public opinion was made evident in many ways. No one at *Time* questioned the validity of the index. The reaction was generally: "What a good idea," unaccompanied by the slightest hint of enthusiasm or action. On a number of subsequent occasions, I urged *Time*'s editors to use the index, arguing that they could make a useful contribution, win positive publicity, and perhaps achieve a slight competitive edge in reporting the public's views with the worthwhile innovation that they had funded so generously. They agreed fully with these arguments; they also agreed that they should and would find occasion for deploying the index, but they never did.

This is one of the many bewildering experiences that led me to write this book. I wanted to address the puzzle of why there is so little interest in — and so much resistance to — the concept of public opinion quality. Presumably, encouraging the best and highest quality of public thought is fundamental to democratic self-governance — not only in the United States but in the many countries of the world that are struggling today to make democracy work.

On the specific question of why *Time* magazine and others never deployed the volatility index, the subculture of journalistic values provides part of the answer. Journalists will devote unlimited amounts of space to trumpeting how poorly informed the public is. But their eyes glaze over when it comes to efforts to grasp and report the subtlety and complexity of the public mind.[30] They will spend millions of dollars on polls to measure the horse-race aspects of presidential campaigns, but find it impossibly expensive to add a few thousand dollars to a poll to learn whether the numbers they report are trustworthy or almost meaningless. They will devote paragraphs and pages of text to explaining issues that interest them, but they are convinced that their readers are not interested in or willing to spend the extra few seconds to grasp the concept of volatility and how to read a simple symbol like an asterisk that might be used to distinguish firm from mushy opinion.

These oddities are not a reason for outrage or incredulity. No one is being irresponsible or obtuse. We are a culture of subcultures. The more successful the subculture is — and journalism is very successful — the more it will fall back on its own interests and values. This is the way the world works, and anyone who does not understand it is doomed to frustration and heartbreak.

3

MASS OPINION VS. PUBLIC JUDGMENT

T he threefold definition of quality (taking responsibility for the consequences of one's views, firmness, and consistency) has some drawbacks. It does not encompass some of the most appealing features
of public opinion — its bursts of generosity, its fierce sense of fairness and
passion for justice, its love of country, its religious faith, and its fidelity
to basic values. Indeed, it does not touch at all on the *content* of public
opinion. So heterogeneous and complex is the United States and so swiftly
changing are our social norms that any definition of quality tied to content might prove too elusive to be useful.

A more serious drawback is that this definition accepts the same
limiting premise as does public opinion polling, namely, that public opinion is the aggregate of millions of individual opinions. This assumption
has long troubled sociologists who see public opinion more closely inter-
woven with social institutions. These scholars are concerned that studying
individuals and then aggregating their separate views does not accurately
gauge social interaction and the influence that institutions exert on society.
In the 1960s, for example, the changing social values of college youth represented only a small fraction of the total number of eighteen to twenty-
five year olds. In quantitative polling terms, the famous "generation gap"
of that period was largely limited to upper middle-class college students
and their parents.[1] But its impact on the culture was far greater than that
of the larger noncollege youth population because the institutional setting
of the students — America's colleges and universities — was such an inherent part of the revolution in values.

Sociologist Kurt Back observes, "It may not be fortuitous that the
technique of public opinion research as we know it has developed in our
society: it is a very individually oriented method, adding up individual
opinions to reach societal characteristics in a way that corresponds to

our individualistic society. The method is a symptom of the values of the society."[2]

These are real limitations, but they are more than offset by the advantages of the definition, both practical and theoretical. It is a practical advantage, for example, to accept the steadily growing assumption that public opinion in America is largely what public opinion polls measure. This conception differs markedly from definitions of the past. V. O. Key defined public opinion as "those opinions held by private persons which governments find it prudent to heed."[3] The implication here is that the opinions of some people count more than others — for example, those who vote, write letters, contribute financially, and are organized into activist and lobbying groups. That not everyone exercises the same influence is a fact of political life all politicians take into account. But equating public opinion with influence on government obscures from view what the public in general believes, irrespective of variations in influence. Once we know how the public as a whole views an issue, it is easy enough to separate the views of any one subgroup, including the influential parts of the public. Key's definition also implies that certain types of opinions count more than others — opinions with a political cast rather than such social and cultural opinions as what people think about their jobs, their marriages, and their religious beliefs. Confining the huge domain of public opinion to issues of interest to government is much too parochial to serve as a general definition.

There are, of course, historic conceptions of public opinion unrelated to opinion polls. But the relevant point is well stated by social scientist Leo Bogart: "The world of public opinion in today's sense really began with the Gallup polls of the mid-1930s, and it is impossible for us to retreat to the meaning of public opinion as it was understood by Thomas Jefferson in the eighteenth century, by Alexis de Tocqueville and Lord Bryce in the nineteenth, — or even by Walter Lippman in 1922."[4]

As a technique of opinion research, public opinion polling is beset with practical difficulties, above all, the failure of so many polls to do justice to the richness and subtlety of public opinion. When public opinion polling is well done, however, it is a far more accurate measure of public opinion than letters to Congress, the intuitive hunches of politicians, the claims of lobbyists about what public opinion is, or the sidewalk interviews conducted by TV newspeople. In fact, even those politicians who have a good intuitive feel for public opinion use this feel to help them formulate questions for future surveys.

Unfortunately, the full capabilities of public opinion polling are mostly hidden from public view. The polls the public sees are those favored (and supported) by the media. Much polling, however, is done by businesses in market research and by political candidates and officials who hold public office. These polls are private. Some are just as trivial and misleading as the media-sponsored instant polls. But many of these private polls are conducted when the stakes are particularly high; for example, testing reaction to a new corporate or presidential initiative. You can be sure that these are not low-cost "quickie" polls built around single, simplistic questions. They are trend-tracking, probing, complex, thorough explorations of consumer or citizen thinking.

The reason for the difference is brutally clear: those who sponsor private polls have much to lose if the polls are wrong; sad to say, the media who sponsor opinion polls have little or no stake in the quality of the poll findings they report—with one exception. The exception is the horse-race poll predictions in the last few weeks of presidential campaigns. And on these polls the media lavish bottomless amounts of money and resources. But otherwise, the validity of a poll finding that makes a good headline is a subject that editors would just as soon not discuss. Because there are no easy ways to prove the validity of poll findings, the editors often opt to avoid the subject. When questions are raised, they mumble something about being sure to mention "the sampling error"—and go on quickly to the next subject.

It may be desirable to say something here about this badly misunderstood question of sampling error. Sad to say, what was once a valid, if partial, assurance of polling accuracy has now become an almost empty ritual. In the early days of opinion polling, the science of sampling—drawing cross sections of voters to represent the electorate or cross sections of consumers—was a chancy affair that struck most people as counterintuitive. "How can a thousand people stand for the whole nation? Why, I've never even been interviewed." For years, comments such as these were commonplace. Then, in the 1950s, the science of probability sampling was carried over from agronomy where it had been developed by a British mathematician (R. A. Fisher)[5] and applied to opinion survey research.

In probability sampling any one person's chances of being interviewed are statistically the same as any other's. The virtue of this method is that when correctly implemented it permits one to calculate the probable error *due to the sampling method.* Most people do not realize that this calculation does not necessarily improve the quality of the sample over that of the old-fashioned method of quota sampling for which the researcher fills quotas for various population groups in the same proportions as they are found in the U.S. census (e.g., 12 percent blacks, 3 percent Jews). A quota sample can be just as accurate and sometimes more accurate than a probability sample. It suffers, however, from the disadvantage that one does not know how accurate it is, whereas with a probability sample one does. That is what the familiar tag line, "This survey has a sampling error of +3 percent or −3 percent" means. (Incidentally, much reporting of sample error leaves out the fine print, namely, that the stipulated range of sampling error is only true most of the time (ninety or ninety-five times out of one hundred) but not all of the time.)

This latter point is a quibble. The more relevant point is that when polls are conducted by reputable professionals nowadays the question of the validity of poll findings has little to do with sloppy sampling. Using sound methods of probability sampling has become standard for the profession. Serious mistakes due to sampling are found only occasionally when polls are conducted unprofessionally.

The primary sources of poor-quality poll findings are those inventoried by Eleanor Singer quoted in chapter 1—dumb questions, obtuse questions, single questions that focus on limited aspects of complex issues, questions without proper context or framework, questions that elicit people's opinions on subjects to which they have not given a moment's thought, and so forth.[6] It is possible that editors who cite the sampling error to give credibility to their poll findings do not realize how misleading their polls may be. But perhaps they do not want to know because knowing would have consequences they do not wish to confront.

When the penalty for poor-quality poll findings is serious loss—of money, prestige, influence, or failed policy—the last thing sponsors worry about is sampling error. Their attention is focused where it should be: "How can we be sure we are measuring the public's real attitudes?" "If the public is ambivalent, what will it take to resolve their ambivalence?" "How can we be sure that the public's opinions will be predictive of their behavior—when they vote or buy the new product?" In later chapters, I will provide some examples of what it takes in private polls to ensure accurate answers to these kinds of questions.

ADVANTAGES

There are two great advantages to defining the quality of public opinion in terms of responsibility for consequences, firmness, and consistency. The first is that the definition leads directly to an objective method for ascertaining quality so that all can agree that a particular specimen of public opinion is either of poor quality or good quality, whether or not one happens to like or disapprove of it. The second and more far-reaching advantage is that the definition enables us to understand how and why public opinion has distinctive value and is not merely a second-rate reflection of expert opinion. Each form of opinion—expert and public—has its own excellences and its own failings. But public opinion is not, as is generally assumed, simply less well-informed expert opinion. It has its own integrity, and different standards of quality apply to it. It is only when we understand the differences between public and expert opinion that we have insight into the special nature of public opinion and the role it plays in democratic society.

To see the first advantage clearly—the value of an objective definition—it is useful to formalize a distinction implicit in the discussion thus far. In what follows, I will use the term *mass opinion* to refer to poor-quality public opinion as defined by the defects of inconsistency, volatility, and nonresponsibility. (People's failure to take the consequences of their views into account is mostly *non*responsible rather than *ir*responsible, which implies a willfulness that is usually absent. The term *nonresponsible* is meant to show that the public is not usually at fault for its failure to take responsibility. Most of the time the public is not given an opportunity to undertake the form of responsibility I am discussing.) I will use the term "public judgment" to refer to good-quality public opinion in the sense of opinion that is stable, consistent, and responsible.

To say that public judgment has been reached on an issue does not imply that people comprehend all of the relevant facts or that they agree with the views of elites. It does imply that people have struggled with the issue, thought about it in their own terms, and formed a judgment they are willing to stand by. It also means that if leaders understand the public's judgments, they have a stable context to work in—either to offer solutions that fit within the public's tolerances, or if they disagree with the public's judgment, to take their case forcefully to the public with full awareness that the public's view will not change easily.

Unfortunately, the umbrella term "public opinion" obscures the distinction between mass opinion and public judgment. It is almost as if we were to use the word *bread* to refer both to the baked loaf one buys from the bakery or supermarket and also to an unbaked or half-baked lump of dough. If consumers were to use the word *bread* for both objects, they would never know when they were buying the baked loaf or the half-baked one. Just so, when we refer to public opinion, we do not know whether we are referring to half-baked mass opinion or to fully developed public judgment.

Words reveal a great deal about a culture. The Eskimos have many words for *snow*. The French have a fabulous vocabulary for food. The fact that our culture has no generally accepted vocabulary to distinguish between raw mass opinion and mature public judgment reveals a blind spot in the way Americans think about this subject.

Unfortunately, there is at present no easy way to distinguish mass opinion from public judgment. I know a number of instances when foreign governments were misled by opinion polls reporting mass opinion that they took more literally than they should have. A number of opinion polls in the 1970s reported that a majority of Americans were opposed to the core of America's NATO commitment — to come to the military aid of our European allies in the event that they were attacked by Warsaw Pact forces. The opinion polls of that era showed that only for Canada did a majority endorse the commitment. (Even England and Mexico failed to receive majority support!)[7] Follow-up on these surveys showed that Americans had not really confronted the issue. Their poll responses merely signified their intense dislike of the idea of military engagement with the Soviet Union for any reason other than to protect American lives and freedom at home. The poll responses gave no reliable clue, one way or the other, to how Americans would actually respond if, for example, France or Germany were attacked. Public judgment on this issue simply did not exist.[8]

There is no mechanical way to predict what the nature of public judgment will be when people finally do confront so difficult a question. Later I will report on some experiments that predict what the public's judgment will be once people begin to move away from mass opinion. These experiments show that it is sometimes possible to accelerate the process of moving from mass opinion to public judgment.

It is not difficult to find out whether an opinion poll is measuring mass opinion or public judgment. Three simple tests can be applied, deriving from the threefold definition of quality. One test is to ask questions in opinion polls in several slightly different ways that do not change the essential meaning of the question. If people change their answers in response to slight shifts in question wording, this is a sure sign that their opinions are volatile. A second test is to plant questions that probe for inconsistencies and contradictions — another sign of mass opinion. A third test is to confront respondents with difficult trade-offs that directly challenge wishful thinking. This approach presents people with the consequences of their views and then measures their reactions.

Because each of the three tests examines a different facet of the same phenomenon, there is no need to keep them rigidly separate or to perform all three tests all of the time. The tests can be conducted separately or blended together. When they are blended together, the results reveal an accurate measure of quality.

4

KNOWLEDGE VS. OPINION

We come now to the most significant advantage of the concept of public judgment. By focusing on public judgment we can crawl out from under the quality-as-information trap. We can begin to shape a concept of public opinion in which quality is defined by evidence that the public has faced up to the consequences of its convictions.

This conception gives public opinion the *gravitās* that theorists of democracy have long recognized to be a prerequisite for genuine citizenship. We begin to understand why public opinion need not be taken seriously when it manifests itself in the form of mass opinion but must be taken quite seriously when it appears as public judgment, even when it is not as well informed as journalists and political philosophers would like. In short, we can begin to develop an alternative to the ideal of the attentive well-informed citizen, so favored by tradition.

For several reasons, developing this alternative model is not a simple task. If one is not careful, it is easy to fall into the opposite trap: the trap of anti-intellectualism and antirational sentimentality, which endows the folk wisdom of the public with special mystical qualities. Ultimately, this is the path of demagoguery, and it is worse than the distortions it seeks to correct. One should never appear to make being ill-informed a virtue. Information is always relevant. It always plays a role, even though it may be of secondary importance.

The role of information can be compared to the role that memory plays for a great pianist. It would be ludicrous to say, "She is a great pianist because she has an excellent memory." On the other hand, the loss of memory would be a disaster, as those acquainted with Alzheimer's disease know all too well. In calling attention to the noninformation components of quality, I am not denigrating information anymore than I would be denigrating memory by pointing to the qualities of creativity, technique, and feeling that make for greatness in a pianist.

One major difficulty in developing an alternative model of quality in public opinion is that being well informed *is* the proper defining characteristic of scientific and expert opinion. We should not apply the same criteria to expert opinion as to public opinion. Generally, for expert opinion we do not have to worry about the same things as for public opinion. Well-educated and trained experts are expected to be well informed; they are rarely self-contradictory or fickle in their views, and the kinds of questions on which we consult experts—questions of fact—do not enmesh them as readily in the value conflicts that beset public opinion. Of course, experts, being human, cannot always set aside their personal feelings; but mainly we judge them on their records on being correct in their special fields of expertise.

At first glance, differentiating public opinion from expert opinion may seem unnecessary. The general view is "Everyone knows the difference between experts and the public. We do not expect the public to be experts, just reasonably informed." But familiarity with the way public opinion is judged makes it plain that a clear-cut distinction between expert opinion and public opinion is sorely needed.

Suppose an engineering expert on bridges is asked whether a particular bridge is safe for heavy traffic. The engineer's opinion, especially after studying the bridge and conducting tests on it, carries more weight than that of the citizens who live in the community. When it comes to questions of bridge safety, we consult the expert, not public opinion.

Here, quality of opinion is clearly defined in terms of knowledge and information. The bridge expert has far more knowledge about bridges than the public. But engineering knowledge may not be sufficient for the expert to know with certainty that the bridge will be safe in the future. Asked the question, "Can this bridge safely carry an anticipated 20 percent increased traffic load over the next five years?" the engineer might reasonably respond, "I do not know the answer to that question." Whereupon the question will almost surely be asked, "Well, can you give us your opinion? Is it your opinion that the bridge will safely carry the increased traffic?" Usually, the expert will then offer an opinion. ("In my opinion, this bridge is not safe. I wouldn't let my family cross it in rush hour conditions.")

In this hypothetical exchange, the expert holds firmly held convictions, but correctly and responsibly refuses to characterize them as knowledge. Part of the expert's expertise is the ability to distinguish personal opinions from knowledge. Conventional standards of what constitutes quality apply quite well to this situation. The trouble comes when we apply this same standard of quality to public opinion, which we always do for the simple reason that we have no other.

When we apply this inappropriate standard, public opinion is inevitably seen in a bad light. It is not difficult to find examples. Here are two from a casual examination of one week of the *New York Times*. One is a report on a Roper poll that queried both the general public and scientific experts in the Environmental Protection Agency (EPA) on the relative dangers of threats to the environment. The greatest threats, as perceived by the public, are "hazardous waste sites" (62 percent) and "workers exposed to toxic chemicals" (60 percent). At that time, the public ranked the "greenhouse effect" (global warming) twenty-third in seriousness. In contrast, the EPA experts ranked the greenhouse effect among its top concerns and hazardous waste sites barely in the top half of its list as a cancer risk and "relatively low" as a risk for other health problems or negative ecological effects.[1]

A high official of the EPA offered his explanation for the differences between the public and the expert rankings. "The most obvious reason is that the general public simply does not have all the information that was available to [the EPA] task force of experts."[2] Later in the interview he added, "People often overestimate the frequency and seriousness of dramatic, sensational, dreaded, well-publicized causes of death," and he went on to comment that if a scapegoat who caused the problem could be identified (for example, a polluting company) the public was especially quick to express their indignation.[3] On these environmental threats public opinion is differentiated from expert opinion both on the availability of information and on the distortions to which the uninformed public is prone.

Several days later, the *New York Times* reported another poll that measured the public's knowledge of politics and civic affairs, comparing it with public opinion measured in similar polls forty years ago. The authors, two professors of political science, expressed their disappointment that the poll's results showed the public to be "only marginally better informed today than forty years ago."[4] For example, they found slightly less than half of the public (46 percent) knew that the first ten amendments to the Constitution are called the Bill of Rights (compared with only one-third [33 percent] who knew this fact in 1954) and that three out of four (75 percent) could correctly name Dan Quayle as vice–president compared with 69 percent who named Alben W. Barkley in 1952. As one of them commented, "It is hard to imagine, if this is the level of information citizens bring to politics, that they have enough context to make informed political decisions."[5]

Other political scientists showed less concern. When asked for his reaction, Professor W. Russell Neuman of MIT commented on his reason for being unalarmed: "What is important is that there are perhaps 5 percent (of the public) who are activists and news junkies who do pay close attention. If they see that something is seriously wrong in the country, they sound the alarm and then ordinary people start paying attention."[6] These two polls are a reasonably good representation of the conventional wisdom held by certain elites: the public is poorly informed; this lack of information is a critical handicap in reaching sound opinions; fortunately, a small part of the general public (the so-called attentive public) make it their business to be well informed, and they resemble us, the experts and elites.

THE DICTIONARY DEFINITION

Why, we might ask, is public opinion judged by standards appropriate to expert opinion rather than by its own special standards? The most obvious answer relates to the meaning of opinion in our culture. Opinion is generally defined in opposition to knowledge. We fall back on opinion when knowledge is lacking.

Using opinion as a substitute for knowledge is a common practice, and this practice gives the word *opinion* its principal meaning. The first meaning of opinion in *Webster's International Dictionary* is a belief that is "less strong than positive knowledge . . . a belief . . . based only on opinion." In this sense of opinion, the more knowledge and information the person holding the opinion has, the better that opinion is deemed to be — and rightly so.

Knowledge in the modern era has come to have a special, almost technical meaning. Knowledge is linked to validation. One *knows* that the earth is round rather than flat because this discovery has been scientifically validated: it has been proven through well-accepted empirical methods. Validated knowledge does not have to be scientific. We validate a small part of our stock of knowledge every day. Suppose you are asked, "Are you wearing your black shoes or your brown ones?" You remember putting on your black shoes, but the chances are that you will glance down before answering. Having done so, you now "know" you are wearing your black shoes because you have validated that knowledge with methods suitable for the occasion. In daily life — whether that of the expert on bridges or the person wearing black shoes — the distinction between knowledge and opinion is largely a matter of validation. The validation is carried out by empirical methods, more or less casual or scientific depending on the occasion.

In our complex society, the pool of validated knowledge is tiny compared to our need to know. We could not survive without depending on opinion — based on information — as a substitute for validated knowledge. A large proportion of our national resources are devoted to educating and training specialists on whose opinions we depend because of the excellence of their information and their skill in interpreting it. The opinions of the general public never count as much as those of the experts when it is expert-type opinion that is needed.

The reason our society judges all opinion by the standards appropriate to expert opinion is that both the dictionary definition and custom support the meaning of opinion as a substitute for knowledge. Therefore, the closer one comes to meeting the standards of knowledge, the better the quality of the opinion is deemed to be. In practice, therefore, expert opinion and public opinion are judged by a single criterion.

But why does this happen? Why does this custom persist? Why does it not change to accommodate the more appropriate meanings of opinion when applied to the public? We know that the meaning of knowledge has changed drastically over the centuries. Does this change have implications for the meaning of opinion? Should its meaning also change? Has it, in fact, changed in various applications and for certain purposes?

For answers to these questions we must take a brief backward glance at the history of the meaning of opinion and knowledge — a fragment of our tradition that I find fascinating and revealing.

THE TRADITION

The meaning of opinion as a substitute for knowledge has an ancient heritage reaching all the way back to pre-Socratic Greek civilization. The familiar distinction between knowledge (*epistime*) and opinion (*doxa*) goes back to Parmenides (b. ca. 515 B.C.).[7] In his only surviving work, Parmenides describes his goddess telling him of two paths, the path of knowledge and the path of opinion: "Both the unshaken heart of well-rounded truth and the opinions of mortals which lack true belief."[8] Parmenides warns us to stay away from the path of opinion, described as that path "along which mortals wander ignorantly, with divided minds and scattered thought, so befuddled and helpless as to resemble the deaf and blind. There are crowds of them without discernment."[10]

The path of knowledge ("the unshaken heart of well-rounded truth") is exalted, whereas the path of opinion is that along which the crowd wanders ignorantly, befuddled, helpless, deaf and dumb, without discernment.

Plato, following Parmenides, identified knowledge with that which does not change. For Plato, who systematized the concept of knowledge, the person who has knowledge uses mind and reason to gain insight into the unchanging nature of being. Knowledge equals being/reason/mind/ eternity. Opinion, on the other hand, emanates not from mind and reason but from the senses and is concerned with the transient world of change and becoming. Opinion equals becoming/senses/body/change. Thus was born the classical tradition with its familiar dichotomies of mind versus body, reason versus sense experience, being versus becoming, and knowledge versus opinion. This tradition has endured for more than two millennia with the knowledge-opinion dichotomy at the very core of it.[10]

The knowledge-opinion split has had an enduring impact on Western culture. The path of knowledge is deemed to be for the few, the path of opinion for the many. The election of paths is fateful because it is both moral and esthetic: the path of knowledge is virtuous and beautiful, the path of opinion lacks moral virtues and is, to boot, ugly.

The ancient Greeks believed mostly in simple dichotomies (one-many, male-female, mind-body). Aristotle began to introduce some finer distinctions. By the Middle Ages, elaborate hierarchies expressing a "great chain of being" replaced the crude either-or dichotomies of the ancients with subtle gradations.

Over the centuries, the idea of a hierarchy with the higher forms of knowledge on top and the lower forms of opinion on the bottom has persisted, even when our understanding of what knowledge is changed from philosophic insight into the eternal nature of truth and beauty to the probabilistic and testable hypotheses of modern science. In the present hierarchy, theoretical physics sits at or close to the top because it combines both the virtues of modern science (knowledge firmly grounded on experimental validations) and the ancient Greek ideal of explanation based on a few unchanging theoretical principles. The other experimental sciences (e.g., chemistry) come next, followed by the sciences based on observation, description, and taxonomy (e.g., botany). The disciplines based on scholarship and historical investigation find themselves somewhere in the middle of the hierarchy. They are followed by the applied sciences and the professions. The status of the poor social sciences is a matter of controversy: for admirers, they snuggle close to the more senior natural sciences; for detractors, they belong almost at the bottom of the hierarchy. The lowest position in the hierarchy is that of public opinion. The opinions of the public are twice blighted: they are merely opinion, not knowledge, and they are held by the plebeian many, not the select few.

The hierarchy is, of course, informal, unofficial. There is no "official" hierarchy for knowledge and opinion, any more than there is for social status. As much as we dislike the idea of people who think they are better than we are, we are all conscious of a social pecking order with the very rich, famous TV personalities, leading sports figures, and political celebrities at the top followed by the rest of us in various gradations all the way down to the bottom. Social hierarchy plays an important role in our culture, and so do the various intellectual/professional hierarchies. There is, for example, a rigid status hierarchy among colleges and universities, with the elite research universities on top and the myriad community colleges on the bottom.

All such hierarchies express powerful status needs. Cultures vary greatly in their choices of symbols of status, but all cultures have them. In the cultures of the West, wealth, power, knowledge, and moral authority are all status symbols, sometimes opposing one another in competing hierarchies, sometimes merging. The most potent hierarchies are formed when two or more such symbols combine. Wealth and power are one familiar combination (e.g., the Kennedy family, the Rockefeller family). Another potent combination is knowledge and moral virtue.

As long as opinion and knowledge are pitted against each other, either as a dichotomy or as occupying the bottom and top positions in a hierarchy, opinion will be deemed inferior to knowledge. Its inferiority is greatly enforced when the knowledge-opinion hierarchy is fused with moral authority. Endowing knowledge with moral virtue was characteristic not only of ancient Greek philosophy but also of Hebraic tradition. It is true that the Bible shows the dark side of knowledge (eating the apple led not to virtuous deeds but their opposite), but the long tradition of Hebrew culture, to this day, honors knowledge, reserves its highest status for the most knowledgeable, and assumes that the wisest and most virtuous rabbis are those who possess the greatest knowledge.

Ancient Greek and Hebrew tradition have become remote influences on American history and contemporary culture — not so that astonishing intellectual-political movement of the eighteenth century known as the Enlightenment. The ideas of the Enlightenment originated in the Old World, but they came to fruition in America. This is the central thesis of historian Henry Steele Commager's wonderful book, *The Empire of Reason.*

"The thesis of this book can be stated quite simply: The Old World imagined, invented and formulated the Enlightenment, the New World . . . realized it and fulfilled it. . . . It was Americans who not only embraced the body of Enlightenment principles, but wrote them into law, crystallized them into institutions, and put them to work. That, as much as the winning of independence and the creation of the nation, *was* the American Revolution."[11]

The central theme of the Enlightenment was faith in reason, and, in Commager's phrase, "addiction to science" as the new form of reason codified into knowledge. It was through scientific knowledge that progress, equality, overcoming poverty, and realizing a common humanity would be realized. The Enlightenment was, Commager writes, "the age of science. . . . Everywhere the scientists were philosophers and most of the philosophers were scientists."[12] Certainly, the two Americans who best personified the Enlightenment mentality, Thomas Jefferson and Benjamin Franklin, were both firm believers in scientific knowledge as the essence of rationality. In his old age, looking back at his lifelong beliefs, Jefferson wrote, "We believed that men, habituated to thinking for themselves, and to follow their reason as guide, would be more easily and safely governed than with minds nourished in error and vitiated and debased . . . by ignorance."[13]

As did most of the other thinkers of the Enlightenment, Jefferson fused reason with virtue and knowledge as a simple whole opposed to error and ignorance. In the eighteenth century, the enthusiasts of the Enlightenment exalted the place of scientific knowledge as the royal road to achieving a utopia on earth. Our contemporary experience of scientific knowledge, in the era of the nuclear arms race and the global threat to the environment, may lead us to respect the skepticism of the Bible more than the unqualified embrace of knowledge so characteristic of the founding fathers. In the hierarchy of the Enlightenment era, as in ancient Greece, knowledge and moral authority are once again merged into an indivisible whole contrasted with ignorance, credulity, and superstition: the world of opinion.

What has changed from the Greek and Hebraic origins of the tradition is the concept of knowledge. For the Greeks, knowledge was philosophical contemplation of eternal truths, for the Hebrews it was Talmudic learning, and for the Enlightenment thinkers it was scientific knowledge almost as we would define it today.

In historical writings, the opposition of scientific knowledge to ignorance and opinion (associated with the uneducated masses) has stimulated a curious set of animal images for public opinion. From the earliest days of our democracy, public opinion has been characterized as a "great beast." In the aftermath of the French Revolution, the German poet Schiller compared the uncontrolled masses liberated by the Revolution to wild beasts, lions and tigers, hyenas and panthers.[14] Observing the contemporary political scene in America, former *Washington Post* editor Barry Sussman writes that politicians regard public opinion as "the great gorilla in the political jungle, a beast that must be kept calm."[15]

It would be a mistake to blame the Enlightenment for debasing the reputation of public opinion. The string of wild animal metaphors and the images of uncontrollable mobs originated in the terror that followed the French Revolution. I wish simply to point out that denigration of public opinion is implicit whenever one defines opinion in opposition to knowledge and then identifies knowledge as the possession of the select few and as imbued with moral authority.

Ironically, however, the Enlightenment also gave rise to the exaltation of public opinion. Indeed, the very term "public opinion" came into widespread use in the early years of the eighteenth century.[16] To the Enlightenment thinkers of the Old World, the enemy was entrenched inherited privilege embodied in the church and in most branches of European royalty in collusion with each other. To oppose these sources of superstition, ignorance, and arrogance, the eighteenth-century *philosophes* developed the doctrine of popular sovereignty. The ultimate authority was seen to reside in the people and, therefore, in public opinion. In America, the public was initially defined as property-owning white males, with the small independent farmer personifying the ideal public for Thomas Jefferson. The European *philosophes* held a narrower view of the public, focusing on the rising bourgeois men of affairs, the professions, and the aristocratic landowners who opposed the monarchy. To endow these emerging sources of power with moral authority, the wisdom of the people was romanticized and elevated to new heights. The voice of the people was discovered to have newly won mystical virtues: The phrase *Vox populi vox Dei* took on new significance.

Thus, the eighteenth century bequeaths to our own a contradictory heritage. In some contexts public opinion is equated with ignorance, with the uncontrolled mass, with wild beasts. In other contexts, public opinion is deemed almost sacred, the voice of God. In present-day America, both sides of the contradiction are alive and well. The public is feared as a beast to be managed and controlled with care. The public is also respected as the voice of the sovereign voter who always has the last word, the consumer who is always right (even when wrong), the responsible jobholder, and the respected citizen.

EXPERT OPINION VS. PUBLIC OPINION

The confusions created by these contradictions persist to the present. Public opinion is regarded with profound ambivalence. Among the general public, respect for public opinion is high. The public holds itself and its powers and privileges in great esteem. Healthy respect for public opinion is also found in those members of the business community who cater to consumers and among members of those branches of the legal profession with everyday experience with the public as jurors. In subcultures that lack daily contact with the public, public opinion often seems remote, mysterious, and abstract. For university professors, laboratory scientists, the foreign policy community, the high civil service, and the upper reaches of the press, public opinion appears fickle, impulsive, disorganized, ill-informed, and unreliable. These elites may be sincerely devoted to the principles of democracy, but their outlook is, simply stated, elitist. They think they know better than the public because they are well educated and articulate. They have superior knowledge, and because they do, they assume in the great classic tradition that they are, therefore, endowed with superior moral virtue.

I will return to this theme in part 3 because it bears on the solution to the mystery I am exploring in this book. I mention it here because it is important to realize that the quality-as-information model of judging opinion has deep historic roots and is endowed with emotion-laden meanings that make clarification more than a matter of mere semantics.

There *is* a logical way to resolve the conflicting traditions surrounding the status and quality of public opinion. Implicit in the discussion to this point is a fundamental distinction between public opinion and expert opinion. Both are "opinion" in the negative sense that they are not validated knowledge — in the same sense that a book on ancient Greek philosophy and contemporary sports bloopers are both categorized as nonfiction. But they differ radically from one another in their positive relation to validated knowledge. Expert opinion relates to knowledge in the conventional dictionary sense: it is a substitute for it. We fall back on expert opinion when validated knowledge is lacking. In principle, expert opinion should be capable of being validated. It should take the form of an empirical proposition. If it does not, it is not "expert opinion." The expert on bridge safety could have said, "We can test the safety of the bridge by letting the traffic build and seeing whether it collapses or not. Then we will know." Opinions are frequently elicited from experts precisely to avoid the undesirable consequences of this type of pragmatic validation.

What we want above all from expert opinion is that it be correct. The best criterion for judging the quality of expert opinion is whether it proves to be right or wrong. ("In my opinion the Democrats will continue to choose losing presidential candidates.") It will take time to validate this opinion, but, in principle, it is capable of being proven or disproven.

Because being correct is so central to the experts' mission, experts generally accept the same constraints that scientists accept in their pursuit of knowledge. Modern knowledge is empirically based. Information is its lifeblood. As we will discuss later, there are other modes of knowing than the scientific. But so great is the prestige of science that knowledge in our day has come to be virtually synonymous with scientific knowledge. In addition, and this is more controversial, scientific or expert knowledge presents itself as value-free. Experts accept the ethos of giving an "objective opinion" whether or not they personally approve of it. If experts are smokers and also research scientists studying the impact of smoking on heart disease and lung cancer, and if they are paid by a tobacco company, their self-respect as experts requires them to give an objective opinion that implicates smoking, even though it may offend their employers, ruin their careers at the tobacco company, and be dissonant with their own personal habits and values. Others may be skeptical about the experts' ability to retain objectivity under such strong cross pressures. But if they let personal bias or career concerns color their opinions, they will have violated their vocations as experts and scientists.

When we contrast public opinion with expert opinion, we see that it has a different relationship to knowledge. Unlike expert opinion, most instances of public opinion cannot be scientifically validated, even in principle, because they do not take the form of empirical propositions. Consider the typical form that expert opinion takes: "It is my opinion that smoking can cause heart disease." "It is my opinion that this bridge cannot safely absorb a 20 percent increase in traffic." "It is my opinion that this man was not legally sane on the night he shot his wife." These are empirical propositions. Most instances of public opinion do not assume this form. Their most typical form is that of a value judgment. Instead of deliberately avoiding values, they focus directly on them: "In my opinion flag burners should be put in jail, whatever the Supreme Court says." "In my opinion, doctors with AIDS should not practice medicine." Expressions of values such as these are like matters of taste: there are canons of good taste and bad taste. So, too, there are good values and bad values. But whatever the method of differentiating them may be, it is not the same as the method of validation that applies to empirical knowledge and expert opinion.

In table 4.1 I contrast the major differences between expert and public opinion.

TABLE 4.1

EXPERT OPINION VS. PUBLIC OPINION

ITEM	EXPERT OPINION	PUBLIC OPINION
Usual form	Empirical proposition	Value judgment
Relation to validation	Can be validated in principle	Cannot (in the usual sense)
Personal preferences	Set aside	Major focus
Chief criterion of quality	Validity	Acceptance of responsibility for one's views

Part Two

THE THREE STAGES OF PUBLIC OPINION

5

THE BUMPY ROAD FROM MASS
OPINION TO PUBLIC JUDGMENT

One must be careful not to denigrate being well informed as a measure of quality in public opinion. This is the dominant norm, and it prevails wherever public opinion is taken into account— in public policy circles, in academic disciplines that study public opinion, and especially among journalists. What some journalists mean by being well informed is, however, too narrow: it is judging people as if they were memory chips. Fortunately, many journalists (and others who hold this point of view) are too sophisticated to reduce being well informed to a sandpile of data. They have a broader concept that includes coherence of outlook and contextual understanding as well as information about the raw "facts." But broad or narrow, concepts of quality-as-well-informed all share one common characteristic that differentiates them from the model of quality-as-public-judgment developed in this book. They all stress the cognitive, information-absorbing side of public opinion. In contrast, the public judgment model stresses the emotive, valuing, ethical side, which includes the cognitive base but moves beyond it.

In the dominant model, poor quality means that essential information is lacking. In the public judgment model, poor quality (mass opinion) means being caught in unresolved cross pressures. The difference is striking. Consider a simple example of how, from the point of view of the two models, one might judge poor quality opinion in two people opposed to the nuclear arms race.

Dominant Model. "You can't take his opinion seriously because he is poorly informed. He doesn't know that you get more bang-for-the-buck with nuclear weapons than with conventional ones. He thinks, erroneously, that the country can save money on the defense budget by substituting

conventional forces for nuclear arms. And he is under the illusion that
nuclear weapons accounts for the lion's share of the defense budget."

Public Judgment Model. "You can't take his opinion seriously because
he hasn't resolved where he truly stands. He is opposed to the nuclear arms
race because he fears for the safety of his grandchildren in a nuclearized
world, and he wants to see the money now spent on nuclear weapons devoted to some more constructive purpose like protecting the environment.
But at the same time, he is an ardent patriot, and he buys into the argument that loyalty to the administration supports its program of nuclear
defense."

In this example, the opinion holder is poorly informed and is caught
waffling between two competing sets of values. But note how different the
two descriptions are, and more importantly, the implied remedy for poor
quality. In the first instance, the remedy is to impart correct information
about the relative costs of conventional compared with nuclear weapons
and to gather accurate statistics about the proportion of the defense budget devoted to nuclear defense. In the second instance, the remedy is to
stimulate resolution of competing priorities and values (loyalty to the administration compared with holding opposing convictions).

The information-driven model leads to a concept of public education as a one-way process: the expert speaks; the citizen listens. Questions
may arise about the best technique for grabbing the public's attention and
conveying the relevant information. But conceptually, the model is simple
and unidirectional: the expert's role is to impart information to the public
skillfully and effectively; the citizen's role is to absorb the information and
form an opinion based on it.

So deeply embedded in our culture is this model that it blocks from
view the process of shifting from mass opinion to public judgment. In the
dominant model, the remedy for poor quality is to communicate more
information. What is the remedy for overcoming mass opinion? How do
you get from it to public judgment? Admittedly, the path is difficult—a
bumpy road full of potholes and roadblocks and detours. The territory
is unexplored because it has been so completely hidden by the more familiar quality-as-well-informed model. But if one steps back to gain perspective, the road from mass opinion to public judgment, as it might be seen
on a map, is surprisingly straight and orderly.

FOCUS OF PART 2

There are three stages in moving from mass opinion to public judgment.
The description of these three stages, the obstacles that beset each, and

some proven methods for overcoming them is the major focus of part 2. Only when the full picture of the three stages is clearly set forth can one appreciate how profound the difference is between this concept and the quality-as-well-informed model.

The purpose of bringing the differences between the two models to light is both practical and theoretical. The practical purpose is to develop a methodology for enhancing quality public opinion. American society possesses a wide range of institutions for conveying information and making citizens better informed. So powerful are these that the danger of information overload is greater than the danger of information malnourishment.

And yet, ironically, there is want in the midst of plenty. As we have seen, Americans are not materially "better informed" than they were forty years ago when people were less well educated and not nearly as bombarded with information. This opinion poll finding suggests that something is dreadfully wrong — either in the definition of what it means to be well informed, or with how information is organized and conveyed to citizens, or, as I am proposing, with the very concept of quality public opinion. If we focus on the new model of quality-as-public-judgment, we will discover new technologies for overcoming mass opinion and new ways to navigate the tortuous path to public judgment.

In the several decades I have been studying the differences between mass opinion and public judgment, it has gradually dawned on me that apart from its practical uses, there is an important theoretical objective to be gained. The "laws of motion" in moving from mass opinion to public judgment are so different from those involved in moving from being poorly informed to being well informed that a whole new light can be shed on the nature of public opinion and particularly on how Americans gradually force themselves to resolve their conflicting values to form a mature body of responsible public judgment. Therefore, a better theoretical understanding of how public opinion deepens in quality and judgment contributes to our understanding of what makes our democracy work.

Before plunging ahead on the journey from mass opinion to public judgment, it would be good to say a word about the *desirability* of the practical objective. There will be some readers who think: "If American attitudes toward capital punishment and abortion and sex education in the schools are examples of public judgment, then the last thing our society needs is new techniques for generating it more quickly and efficiently. These are divisive, emotion-laden issues on which large parts of the public hold wrong-headed views. If my only alternative is mass opinion, then I'll take that. If people are inconsistent and hold mushy points of view, they are easily persuaded to shift one way or the other, leaving room for leadership to do what is right without 'consulting' the public."

This is not a trivial argument. Moreover, in one form or another it is held by many of our elites. But it is untenable when examined closely. First of all, not all instances of public judgment are divisive and controversial. Most, in fact, help the country to move toward the kind of consensus on which successful political action must be based. Examples include: public support for the foreign policy of the postwar period, with its willingness to offer reconciliation to former enemies and to devote considerable resources via the Marshall Plan to reconstructing the economies of our allies. It includes also the post-Sputnik consensus that America had to improve its technical and math education in the schools to meet the Soviet challenge in space, and the post-Afghanistan consensus supporting both Presidents Carter and Reagan in their policies of increasing the U.S. defense budget. The country is now in the throes of forming a national consensus on the importance of doing more to protect the environment (see chap. 6). It will take several additional years before public judgment on this issue has jelled, but the direction is clear.

In our system of representative democracy, settling for mass opinion instead of public judgment is not viable. If the United States were not so active a democracy, perhaps this alternative might work. In countries like Japan or Germany, where there are strong traditions of authority, the point of view of elites carries much more weight than does public opinion. In fact, elites often shape public opinion. In the United States, however, elites still exert much less influence than in these other countries despite the creeping expertism that we have already noted. Sooner or later public opinion makes itself felt, sometimes directly as in the public pressure that undermined the policy of support for the Contras in Nicaragua in the Reagan administration and persuaded President Reagan to withdraw the marines from Lebanon after a number of marines had been killed by a terrorist bomb.[1]

More often, public opinion makes itself felt indirectly through watershed elections. The election of 1980 is a good example. The country turned to the right-wing populist Ronald Reagan out of disillusionment with the policies of liberalism that had characterized both political parties in earlier years (including the Nixon and Ford administrations). The public forced the change in the country's direction.

If Americans had a choice, if, that is, American culture and its institutions supported governance by elites with the public staying out of the political process except on rare occasions (as in present-day Japan), then perhaps an apathetic, malleable public mired in mass opinion might be a thinkable option. But given the system as it now exists, there is no way to keep the public out. If the public is bound to have the ultimate last word—and it is—it is far better that it be based on responsible public judgment, however prickly, than on mass opinion, however malleable. (I will return to this theme at the end of the book.)

FROM MASS OPINION TO PUBLIC JUDGMENT

In the quality-as-public-judgment model, there are three stages of evolution. The first is "consciousness raising." The second is "working through." The third is "resolution."

Stage 1. Consciousness raising is the stage in which the public learns about an issue and becomes aware of its existence and meaning. I call it consciousness raising because this term, borrowed from the women's movement, is more accurate than "creating greater awareness." Consciousness raising means much more than mere awareness. One can be aware of an issue without feeling that it is important or that anything needs to be done about it. When, however, we speak about consciousness raising on the environment, for example, the intention is clear. When one's consciousness is raised, not only does awareness grow but so does concern and readiness for action.

When, in chapter 6, we describe the consciousness-raising stage in greater detail, there is no need to elaborate the subject endlessly. Consciousness raising is a process that our society understands well and that our institutions perform well. More surprising, perhaps, are the number and variety of obstacles that prevent consciousness raising from proceeding smoothly. These obstacles are worth citing and illustrating.

There are several clear-cut features of the consciousness-raising stage. It is largely media driven. Events are a major factor in expediting the process (e.g., the accidents at Three Mile Island and Chernobyl raised people's consciousness about the safety problems of nuclear power very quickly). Sometimes consciousness raising proceeds with agonizing slowness, but, unlike the other two stages, it is often accomplished with great speed and in "real time" (i.e., in the time it takes to convey the relevant information). And the public whose consciousness is raised can be in a passive and receptive frame of mind without needing to exert any special effort.

In recent years we have seen large-scale consciousness raising on a variety of issues including:

- the dangers of AIDS
- the difficulties that beset primary and secondary education
- the threat to U.S. competitiveness from Japan

- the end of the cold war with the Soviet Union
- the importance of nutrition and physical fitness
- the dangers of drug addiction
- the mounting threats to the environment
- the dangers of being dependent on the Middle East for our oil supplies.

In chapter 6 I describe this first stage of the public judgment process.

Stage 2. For the second stage, I borrow a term from psychology, "working through." When the consciousness-raising stage has been completed, the individual must confront the need for change. The change may be slight or it may be very great. A woman who has undergone consciousness raising in her marriage may be faced with the prospect of separation or divorce or confrontation with her husband. A man whose consciousness has been raised about the dangers of cholesterol may be faced with the need to make drastic changes in his diet. Many changes are less demanding and traumatic. Having heard about the dangers of ozone depletion from aerosol dispensers, a consumer may be willing to switch to a different type of dispenser for insect repellent or shaving cream even though it may be less efficient. Often it is not people's overt behavior that must change, but their attitudes: the man caught in the cross pressures of loyalty to his president and the desire to switch national priorities is obliged to face up to his ambivalence and stop waffling — to come down on one side of the issue or the other.

As observers of human psychology know well, all change is difficult. When people are caught in cross pressures, before they can resolve them it is necessary to struggle with the conflicts and ambivalences and defenses they arouse. Change requires hard work. Rarely does the course of change proceed smoothly. Rather, it is full of backsliding and procrastination and avoidance. "Two steps forward and one step back" is the apt common description for the process. Psychologists call it "working through," especially when one is reconciling oneself to a painful loss.

To an extraordinary degree, the requirements of the working through stage differ from those of consciousness raising. When working through, people must abandon the passive-receptive mode that works well enough for consciousness raising. They must be actively engaged and involved. Rarely is working through completed quickly. Typically, it takes an irreducible period of time — much longer than the time needed to convey and absorb new information. The length of time depends on the emotional significance of the change to the individual.

Though events can sometimes affect the working-through process, they are not critical to it: working through is a largely internal process that individuals have to work at and ultimately achieve for themselves. Nor is working through media driven or information dependent as is consciousness raising. Generally, people engaged in working through may have all the information they need long before they are willing to confront the cross pressures that ensnare them. And, finally, unlike the consciousness-raising stage, our society is not well equipped with the institutions or knowledge it needs to expedite working through. Our culture does not understand it very well and by and large does not do a good job with it. In brief, then, there is a wrenching discontinuity between consciousness raising and working through that is a major source of difficulty in any effort to improve the quality of public opinion.

Stage 3. Stage 3 is resolution, the result of successful consciousness raising and working through. In later chapters the reader will be supplied with an abundance of examples of issues that travelled all the way from mass opinion to resolution and hence to public judgment. (To say that public judgment has been achieved is just another way of stating that the public has completed its journey through the three stages.)

The most important point to make about stage 3 is that resolution is multifaceted. On any issue, to complete working through successfully, the public must resolve where it stands cognitively, emotionally, and morally. These facets of resolution are interrelated, but they each require hard work in their own right and are surprisingly independent of one another.

Cognitive resolution requires that people clarify fuzzy thinking, reconcile inconsistencies, break down the walls of the artificial compartmentalizing that keeps them from recognizing related aspects of the same issue, take relevant facts and new realities into account, and grasp the consequences of various choices with which they are presented.

Emotional resolution means that people have to confront their own ambivalent feelings, accommodate themselves to unwelcome realities, and overcome their urge to procrastinate and to avoid the issue. Of all the obstacles to resolution, none is more difficult to overcome than the need to reconcile deeply felt conflicting values.

In arriving at moral resolution, people's first impulse is to put themselves and their own needs and desires ahead of their ethical commitments. But once they have time to reflect on their choices, the ethical dimension comes into play and people struggle to do the right thing. Issues such as AIDS and homelessness and health care for those who cannot afford insurance cannot be resolved until the ethical dimension has been considered and dealt with, one way or the other.

Each one of these dimensions is beset with obstacles.

6

CONSCIOUSNESS RAISING

The broad outlines of consciousness raising, American-style, are familiar. Daily, we are bombarded with advertising messages, public relations stories, advocacy group claims, and news reports of events local and global, trivial and momentous. We ignore most of them and glance casually at those that manage to catch our interest. To avoid information overload, we screen out all but the tiniest fraction of the messages beamed at us.

But some events are so dramatic or important to our lives that they penetrate the screen, lodging themselves in our consciousness: earthquakes, acts of terrorism and hostage taking, airplane crashes that take hundreds of lives, major oil spills, nuclear accidents, new medical breakthroughs, and scandals in high places. The symbols are familiar: Three Mile Island, Chernobyl, the 1989 San Francisco quake, the Exxon Valdez, Saddam Hussein's invasion of Kuwait—it is easy to recall these and other images from the recent past that raised the nation's consciousness.

Sometimes the agency of consciousness raising is not an event, but a book or article such as Betty Friedan's *Feminine Mystique* that introduced the very concept of "consciousness raising," or Rachel Carson's *Silent Spring* that did so much to make the nation aware of the threats to the environment, or Ralph Nader's *Unsafe at Any Speed* that launched the consumer movement. Most consciousness raising does not depend on seminal books or dramatic events. Consciousness raising is the bread-and-butter business of the press, which it carries out with great vigor and proficiency day after day, year after year. Whether it is a series of articles or TV shows on rising health-care costs, or the cancer-threatening effects of Alar on apples, or the abuses of the savings and loan industry, or influence peddling in Congress, the media are on the job. They recognize consciousness raising as an important part of their function, and treat it accordingly.

66

Consciousness raising does not always advance expeditiously. Later, we will examine instances where the idiosyncrasies of the press and the experts grossly distorted the process. But examples of "normal" consciousness raising are so abundant that it will be useful to illustrate several of them. Consciousness raising has some distinctive features that must be kept in mind if we are to understand how mass opinion eventually makes its way to public judgment.

AIDS

Let us start with an example of an issue — AIDS — that has completed the consciousness-raising stage and is now deeply mired in stage 2, working through. AIDS is a particularly useful example because consciousness raising about its dangers has advanced much more quickly than other threats to health, such as smoking or high cholesterol. The speed-up permits us to see the special features of the consciousness-raising process more clearly than in issues in which it unfolds more slowly.

As recently as 1980, AIDS was not even recognized as a disease. In 1981, however, three hundred cases were reported and the disease was named. At first, little was known about it except that it was associated with the homosexual life-style; it crippled the immune system and always proved fatal, striking down otherwise healthy young men in their twenties, thirties, and forties. By the next year public health officials and others had grown alarmed. The number of AIDS cases was doubling every six months. A lethal epidemic seemed to be in the making. Dr. James Curran, of the Centers for Disease Control, warned that AIDS had become "a matter of urgent public health and scientific importance."[1]

In 1982 and 1983, information about AIDS began to accumulate, and what the public learned fed people's fears. They learned that AIDS could be spread in a variety of ways — not only through homosexual activities but also through needles shared by drug users, through blood transfusions with blood taken from infected people, to babies from infected mothers, and, under certain circumstances, through heterosexual activity.

No public opinion poll questions were asked about AIDS until 1983. This is not unusual. Poll questions are commissioned by the media when an issue begins to assert itself. A perspicacious editor or poller will often detect an issue before it has fully developed. But in the case of AIDS, this did not happen — partly because of the rapidity with which the AIDS crisis developed. In 1983, twenty-one poll questions were posed to the public; by 1988, the number of poll questions about AIDS had swelled to 774.[2]

The first poll question, asked by the Gallup Organization on June 10, 1983, revealed that 77 percent of the public had already heard about AIDS. By 1985, the number of Americans who had heard about AIDS had grown to 98 percent — an extraordinary level of news penetration.[3] (It is doubtful that this many adult Americans know who the president of the United States is, or who won World War II, or even that there was such a war.)

This is a good place to remind the reader that consciousness raising and awareness are not synonymous. For consciousness raising to occur, the level of concern must be beyond mere awareness. People can be aware of a problem without taking it seriously or feeling that something must be done about it (for example, the high noise levels in large cities from construction and indiscriminate horn honking of automobiles, taxis, ambulances, police sirens, and fire trucks). About AIDS, the public has definitely gone beyond awareness to high levels of concern. In 1985, the threat of AIDS ranked slightly behind cancer as the most urgent health problem facing the country. Two years later AIDS clearly became the number one threat to health in the public's thinking, swelling from 31 percent in 1985 to 70 percent in 1987. In relation to cancer, Americans placed AIDS as the more urgent threat to health by an almost six to one margin (70 percent to 12 percent)![4]

In addition to heightened awareness and level of concern, the public's knowledge about AIDS also increased. In 1985, the majority of Americans (55 percent) held the erroneous conviction that one could catch AIDS from donating blood.[5] By 1987, two-thirds of Americans (66 percent) knew this perception was not true.[6]

The pattern of these data shows convincingly that full consciousness raising among the public was achieved in the five-year period between 1982 and 1987: the public became vividly aware of the disease, its level of concern shot up, its misperceptions dwindled, and its level of knowledge increased sharply. (Some gaps in the public's knowledge remain: for example, people have little understanding of the high costs involved in treating AIDS patients.[7])

According to the conventional model of quality — being well informed — the objective of informing the public has been achieved. Political scientists and journalists who like to trumpet the public's ignorance should rejoice in this tidy example of a well-informed public. But one would do well to restrain enthusiasm. For as soon as one probes beneath the surface it becomes all too clear that mass opinion still dominates the issue of AIDS with the public still years away from genuine public judgment.

The public is bogged down in innumerable conflicts of values and other obstacles that are sure signs that the working-through struggle has not been fully engaged.

The public is conflicted about virtually every aspect of public policy for dealing with AIDS — whether or not clean needles should be given to drug addicts,[8] whether individuals with AIDS who persist in practices that expose others to the disease should be quarantined,[9] whether employers have the right to test employees for AIDS,[10] whether or not to make changes in personal life-styles to reduce the risk of AIDS (such as using condoms),[11] whether there should be mandatory screening to determine who are the carriers of the AIDS virus,[12] whether test results should be reported to the government or employer,[13] whether insurance companies should have the right to jack up the price of premiums for at-risk groups or refuse them insurance altogether, or whether people carrying the AIDS virus should be obliged to tell their insurance companies.[14]

Further, people are confused about the dangers to themselves personally. The vast majority (84 percent) state unequivocally that they do not feel at risk.[15] Yet, two out of five (41 percent) admit they are worried that they or someone they know will get AIDS,[16] half (50 percent) agree that they are personally concerned about getting AIDS,[17] two-thirds (65 percent) of all adult women admit that their level of concern about catching AIDS has increased over the last year,[18] and almost everyone (89 percent) acknowledges that people in general have grown more frightened about AIDS.[19]

Moreover, people are confused and mistrustful about the information they receive. In one study, two-thirds of those interviewed (66 percent) said they would avoid sharing a bathroom with someone who has AIDS,[20] even though they have been informed that this is not a way one can catch the disease. Most people say they believe that you cannot get AIDS from food (74 percent),[21] or from a drinking glass (66 percent),[22] or from a person who coughs or sneezes in your direction (65 percent).[23] And yet two-thirds (67 percent) also insist that food servers and food preparers in restaurants should be required to be tested for the AIDS virus.[24]

This mistrust of public information is not a fear that the government or medical community is holding back important information, but rather that we have incomplete knowledge.[25] Much too often people read or hear of a new study showing some previously innocuous substance or behavior to be the cause of a dreaded disease. Many are afraid that as scientists learn more about AIDS, similar findings will surface showing that AIDS *can* be transmitted by the more common ways people are infected by a disease (e.g., eating contaminated food or using unclean bathrooms).

The public's attitudes on policies designed to deal with AIDS are volatile, as revealed by the different answers people give in polls that use slightly different question wordings. On the sensitive question of testing workers for AIDS, if the question is worded "employers have the right to test workers for AIDS," clear majorities agree.[26] Yet, if the question is worded, "All present employees in an organization should be required to have an AIDS test," clear majorities say they oppose this policy.[27]

By 1987, when everyone knew about AIDS and believed it to be the most urgent threat to health facing the nation, fewer than 15 percent said they had taken or planned to take any action to reduce their chances of catching AIDS. Among the leading actions that were taken were avoiding public restrooms, avoiding casual contact with gay persons, stopping the donation of blood—actions people knew to be irrelevant.[28] By 1988, more people reported a readiness to take action.[29] But the overall pattern could hardly be more clear. On AIDS, although consciousness raising has been achieved, the public is far from stable, consistent, responsible, thoughtful judgment.

THE GREENHOUSE EFFECT AND RELATED AIR POLLUTION PROBLEMS

Let us now turn to an issue that is at a less-advanced stage of consciousness raising—the threat to the environment posed by the so-called greenhouse effect.

The greenhouse effect takes its name from its similarity to what happens in garden greenhouses. The glass in any properly functioning greenhouse serves a dual purpose: it lets sunlight in (glass is transparent to incoming light), but it also prevents heat from escaping (glass is solid and, at least for a while, traps and holds the heat). Scientists hypothesize that a process of this sort is taking place on a global scale—but with much less benign effects.

The difficulty with communicating information about the greenhouse effect and related environmental problems to the public is that a multiplicity of technical terms exist for describing different aspects of the same phenomenon. Sometimes scientists will refer to acid rain, sometimes to the hole in the ozone layer, sometimes to smog and ground level ozone, and sometimes directly to the greenhouse effect. All of these terms are justified because they describe different effects of the same problem—changes in atmospheric composition caused by the burning of fossil fuels, the destruction of the world's rain forests (mostly through burning) and the release of other chemicals (e.g., methane and chlorofluorocarbons) into the atmosphere.

Oxygen and nitrogen compose 99.9 percent of the world's atmosphere, which has remained relatively stable for the last one hundred thousand years. The other 0.1 percent is made of various trace gases — carbon dioxide, sulfur dioxide, nitrogen dioxide, methane, and chlorofluorocarbons. Surprisingly, these minor trace gases are the culprits threatening dire changes in the global environment.[30]

The threat works as follows: Carbon dioxide and other "greenhouse" gases such as methane create the equivalent of the glass effect in a greenhouse. Scientists have shown that the concentration of carbon dioxide in the atmosphere has increased by about 25 percent since the start of the industrial revolution. These increases have produced a more efficient greenhouse — one that lets more sunlight in and less heat out. As a result, the world faces the prospect of global warming — an increase of as much as 3 to 8 degress Fahrenheit by the year 2050, according to some predictions.

The ramifications of such a climatic change could be devastating on a global scale — fertile farmland turning into parched desert; coastal land destroyed as the sea level rises; the habitats of plants, fish, and other wildlife threatened; cities such as Denver, Washington, D.C., and New York experiencing three months of temperatures higher than 90 degrees, which would lead to frantic relocation as people around the world scrambled to find a more habitable environment.

In addition to producing greenhouse gases, the burning of fossil fuels — primarily from car emissions, industrial manufacturing, and smokestack utilities — also creates ozone. Ground-level ozone holds microscopic particles of hydrocarbons, nitrogen oxide, and sulfur dioxide. Together, this sun-cooked melting pot of noxious chemicals, usually referred to as "smog," causes eye irritation, impaired lung function, and damage to trees and crops. When it rains, these chemical particles adhere to water droplets creating "acid rain" that damages trees and other vegetation and destroys the delicate ecosystems of lakes and rivers.

The last piece of the story is atmospheric ozone depletion. When ozone is near ground level, it has negative effects (as described above). But when that same ozone is 10–15 miles above the earth's surface, it is good because it serves as a protective shield against the harmful ultraviolet rays of the sun. Any decrease in stratospheric ozone is disturbing because of its potential harmful effects: increases in the incidence of skin cancer and cataracts in humans and damage to plant life, including major agricultural crops and phytoplankton, the starting point of the food chain in the oceans.

Chlorofluorocarbons primarily used as refrigerants, aerosol propellants, solvents, and blowing agents for foam production are the major culprits responsible for ozone depletion. Originally, they were thought to be ideal because they lack toxicity and are nonreactive in the lower atmosphere. Yet, because of their inert nature, they travel unchanged into the upper atmosphere where they act as a catalyst in chemical reactions that break down the ozone layer surrounding the earth. Because their role is catalytic (a catalyst accelerates chemical reactions but is left unchanged when the reaction is completed), the damage they cause to the ozone layer is significant.

Scientists disagree about the seriousness of the problem, the risks it poses, and the time frame within which harmful effects are taking place. Not all regions respond to these problems in the same way. Places like Los Angeles and Denver are painfully conscious of bad air quality. Their geography and geology create basinlike effects that trap noxious gases and chemicals, preventing them from being dispersed by normal wind patterns and rainfall during high-risk periods. Residents "see" the smog and experience the harmful effects firsthand. (Just talk to a Los Angeles jogger midsummer about air quality!)

I will use the term "the greenhouse effect" as shorthand for the full range of newly emerging air pollution problems, including acid rain, smog, the hole in the ozone in the upper atmosphere, and so forth. It is useful to see the greenhouse effect (in this expanded sense) in the context of people's concerns about air pollution that have troubled the public since the 1960s. It was in the sixties that the symbolism and imagery associated with smokestacks became transformed. This transformation might be taken as a historical marker to date America's transition from an industrial to a postindustrial society. Before the mid-1960s, smokestacks darkening the atmosphere with their black-gray, grime-laden emissions were hailed as a sign of prosperity. In cities like Pittsburgh in the pre-1960s era, the smoke did not mean pollution, it meant jobs. Then the imagery abruptly changed. The smoke came to mean pollution and threats to health. Pittsburgh cleaned up its act. Detroit, under the terms of the Clean Air Act of 1970, did likewise. And the public began to relax, feeling that the problem had been solved.

It was in this context that new forms of the air pollution threat began to emerge. At the very start of the 1980s, polls began to query Americans about their consciousness of acid rain. In January 1980, only 26 percent could give a correct definition of acid rain.[31] By 1986, however, three-fourths of Americans (76 percent) were aware of the problem.[32] And by the end of the decade, virtually all Americans were knowledgeable about it. In the course of the decade, an impressive 80 percent had had their consciousness raised in the sense of going beyond awareness to the demand that urgent government action be taken, virtually irrespective of costs.[33]

Awareness and concern over the greenhouse effect family of problems developed in two distinct phases. The first might be called the "aerosol can" scare. In the 1970s, scientists first suggested that the earth's ozone layer might be deleteriously affected by chemical emissions. One of the leading villains, in the view of scientists, were ordinary aerosol cans used by consumers to spray bugs and armpits and to shave. In 1974, Roper asked a national cross section of consumers whether "the gases from aerosol cans destroying the protective ozone barrier around the earth will or will not be a serious problem for your children or grandchildren in the year 2000." Almost three out of ten (28 percent) answered that it will be a serious problem.[34] Roper continued to ask this question every two years up to 1980. By the end of his 1980 poll, the results showed that people's level of concern had barely budged. In that year, once again three out of ten Americans (30 percent) thought that the aerosol can problem was serious (the 2 percent increase from 1974 to 1980 is not statistically significant).[35]

The continued lack of public concern was countered by an increased concern among scientists. America's meteorological satellites collect continuous data on global changes in the earth's atmosphere, vegetation, and climate. In 1980, the Nimbus 7 satellite gave scientists a record of a growing "hole" in the ozone layer over the Antarctic. Here was the first hard evidence to support the theory that chlorofluorocarbons were breaking down the ozone layer.[36]

At the same time, the majority of the public, surrounded as they were by gas-guzzling automobiles, chemical factories, smokestack utilities, and other major sources of pollution, simply did not find it credible that the act of shaving and using hair spray was the critical factor destroying the environment for their grandchildren. Still, the lack of growth of concern does not mean that people were unwilling to take action — under certain conditions. When in 1982 Roper asked people whether aerosol cans should be banned or continue to be sold, by a two-to-one margin people opted for the ban (60 percent to 30 percent).[37] In part they did so because they were told that "cans with compressed air or pumps can be easily substituted" for the aerosol can. Nothing was said about costs or convenience. Under these circumstances, the typical attitude was, "Why not ban them, better to be safe than sorry." As we shall see in other examples, the better-safe-than-sorry attitude prevails on most threats — until costs, inconvenience, and other sacrifices enter the picture. Then, consumer attitudes are much more sharply divided, especially for costly action against abstract future threats.

The term "greenhouse effect" was introduced around the start of the

1980s. In March 1981, the Opinion Research Corporation (ORC) conducted the first poll using the term. It showed only 14 percent of the public had heard or read very much about the greenhouse effect.[38] Seven years later, this number had risen substantially. By fall 1988, a majority of Americans (58 percent) were familiar with the term,[39] and most of them were able to choose the correct definition of it on a multiple-choice question ("the gradual warming of the earth's environment as a result of the release of carbon dioxide and other pollutants into the atmosphere").[40]

Something odd happened in the summer of 1988 that reveals the importance of events to consciousness raising. The summer of 1988 was one of the hottest summers on record. During the peak of the heat, a prominent scientist, Dr. James E. Hansen, director of the Goddard Institute for Space Studies, testified before Congress on the seriousness of the greenhouse effect. Dr. Hansen stated firmly and without qualification his concern that the greenhouse effect must be taken seriously, and, among its other effects, people could expect fiercely hot summers as early as the 1990s. "It became quite clear this summer," Dr. Hansen said, "that what we had been predicting is just what is happening."[41]

Dr. Hansen's testimony received special attention when he complained bitterly to the press that the Office of Management and Budget (OMB) had attempted to muzzle him and had changed his testimony to play down the seriousness of the greenhouse effect. If that was OMB's intention (presumably to prevent a groundswell of demand for costly solutions to the problem), it had the opposite effect. Polls showed that the oppressive heat dramatized the seriousness of the greenhouse effect—at least for a brief few weeks in August. A Gallup poll conducted in August showed that three out of four Americans (74 percent) had closely followed the news story linking the "hot weather this summer with the greenhouse effect."[42] And a series of opinion surveys showed that during the summer the number of Americans who regarded the greenhouse effect as a serious problem swelled (including some who did not know what it was but said it sounded hot to them).[43] By fall 1988, when the weather cooled, so did people's concerns; by September, the number of Americans who saw the greenhouse effect as a serious threat had dropped from its summer high of 77 percent to 53 percent.[44]

NORMAL FEATURES

These two examples illustrate many of the features of what I am calling "normal" consciousness raising. (Distortions of the norm will be discussed in chap. 7.) Among the many characteristics of normal consciousness raising, six are particularly noteworthy.

Time Variability. Perhaps the most striking feature of consciousness raising is the vast range of variability in the amount of time needed for consciousness raising. It varies from minutes to decades. "Giant oil spill pollutes Alaska's waterways." "Terrorists take new hostages." "Devastating earthquake hits San Francisco." These consciousness-raising messages can be conveyed in real time in a matter of seconds. Of course, the fact that information can be conveyed in real time does not mean that consciousness raising is completed. But on particularly dramatic and clear-cut subjects, people can move in minutes (with sufficient information) from total lack of awareness to full consciousness.

On other types of subjects consciousness raising takes much longer. Subtle forms of discrimination against women in the workplace, the importance of nutrition to good health, the dangers posed by the greenhouse effect — topics such as these have required years to achieve widespread consciousness raising. It is the difference between being hit by a two-by-four and being vaguely aware of events occurring on the periphery of one's conscious attention and interest. (More on this subject later.)

In our two examples, consciousness raising on AIDS was completed within four to five years from the time the syndrome was named; consciousness raising on the new wave of air pollution problems has been underway for three times as long and is still unfolding. At the start of the 1990s, fewer than six out of ten Americans are aware of and deeply concerned about the greenhouse effect, in contrast to the nearly universal level of awareness and concern that accompanies the onslaught of AIDS.[45]

Many factors contribute to time variability. As a rule of thumb, the time factor can be considered the most sensitive barometer of the degree of difficulty linked with achieving consciousness raising. Each degree of difficulty adds to the time required.

Cogency of Events. Nothing advances consciousness raising as forcefully as events that dramatize the issue. Nothing retards it more than the lack of such events. Consciousness raising on the greenhouse effect got a swift boost from the oppressive heat of the summer of 1988 — especially when Dr. Hansen explicitly linked the two. His linkage proved highly controversial: the hot weather of 1988 could readily be explained without recourse to the greenhouse effect, and many scientists who agree with Dr. Hansen on the seriousness of the threat part company with him in tying the 1988 summer heat to it. But for a committed scientist who wanted to grab the public's attention, the summer of 1988 was made to order.

Sadly, dramatic events to underscore the seriousness of AIDS have not been lacking. The death from AIDS of celebrities added to the deaths of thousands of vigorous young people (mostly men) have made the dangers of AIDS real to almost all Americans.

The use of events to advance consciousness raising seems so self-evident that it barely deserves mention. And yet, there is something unobvious about it. Why should it take a disastrous happening to persuade people that a problem is serious when so much other evidence is usually available? Does an airplane have to crash and kill hundreds of people to get action on air safety when droves of experts can document the dangers in other ways? Why did the savings and loan industry have to undergo massive failure before the authorities paid attention, when the abuses that led to the failures were there for everyone to see? Why did the dangers of operating nuclear power plants with casual safety procedures and under-trained personnel persist unattended for so long, receiving proper attention only after the terrible accidents of Three Mile Island and Chernobyl? Why does the worst have to happen before people pay attention?

These are questions that elude satisfactory answers. A number of explanations are possible. In the study of consciousness raising, one is often struck by what appears to be poeple's lack of imagination. This trait is not confined to Americans. Russians, Frenchmen, Germans, Japanese, Tasmanians — all peoples seem to share it.

It is not a universal characteristic, though it does characterize the large majority. A significant minority of persons exists — men and women, well educated and uneducated, young and old — who are able to imagine what might happen without it actually having to happen. All they require is an explanation that makes sense in their frames of reference. For some, this frame of reference is quantitative and statistical: if the chances of heavy smokers contracting cancer or heart disease are far greater than those of nonsmokers, this group will fully accept the evidence without needing to experience a heart attack to make the dangers of smoking real for them. Others bring to bear a more qualitative framework: anecdotes, or personal experience, or explanations that fits their world views are more persuasive than statistics or other forms of scientific proof.

It is clear that a minority among us is capable of foresight. What is surprising is that the majority do not seem to be. Rarely do we act on *potential* threats. Unless disaster strikes, we seem incapable of farsighted preventive action.

What appears at first glance to be lack of imagination may be something quite different. We may simply be too distracted, too harassed, too busy to pay attention to everything that deserves it. Experts are constantly crying wolf. Cranks grab greedily and indiscriminately at our attention. Dangers come packaged in hype that needs to be discounted, because those who wish to inform us have learned that a sensible, moderate approach gets them nowhere. There are simply too many dangers, too many crises, too many topics competing for our limited capacity to care and to take action. Perhaps our way of setting priorities is to push everything aside that is not an emergency or a quasi-emergency.

But whatever the explanation, the public appears excessively practical: the unwillingness of the majority to pay serious attention to anything that has not actually happened may one day make remedial action too late to take.

Perceived Applicability to Self. It is also a truism that people pay more attention to issues relevant to their lives than to those that are not. On so-called women's issues, for example, the problems of working mothers, discrimination against women in the workplace, day care provisions for mothers where they work, consciousness raising among women who are at risk for these problems is higher than it is among men and women who are not at risk. A *New York Times* journalist notes with astonishment that Americans pay less assiduous attention to news of hanky panky in Washington than to issues that touch their lives more directly. He quotes a Gallup poll showing that only 15 percent of Americans closely followed reports about congressional misbehavior, in contrast to almost half of the public who avidly pursued debates over abortion or flag burning.[46] Consciousness raising depends directly on people's ability to apply the issue to their own lives.

For AIDS and the greenhouse effect, personal relevance has played a dominant role in the unfolding of consciousness raising. When AIDS first appeared, it was mainly the homosexual communities in cities like San Francisco and New York that paid it heed. But as soon as word began to spread that blood transfusions and heterosexual intercourse could result in the transmission of AIDS, consciousness raising zoomed upward. As the disease spread, the number of people who knew someone with AIDS increased sharply,[47] and as long as people remain unsure about the risk of contracting AIDS and the extent of danger to the general population, concern about the disease will persist at high levels.[48]

On the greenhouse effect, those whose consciousness was raised early included environmentalists and people who moved recently into high smog areas. These new arrivals were more sensitive to the problems of pollution than long-term residents who, in the manner of humans everywhere, had habituated themselves to their flawed environment.[49]

It is clear from the research data that mere exposure to the same messages does not mean that all of those exposed will respond in the same fashion. Students of communications research have long been aware of how selective people's attention can be, and no force is more selective than personal relevance.[50] At the same time, AIDS and the greenhouse effect show that people don't have to be directly affected to show interest and concern. The almost universal levels of consciousness raising on AIDS demonstrates that you do not have to be gay or a swinging single or a drug user to know and to care about those who become the victims of the AIDS virus.

Concreteness and Clarity. A fourth factor influencing the tempo and ease of consciousness raising relates to the clarity and concreteness with which the issue presents itself. The budget deficit is abstract and unclear. The effects of inflation on food and gas prices is clear and concrete. In the examples above, AIDS has an extraordinarily abstract name (Acquired Immune Deficiency Syndrome), but its effects are all too clear.

Nothing has retarded the evolution of consciousness raising on the greenhouse effect more than its lack of clarity and concreteness. At various times, different causes, consequences, and terminology have been used to describe the problem, making for mass confusion. In the 1970s, the culprits were aerosol cans in relation to ozone layer damage and auto and industrial emissions in relation to smog. Smog and ozone damage were not linked with one another, at least in the public mind. It was much easier to understand smog because it was visible. Ozone damage from the use of aerosol cans was invisible and abstract, its putative harm projected into the long-term future. Then, suddenly, in the late seventies and early eighties, a series of new terms and culprits was introduced: the greenhouse effect, acid rain, the destruction of tropical rain forests, the concept of holes in the ozone. The latter term is particularly confusing. If the ozone layer in the upper atmosphere thins, this is bad. Yet, the public is also told that too much ozone is bad. Confusion occurs because the media fail to point out that ozone is good or bad depending on where it is located. Ozone is good if it is located in the stratosphere where it serves as a protective umbrella to filter out harmful ultraviolet rays. But ozone is bad if it is at ground level where people breathe.

What scientists mean by a hole in the ozone is also misleading imagery. They do not literally mean a gap or an empty space in the atmosphere like a tent with a tear in it. They mean that the composition of the atmosphere in certain regions, such as the Antarctic, is solely carbon dioxide and other pollutants, which permit harmful sun rays to penetrate more readily. From a commonsense point of view, the so-called hole is not an aperture but a concentration of pollutants.

The public is also unclear about precisely what damages we should be seeking to avert. Dr. Hansen stressed warming. Other scientists stress the effects on health such as a rising incidence of skin cancer and cataracts. Others focus on the harmful effects on children and the elderly. Others fear premature lung damage. Still others emphasize the economic effects on farming, raising the specter of America's fertile breadbasket becoming a desert.[51]

In brief, an inherently abstract and difficult issue has been made even more abstract and difficult by treating it in a fragmented way with confusing and misleading semantics. A recent poll asked people which environmental threats worry them the most. Four of the threats they cited relate to air pollution. The poll findings show widely varying levels of concern. A 51 percent majority said they worry most about "loss of natural habitat for wildlife." Slightly less than half (48 percent) worry most about "contamination of soil and water by radioactivity from nuclear facilities"; 43 percent worry about "damage to the earth's ozone layer"; 40 percent worry most about "loss of tropical rain forests"; 34 percent worry about the ravages of acid rain; and at the bottom of the list, a mere 30 percent say they worry most about "the greenhouse effect or global warming."[52] Although all of these threats are interrelated, public consciousness raising has not yet made the connections among them.

Credibility. The credibility of the sources of information the public receives is a fifth influence on consciousness raising. Lack of credibility can retard consciousness raising severely. During the energy crises of the 1970s, for example, efforts to persuade the public to conserve energy and to support a new national energy policy were undercut by the public's profound mistrust of the information they received from the oil companies *and* from the federal government. The public was convinced that the oil companies and the government were in collusion to raise oil prices. They disbelieved the information from both sources because they were persuaded that the oil shortages were a fake. Opinion surveys reported that people were convinced that plenty of oil was available and that it would reappear as soon as prices went up.[53] The government and the oil industry never fully regained the public's confidence in this arena, and as a result the country still lacks a sensible energy policy.

By way of contrast, for AIDS, the various sources of information — the Centers for Disease Control, other government agencies, the medical profession — all enjoy high levels of credibility. Where the public has doubts, these are not suspicions of the good faith of those conveying information about AIDS. Nor is there any suspicion of conspiracy or cover-up. People's doubts are confined to questions about how firm and certain the knowledge of the experts is. Are they 100 percent sure AIDS cannot be contracted from toilets used by people who have the disease or through food contaminated by AIDS carriers? How can they know for sure? Experts have been wrong before. Why not avoid the toilets and test the food handlers? Better safe than sorry.

The greenhouse effect *is* plagued by mixed messages illustrated in two *New York Times* articles. The first, a front page article entitled "Skeptics are Challenging Dire 'Greenhouse' Views," focused on the striking disagreement in the scientific community about predicted effects of greenhouse gases on global warming and other climatic factors.[54] The dispute revolves around skepticism about the accuracy of computer simulation models as the basis for taking expensive and draconian measures to limit the emission of greenhouse gases.

The second article by the same author appeared the next day. Its title was "Study Supports Global Warming Prediction."[55] Based on direct measurements of atmospheric heat and water vapor, the study confirmed many of the results of the disputed computer model. The article also cited the continued dispute among the experts.

Under these confusing conditions, how can one expect the public to take a clear-cut position? A person reading just the headlines in the *New York Times* on both days would get two contradictory messages. And taking the time to read the articles thoroughly would not have dispelled the confusion.

The greatest threat to credibility comes from the strategy that policy makers have adopted. Experts agree that the major sources of the greenhouse effect are vehicles and fuel, manufacturing processes, the use of industrial solvents, and other industrial uses of chemicals.[56] These pollutants also contribute to acid rain and the depletion of the ozone layer. Three-quarters of the 23 million tons of chemicals that are thrown into the atmosphere annually, are, according to the EPA, emitted through vehicles and industry.[57] Officials also agree that it will be extremely difficult to achieve further major gains in these areas. The feeling is that most of the gains that can be derived from fuel efficient cars, the use of scrubbers and other devices on utility smokestacks, and other pollution-reducing actions have already been achieved. The EPA and independent scientists have, therefore, turned their attention to the thousands of lesser sources, such as aerosol cans, starter fluids for backyard barbecues, and household cleaners. Their bureaucratic eye is trained not on the utilities and the chemical companies and the proliferation of cars and trucks, but on bakeries where bread-baking emits alcohol vapors from the yeast used to raise dough and on dry cleaners where vapors are also suspect.[58]

So we are back to the great aerosol can dispute of the 1970s. The public may not know the precise statistics, but it suspects that the big polluters will be ignored while consumers will be harangued that life on earth is threatened by their use of household cleaners and charcoal lighters. The same mistrust and lack of credibility that prevented the nation from developing a sound energy policy may well block the development of sound policies for dealing with the greenhouse effect. The well-meaning efforts of the government to raise the public's consciousness may be frustrated by their lack of sensitivity to the issue of credibility.

Publicity. A brief word ought to be said about the importance of advocacy groups and the publicity they generate for the causes they embrace. Consciousness raising is largely a matter of publicity. This is the sixth factor to consider. With enough publicity, even the most difficult task of consciousness raising can be achieved. There are obstacles, of course. If credibility is low or if the pains and gains are difficult to communicate, consciousness raising will take longer and will require more publicity. But in the end, it is the quantity of publicity that counts — *at least as far as consciousness raising is concerned.*

This is an important qualification that refers back to our basic distinction between consciousness raising (stage 1) and working through (stage 2). For consciousness raising, one must perform two basic tasks: make the public *aware* of an issue and arouse their *concern* that something be done about it. These two tasks are performed well by publicity. The most effective publicity is the exploitation of events that dramatize the issue (e.g., the Iraqi invasion of Kuwait that underscored the nation's dependence on Mideast oil).

In recent years, the importance of publicity for consciousness raising has become self-evident, with the result that all effective advocacy groups find themselves in the publicity business. Often these are partisan efforts. But sometimes they are not. In May 1988, the federal government sent out 150 million copies of the pamphlet "Understanding AIDS" (outlining the dangers of AIDS) to the 107 million households in the United States served by the postal service. (The now retired Surgeon General C. Everett Koop was the overseer of the English and Spanish versions used.)[59] A Gallup survey conducted a month after the mailing showed that the pamphlet was received by 63 percent of U.S. households and read by someone in more than one-half of them.[60] In later chapters we will examine some of the consciousness raising efforts of nonpartisan public interest groups. For present purposes, the single point that should be emphasized is that publicity creates consciousness raising, and publicity can be bought because it is largely a matter of money and effort, which means that consciousness raising can be bought — and is, every single day.

7

TRANSITION OBSTACLES

With this picture of consciousness raising in mind, we now turn to stage 2 — working through. In shifting focus, we move from light to murkiness. We shift from an activity that is reasonably well defined and carried out by powerful institutions with massive resources.

The working-through process is another matter altogether. It is neither clear nor well defined, and our institutions have no commitment to accomplishing it. Indeed, they do not even recognize it as a separate stage in the development of public opinion. Consequently, working through is burdened by obstacles, many of them imposed inadvertently. Reducing them is one of the keys to improving the quality of public opinion.

THE TRANSITION TO STAGE 2

Some of the most serious obstacles are encountered in the transition from consciousness raising. Indeed, the success of working through depends largely on how consciousness raising has been accomplished. The way consciousness raising is done can either help working through, or retard it. The transition from stage 1 to stage 2 can be smooth and easy, or it can be rocky and difficult.

It is smooth and easy when, in the process of making the public aware of a problem, the media also present what might be done about it. If the media offer either a credible solution or a range of choices, then the stage is set for the public to go to work, and stage 2 can progress speedily (especially if stimulated by events). In 1957, when the Soviets launched *Sputnik*, our media, our government, and our experts all converged on the same interpretation and solution. *Sputnik* proved, it was held, that America had fallen behind in the exploration of space; the failure was attributed in large measure to neglect of math, science, and engineering in the nation's schools and colleges. The solution lay in reordering our priorities and improving our academic performance in these fields.

The public accepted this interpretation and supported it wholeheartedly. In retrospect, the speed with which a national consensus was built is impressive. The public might have responded in so many other ways: with recriminations; with endless debate; with fear; with mistrust and cynicism; with running off in disarray; with politicizing the issue to make constructive action impossible. If the consciousness raising that accompanied *Sputnik* had been less efficient, it is likely that one or more of these other reactions would have occurred and working through would have been delayed by years or resulted not in consensus but in polarization.

We see a similar pattern in the aftermath of the Soviet invasion of Afghanistan. When Ronald Reagan ran for president in 1980, he linked that event to a series of other high-profile events, such as Fidel Castro's defiance of American power, the Ayatollah Khomeini's taking of American hostages, and heaping insults on the United States as "the great Satan." Mr. Reagan told Americans that there was no need for them to accept being humiliated and pushed around and that for America to "stand tall" again a large increase in the defense budget was needed. Because Jimmy Carter's administration had already begun to increase the defense budget, the issue never became a partisan one.

Historians will long argue about whether the Reagan response was the correct one. But it was so credible to the American public that it was accepted uncritically. In the aftermath of the Vietnam War, Ronald Reagan interpreted a series of events that greatly disturbed the American people in a fashion that articulated what average Americans were feeling. He abetted consciousness raising about America acting like a "pitiful, helpless giant." Mr. Reagan handed the American people a simple, doable antidote to their anxieties — raise the defense budget. Republican polling after the campaign showed that the appeal of this interpretation was second only to economic stagflation in winning Mr. Reagan's decisive 1980 victory.[1]

These two examples of speedy working through are dramatic but atypical. They show it *can* happen. But it does not happen often, even when consciousness raising culminates in proposed solutions or choices citizens can understand. The more typical pattern is to be seen in the AIDS example reviewed in chapter 6.

In the early period of consciousness raising about AIDS from 1983 through 1987, media attention was focused on making the public aware that an epidemic was in the offing and also on the controversies about how the disease was transmitted and who was or was not at risk. The public was only dimly aware of the civil liberties and economic issues the AIDS crisis raised. In subsequent years, the media began to bring these to light. Do employers have the right to test workers for AIDS? Under what conditions is it acceptable to quarantine AIDS victims? Should drug addicts be given free needles to stop the spread of AIDS through needle sharing? These questions raise deep conflicts of values between protecting communal health values and protecting civil liberties, between actions to slow the spread of AIDS and violating people's deepest convictions about not condoning or encouraging the use of drugs. The public is gradually confronting these agonizing choices. It will still take years before they are resolved. It is possible that a medical solution to AIDS will be found before they are resolved.

The point here is that in the case of AIDS, unlike examples to be presented later, the media helped constructively to make the transition to working through a smooth one. Once people are aware of their choices and the ethical and practical dilemmas that accompany them, the public can begin to come to grips with them. Yet even here the transition is far from complete. Some AIDS-related issues have not yet surfaced in a fashion that the public can address. One issue is the huge economic costs in caring for AIDS victims who do not have the means or the insurance coverage to defray these costs. The press has yet to focus sufficient attention on these aspects of the AIDS issue and has not presented viable choices for the public to ponder so that working through can take place.

THE DOMINANT PATTERN

In the examples above, consciousness raising was capped with proposed solutions or choices for the public to consider. The consciousness-raising stage was completed in a fashion that expedited the transition to stage 2. Unhappily, this is not the dominant pattern. More typically, awareness and urgency are sought by the media virtually as an end in themselves without preparing the ground for stage 2. In these instances, the issue is not well launched into working through, and the transition is a rough one.

More specifically, an issue is poorly launched into stage 2 if

- people do not understand what the possibilities for action are,
- or if they are given insufficient and inadequate choices,
- or if they do not grasp what the consequences of the various choices would be,

- or if their attention is diverted away from the issue before they have a chance to come to grips with it,
- or if they are given contradictory information about it,
- or if they believe those who propose the action are acting in bad faith.

It may seem odd, but the news media can inadvertently create every one of these obstacles and *still* achieve a high level of consciousness raising among the public. And because consciousness raising is their main goal, they can be indifferent to the obstacles they raise, brushing them aside because they do not want to be bothered with them. If there is an important news story to cover that should arouse public concern and alarm, the media are superb at beating the drums and getting everyone agitated. But once people are whipped into a state of high anxiety, the news media then move on to the next task of consciousness raising, as if arousing people's concerns were an end in itself. Just as people are starting to wonder, "What in the world should we do about this problem?" the news media move on to the next story.

By shifting restlessly from one story to another, the news media leave the public either in a state of moral frenzy or in a passive posture of being entertained and diverted. One week it is the Exxon Valdez oil spill in Alaska, the next week the hostages in Lebanon, the next the murder of citizens who interfere with the drug traffic in their neighborhoods. You barely begin to focus on one issue before it is gone and replaced by another. In each instance consciousness raising is achieved, but the task of stage 2 is greatly complicated. It is hard enough for the public to come to grips with painful choices even when the ground is well prepared. When it is not, the task is made doubly difficult, and working through can be delayed for years.

The analysis of what constitutes quality in public opinion is largely a matter of understanding the obstacles that stand in the way of working through. A theory of public opinion is obliged to identify and describe the various types of obstacles that arise as public opinion moves on its journey from mass opinion to public judgment.

The press itself could benefit from consciousness raising about the obstacles it creates. The press is like the 800-pound gorilla that sits anywhere it wants, oblivious to those who are sat upon. There is no deliberate effort on the part of the media to retard working through. On the contrary, the media want to contribute to resolving the great issues of our time, consistent with their larger vision of contributing to democratic values.

Working through is now such a hit-and-miss affair because the media have little concept of when they are helping it and when they are hurting it. They operate, as we have seen, on the basis of the conventional model: one informs the public via consciousness-raising methods, which lead directly to resolution. Because the media make no provisions for a working-through stage, they can hardly be expected to be careful not to mess it up. If they became more conscious of how much anxiety and disarray and confusion they create inadvertently, they might be more sensitive to public needs without being deflected from their own mandate. The obstacles described next are, with few exceptions, not the result of media ill-will or bad faith but simply of inadvertence touched with arrogance.

Two categories of transition obstacles will be discussed. In each, the role of the press cannot be understood without reference to the role of technical experts and governmental authorities. On major policy issues, it is these sources that feed the press the information the press transmits to the public. The worst transition obstacles are those that combine the incidental distorting tendencies of the media with the often deliberate distorting tendencies of the experts and authorities.

FAULTY AGENDA SETTING

The biggest obstacles that bedevil the transition from stage 1 to stage 2 relate to what is sometimes referred to as the "agenda-setting" function of the press.

A sizable body of research literature on the effects of mass media exists. This literature describes a controversy that has raged for decades on the magnitude of the effects of the mass media on the public mind. Just how great are these effects? Systematic efforts to answer this question began in the 1920s. At that time, the dominant theory was that the mass media were all-powerful. The propaganda efforts in World War I on both sides were cited as evidence that the newspapers could make the public believe at will all atrocity stories that painted the enemy as "brutal and immoral."[2] In the 1930s, the influence of the movies on children and the spreading power of radio reinforced the view that the media could manipulate people at will and get them to believe and to do anything those who controlled the media wanted.[3]

The theory held that as modernization advanced and as a directionless mass society replaced the traditional society of the past, the masses of people would become ever more susceptible to the mass media.[4] In the post–World War II period, this theory was replaced by more discriminating research that documented the selective influence of the media. The effects of the media were seen to depend on many factors, including people's social status, their personal relations with others, and the relevance of the story to the public's needs and interests.[5]

The influence of the media was seen to be more indirect than had been presupposed. Researchers found it difficult to pin down effects attributable solely to media influence. The pendulum swung from the earlier view that the media were all-powerful to the view that the media's influence was surprisingly limited. The media, it appeared, simply amplified other influences and trends in the society. Communication researchers came to the tepid conclusion that "mass communication only had limited effects on some people under some circumstances."[6] But the public—and some within the research community—never bought into this vision of media impotence. Skepticism about this conclusion impelled some researchers to develop new theories and research strategies. Researchers now suspect once again that the media have far-reaching effects.

They pay particular attention to the "agenda-setting" function of the press. Scholars in the field trace this concept to a suggestion by political scientist Bernard Cohen, who in 1964 wrote, "The press may not be successful much of the time in telling people what to think, but it is stunningly successful in telling its readers what to think *about*."[7] Leading researchers in the field such as Maxwell E. McCombs and Donald L. Shaw have developed data suggesting that the press plays the decisive role in communicating to the public just how much importance is to be attributed to an issue. It does so by selecting which stories to cover, how much attention is to be given to each, how long they are to be played, and how they are to be interpreted.

Those who poll the public take this agenda-setting function of the press for granted. People may have personal experience of a few select issues such as crime, inflation, and high interest rates, although even here they have no clear sense of how general their experience is until it is reported in the media. But average Americans are not privy to goings-on in Moscow or Beijing or Baghdad until they see it on the tube or read about it in the newspapers. Most matters of concern to people do not come from personal experience—not the shenanigans of the savings and loan industry, or the toll from AIDS, or the effects of "junk bonds." What people know about these matters comes mainly from the media.

In an era of information overload, it is the media's judgment of just how important an issue is that makes the critical difference to how seriously average Americans will take it and what action they will be willing to support—especially if the action involves inconvenience, discomfort, or pain in the pocketbook. Here is where the power of the media can hardly be exaggerated. The most serious transition obstacles are created either when the media underestimates the importance of an issue or exaggerates it.

In this century, perhaps the most dramatic example of media underestimation relates to the press's coverage of the Holocaust in World War II, one of the biggest stories of the century. As we now know, Hitler's "final solution" resulted in the murder of six million Jews, Poles, and other victims—one of the most momentous events in human history. The Holocaust began in 1938, initiated on *Kristallnacht*. It proceeded remorselessly up to the defeat of Germany in 1945. But Americans knew virtually nothing about it until the war had ended. In the first stages of the Holocaust, news coverage was good. Coverage of the Kristallnacht was so extensive that when Gallup in a national survey at the end of 1938 asked a cross section of Americans what were the most interesting stories of the year, the persecution of the Jews by the Nazis was ranked highly.[8]

Curiously, press treatment of the story fizzled out shortly thereafter. For a number of reasons that bear directly on how the process of consciousness raising works, the full horror of the Holocaust did not enter American consciousness until the late 1940s.

One reason was the attitude of American officialdom. Throughout the late 1930s, as President Franklin Roosevelt became convinced that America would ultimately have to take military action to stop Hitler, he found himself contending with a strong isolationist movement in the country, and he feared being vulnerable to isolationist attack. Roosevelt was much taken with the new public opinion polling techniques that George Gallup had popularized, and he had a number of polls conducted about American attitudes toward accepting Jewish refugees. He found, not to anyone's surprise, a strong strain of anti-Semitism and xenophobia in the country.[9] (One of its strangest manifestations was a persistent rumor enthusiastically spread by affluent Republicans that Roosevelt's real name was Rosenfeld.) The president's polls showed him that he could expect fierce resistance to any efforts to accept large numbers of Jewish refugees. The country was still suffering from the bleak depression of the 1930s, and Americans were not in a generous, welcoming mood. A Gallup poll in 1938 reported that almost three-quarters of the public (72 percent) felt that "we should not allow a larger number of Jewish exiles from Germany into the U.S."[10] A year later, almost as many people (61 percent) opposed "permitting 10,000 refugee children from Germany—mostly Jewish—into the U.S."[11]

Roosevelt's greatest fear was that if America put up too much of a fuss about the Nazi persecution of the Jews, Hitler would turn around and say, "if you love the Jews so much, take them. You're welcome to them." Roosevelt knew that if that happened, the country would not be willing to assume that responsibility. Under these circumstances, it became Washington's policy to minimize the story of Nazi persecution of the Jews in every possible way.

One quite effective way related to press inquiries. America's foreign correspondents in Germany, young men at that time like Richard C. Hottelet and Daniel Shorr, were aware of the Nazi persecutions and filed many stories about them. But their editors back home did what editors always do. As gatekeepers of the news, they exercised their editorial judgment. Checking the stories with official sources in the State Department, they either received no confirmation of the validity of their correspondents' stories or outright discouragement. As a result, they either failed to carry the stories or placed them in obscure positions in the back of the paper — a sure message to the reader that the story was unimportant.

The tendency to treat the Holocaust as nonexistent or unimportant was further reinforced after Pearl Harbor. Not only did war stories now push all other news off the front pages, the Japanese were now enemy number one. Given a choice of Japanese or Nazi atrocities, the Japanese horror stories were preferred. As a result, polls showed that the public viewed Japan over Germany as "our chief enemy" (53 percent compared with 34 percent),[12] with Germany seen as "the country we can get along with better after the war" (67 percent compared with 8 percent).[13] In addition, the Japanese were seen as "more cruel at heart" (82 percent compared with 18 percent)[14] than the Germans and more approving of "the killing and starving of prisoners" (63 percent compared with 31 percent).[15]

The story of the press's coverage of the Holocaust unfolded at a conference held at Harvard University in 1988 on the subject of the American press and the Holocaust.[16] It was attended both by former officials of the Roosevelt administration and by members of the press who had been foreign correspondents in Germany before the attack on Pearl Harbor brought America directly into the war. There was particular concern at the conference to bring to light a faithful rendition of the facts. Although criticism of the Roosevelt administration was implicit, the participants took pains to emphasize that Franklin Roosevelt had made many efforts to save the lives of Jews, and that, in sharp contrast to the State Department, Roosevelt was personally uncontaminated by anti-Semitism. Nonetheless, the story illustrates how government authority works together with the exigencies of the news media to affect consciousness raising.[17]

In most instances, big stories and major events get told in one form or another. But as this anecdote shows, this is not always so. A more recent example is the savings and loan debacle — the most costly boondoggle in American history. The media were at least two or three years behind on giving this story the prominent coverage it deserved. Had the media been more alert, taxpayers might have been saved hundreds of billions of dollars. The key point is that events, however large and important, are always filtered and editorialized. Not only the content of the events but, more to the point here, the importance with which stories are to be treated, depend directly on the media's editorial interpretation.

The Holocaust was minimized in importance. The savings and loan story was neglected. More frequently, events are hyped and given too much attention. Whether they are given too much importance or the right amount or too little is a matter of subjective judgment. But it is always the media who make that judgment.

8

THE EXPERT-PUBLIC GAP

F aulty agenda setting is not the only transition obstacle the public encounters. Even when the media's consciousness raising succeeds brilliantly, the transition to working through can be blocked by another
set of obstacles — those created by the experts and other elites. In present-
day America, a serious gap exists between the point of view of the experts
and that of the general public. The gap is wide and deep. It covers not
only differences in levels of knowledge but also in values, frameworks,
and modes of expression.

In the introduction, I cited Professor Key's lament of many years ago
that no aspect of his subject had left him more mystified than the relationship of elites to public opinion. What puzzled Key most were the motives
and values of the elite subculture and how these related to the general
public.[1] Key's puzzle remains unsolved. Little is known today about the
interaction between the views of elites and those of the general public.
Fortunately, the work of the Public Agenda and Kettering foundations to
bridge the gap between the elites and the public sheds light on the puzzle.

The work of these organizations reflects that the differences between
the general public and the elites are not confined to levels of knowledge
or degrees of articulateness. They are broader than that. American leadership is recruited from the specialized worlds of the legal profession, business management, finance, the foreign policy community, the higher ranks
of the civil service, academia, the sciences, the church, journalism, and
so on. Their knowledge and interests are specialized. Their day-to-day
contact with the general public is meager. They belong to distinct subcultures, each with its own outlook. Often they are graduates of elite colleges
and universities, which indoctrinates them with a noneradicable feeling
of superiority to the general public. Without questioning the depth of
their attachment to democracy, in their personal lives many have adopted

the outlook of a ruling social class, and though their attitudes may be benign, their life-styles create a vast social distance between themselves and average Americans.

Many of them are aware of how remote their contact is with middle America and are eager to learn how they can better communicate their views to the larger public. They assume that they have much of value to communicate to the public, without imagining that the public has much of value to impart to them. One of the most severe drawbacks of the conventional model of quality-as-information is that it always assumes a one-way flow of wisdom from those with more information to those with less.

The relationship between leadership elites and the general public is a weak link in our democratic system and the source of endless misunderstandings. Perhaps the greatest misunderstanding arises from the fact that each side approaches issues from a different point of departure. This makes it difficult for them to communicate with each other, especially when those in leadership do not know what the public's point of departure is and how it differs from their own.

The purpose of this chapter is to illustrate this point. It is important for the reader to grasp it concretely, for there is no more serious obstacle to strengthening the quality of public opinion in America. In what follows, I want simply to present concrete examples of misunderstandings between experts and public that originate in the differing points of departure each side takes to various issues. These misunderstandings make it nearly impossible for the public to perform the difficult task of working through that people *must* undertake before any important public issue can be resolved.

THE GREENHOUSE EFFECT

The first set of examples is taken from an issue we have already examined in detail — the greenhouse effect. The reader will recall the squabble between Dr. Hansen and government experts in the Office of Management and Budget (OMB) regarding the seriousness of the greenhouse effect and the extent to which it has been scientifically validated. This kind of expert disagreement is quite common. It has marked consequences for public opinion. When experts disagree openly and contentiously, the public is confused and does not know which side to believe. If the costs of taking precautions are trivial (as with accepting some substitutions for aerosol cans), people will fall back on their "better-safe-than-sorry" positions. But if the costs and discomforts are substantial, the public will seize upon the disagreement among the experts to stall and evade the issue as long as possible, postponing the hard work of stage 2.

A second expert-generated obstacle illustrated by the greenhouse effect concerns semantic confusion. Nothing could be more confusing to the public than the contradictory ways in which words like "ozone" are used. As noted in chapter 6, sometimes ozone is used to refer to the protective barrier in the earth's upper atmosphere that helps to prevent the atmosphere from developing so-called holes. But sometimes ozone designates the noxious result of pollutants at ground level, the major cause of smog. Ozone is "good" when it is in the upper atmosphere and "bad" when it is close to the ground. But this clarifying point is rarely mentioned. So people do not know whether ozone is good or bad. This may not be the central issue in the greenhouse effect, but it certainly muddies understanding.

Another expert-generated obstacle illustrated by the greenhouse effect relates to the strategy experts have chosen for dealing with it. As we have seen, having concluded that there is little further to be gained by targeting the major sources of the greenhouse effect—vehicle emissions and industrial practices—the EPA and state agencies have decided to clamp down on multiple minor sources such as backyard barbecues.[2] We are returning to the aerosol can syndrome of the 1970s and its lack of credibility. This new strategy may win some compliance on the better-safe-than-sorry principle, but as soon as larger sacrifices are required, the public will balk. It will do so because it finds it difficult to believe that its tiny transgressions have such large consequences. More importantly, it will quickly understand that the major sources of the problem, large industrial corporations, are not being targeted. The public's suspicions, ever ready to be incited, will generate public cynicism. "Why should we sacrifice while the big guys are getting away with murder?" will be the public's reaction. The issue will swarm with ugly controversy rather than serve as a basis for swift communal consensus against a common threat.

These three types of obstacles—experts disagreeing among themselves in public, language used in a confusing way, and strategies adopted that are insensitive to the public's need for credible solutions—are common to many issues.

PRISON OVERCROWDING

The issue of prison overcrowding is an excellent illustration of how the point of departure of elites differs from that of the public. Most elites assume that prison overcrowding is, as the court decrees it, "cruel and un-usual punishment." They also assume that the public would concur with this conclusion if public education graphically demonstrated the negative effects of such overcrowding. To test this hypothesis, the Public Agenda Foundation conducted a study in the state of Alabama.[3] A cross section of Alabama citizens were shown a specially prepared video dramatizing the ills resulting from prison overcrowding. The Alabamans were asked a number of questions before and after they saw the video. Before they saw the video, six out of ten (61 percent) of the Alabama citizens rejected the conclusion that "putting someone in an over-crowded prison amounts to cruel and unusual punishment." Significantly, even after being exposed to the effects of overcrowding, an equal number (63 percent) rejected this conclusion.[4] In other words, the majority rejected the expert's premise both *before* and *after* being exposed to the public education campaign. The sizable majority who were opposed to building more prisons in Ala-bama before they saw the video (69 percent) maintained this conviction even after seeing it.[5]

The video did, however, have an impact. Citizens are not rigid in their views about punishing and rehabilitation. They simply do not buy the expert premise that prison overcrowding is a social ill that must be addressed. The public's view is that prison is both a punishment and a deterrent, and to serve these purposes the prison experience should be ex-tremely disagreeable. Efforts to reduce overcrowding strike the public as tantamount to reducing both the punitive and the deterrent effects of prison. After the video, there *was* substantial support for alternatives to prison for nonviolent offenders, such as restitution, house arrest, community ser-vice, and intensive parole. Citizens concluded that these were sufficiently rigorous and more likely to rehabilitate nonviolent offenders than a stay in prison.[6]

Thus, Alabaman voters reject outright the starting point of the ex-perts that the principal reason for building more prisons is to reduce the "cruel and unusual" punishment of overcrowding. The crime issue is a top priority for all Americans, especially its drug-related aspects. People are anxious about the high levels of drug-related crime. They are severely criti-cal of the criminal justice system as being too lenient and as biased in favor of the criminal and against the victim. If, in the consciousness raising that accompanies the crime issue, emphasis is placed on strategies that strike Americans as continuing to show more concern for the criminal than the victim (building more prisons to reduce overcrowding), most Americans will simply block out the message. It so lacks credibility that it deflects people from the task of engaging the hard choices involved in combating crime and drugs. It arrests people at the level of mass opinion, stopping thought that might address the crime issue more productively.

FREEDOM OF EXPRESSION

An interesting example of a subtle conflict of interest between experts and the public and their different points of departure is seen in the issue of freedom of the press. The conflict between journalists and the public comes from their different positions as producers and consumers of information.

The position of journalists is familiar. They work with the First Amendment every day, and their professional training familiarizes them with the advantages of a free press in a democracy. Naturally enough, they define freedom of the press from their perspective as producers of "free speech."

A second element of the press subculture, almost as deeply entrenched as the emphasis on freedom of the press, is a widely shared conviction that the public does not understand just how important this essential American liberty is. Over and over again, journalists interviewed for a study on freedom of expression cited studies that showed that the public could not identify or recognize the First Amendment.[7] And to be sure, when average citizens are asked to sign a petition in favor of the First Amendment (though not identified as such), they refuse. In opinion polls, the public frequently calls for greater regulation of the press. For the experts these facts demonstrate that the public has an adversary relationship to the role of the press in a free society.

Part of the problem is that the press confuses the public's lack of familiarity with the language of the First Amendment with lack of support for its ideals. The general public is fiercely protective of all rights associated with free speech. The fact that people cannot quote or identify the First Amendment does not prove that they are opposed to freedom of the press, any more than the fact that people cannot quote the Second Amendment necessarily means that they want soldiers quartered in their living rooms.

The biggest gap between the press and the public is on the very definition of what freedom of the press means. The public's clear understanding of what freedom of the press means to it is misunderstood by journalists. Average Americans do not think of themselves as producers of free speech who need to be protected should they decide to publish a newsletter or to speak on a street corner. Instead, they see themselves as consumers, viewers, and listeners; their concern is access to information, not their ability to voice their views freely. To paraphrase how one citizen put it, "Isn't that what freedom of the press means, getting to hear all sides of the argument?" From the public's point of view certain types of regulation (such as the fairness doctrine and equal time on the electronic media) are perceived as increasing their freedom of speech by insuring that all points of view will be presented.

When opinion polls report that the public desires greater regulation of the media, there is a built-in misunderstanding. Experts and journalists automatically assume that the public is calling for censorship of unpopular ideas, and the press instantly wraps itself in the mantle of the First Amendment. The public, for its part, perceives itself as calling for greater freedom of expression by asking for regulations that will prevent the media from foisting a one-sided point of view on them. Each side brings a different point of departure to the table.

THE WATER PROBLEM IN THE WESTERN STATES

Consider another example of how differences in the frameworks of public and experts create an almost unbridgeable gap of misunderstanding. Several years ago, I was involved in a project with the Western Governors Association.[8] The governors were concerned about the water shortage in the western states. So were the citizens of these states. But the outlook of the citizens differed from that of the governors and their experts. Each side started from its own premises, its own point of departure. The governors' experts perceived the problem as (1) regional, (2) impersonal, and (3) economic. If water is a scarce resource in the region, then it should be treated in the classic economic manner, using price to allocate it fairly and impersonally.

This typical expert approach to the problem outraged the citizens of the western states. First of all, they do not see the problem as a "western" or a "regional" problem. Their point of reference is closer to home; they think Colorado, Denver, Phoenix, and Laramie. They see the issue in terms of their own state, their city, their community. Nor do they see water as an impersonal market commodity. It is not *the* water; it is *my* water. "They want to sell *my* water." "Some speculator is going to make a killing on *my* water." "The government is going to tell me when I can and when I can't use *my* own water." These are typical expressions of citizen sentiments. They are full of outrage, incomprehension, and mistrust.

The issue here is not who is right or wrong. It is simply that the gap between the experts and the public is so vast that the transition between consciousness raising and working through is effectively blocked. The citizens of the western states have had their consciousness raised about the threat of a water shortage. But they are presented with an unacceptable solution — rationing by price — which enrages them rather than engaging them constructively in debate about how to solve a communal problem.

The western water problem symbolizes a larger conflict of values with many forms of expression. It is the conflict between communal and market-based values. Should everything have a price tag on it? Where do you draw the line? How do you strike the balance? Must those who cannot afford to pay the price abandon all rights, all hopes? What about the bare necessities — food, water, clean air, shelter, the care of helpless children, old people, sick people, and the infirm? In a democracy, striking the right balance between communal and market-based values is a task that cannot be delegated to experts. The fundamental judgments must be made by the citizenry or the very idea of democracy is mocked. Such decisions must be made thoughtfully, carefully, and responsibly. In every instance, the conflicts must be worked through. Making these kinds of decisions is what working through to public judgment is all about. Preparing the ground for the citizenry to make such decisions prudently and responsibly is what democratic leadership is all about.

The experience of conducting polls with cross sections of citizens bears out a principle well known to psychologists: if people have a preoccupation or major worry they will not listen to you until and unless you have addressed their concern. If political leadership wants to reform social security, for example, by taking something away from older Americans so that younger people can have more, they must first address the concern of older Americans that if you take as much as a nickel away from them you are robbing them of the money they personally invested in paying social security taxes, and you are threatening them with destitution: a nickel today, tomorrow the specter of homelessness. Never mind that these fears may be irrational and erroneous (the taxes of today's social security recipients pay for only a small fraction of the money they receive). Older Americans will fiercely rebuff any proposed reforms, however reasonable and fair they may be, unless their fears of being robbed and made destitute are first addressed. If these fears are addressed, they will listen and respond reasonably. Similarly, Americans will not agree to assume a larger share of the burden of health care costs until and unless their fears of being wiped out by catastrophic illness are addressed. The people of the western region will not consider economic schemes for allocating water until and unless their fears are addressed. If most of the experts think one way and most of the public think another, the result will be stalemate, divisiveness, and polarization. Leadership will be frustrated. Among the public, mass opinion will persist. The quality of our democracy will suffer. And all the while, consciousness raising will proceed as if it were an end in itself not simply a preparation for the next critical step of working through.

9

THE COMPETITIVENESS ISSUE

O ur next example of expert-generated transition obstacles is the most important one—and the most revealing. Its importance derives from the issue itself. How to counter the fierce economic competition from Japan, other Pacific rim countries, and Western Europe poses one of the most serious challenges to America's future that the nation has ever faced. For our purposes here, the competitiveness issue is also important because it illustrates in rich detail the nature of the public-expert gap and how it can effectively block the public from working through its thoughts and feelings.

Chart 9.1, from *USA Today*, is typical of news imparted to the public in a steady stream from the late 1970s to the present. The chart depicts an all-too-familiar tale: how the United States was way ahead of Japan in world trade on an important product (semiconductors) and how the Japanese steadily gained ground, first catching up to the United States in world share of market and then surpassing us. In 1982, we had the bulk of the world market in semiconductors, and Japan had a one-third share of market. A mere six years later, at the end of the 1980s, our positions were reversed, with Japan having more than one-half of all the world's trade in semiconductors, whereas we had now slipped to a one-third share.

A similar pattern of Japanese gain in share of market at U.S. expense occurred frequently throughout the 1970s and 1980s, affecting products and industries as diverse as automobiles, cameras, radios, steel, bicycles, television sets, VCRs, motorcycles, machine tools, optical equipment, personal computers, fax machines, microwaves, farm equipment, and banking. In 1971, after more than one century of favorable trade balances, the United States began to import more than it exported, and, except for a few years in the 1970s, the trade deficit has persisted ever since at levels in excess of one hundred billion dollars a year. It has persisted at these

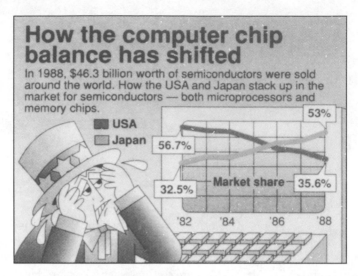

Chart 9.1. How the computer chip balance has shifted. Courtesy of *U.S.A. Today*, Aug. 30, 1989, p. 1B. Copyright 1989, USA TO-DAY. Reprinted with permission.

high levels despite serious devaluation of the dollar, which made American goods cheaper abroad (while raising the cost of imported products for Americans). Because the United States runs a high federal budget deficit, living off borrowed money (much of it from Japan), the nation has not yet felt the full brunt of its loss of competitive strength in world markets—a threat to America's future standard of living, ability to create good jobs, social stability, and economic independence.

To date, the public's response to the threat shows all the signs of failure to work through the issue. There is little sense of national crisis or danger, no public outcry for action, no consensus on what needs to be done, no public pressure for action at either the level of government or the private sector to increase the national savings rates, enlarge the pool of engineers and technicians needed for the future, improve education, curb Wall Street practices that force business to take a short-term point of view, improve the quality of American products, mobilize the American workforce, mobilize and channel technological development, educate the public to the true nature of the threat, and/or take any of the other actions that might reverse the trend. There are some individual efforts here and there from private groups, government officials, individual corporations, business leaders, economists, and journalists. But individual efforts are not the same as public consensus.

Presidential campaigns sometimes bring issues to the fore and advance working through by national debate. Some observers expected the presidential campaign of 1988 to be the ideal occasion for initiating a national debate on what strategies the country should adopt to address the competitiveness issue. But this opportunity slipped by, and every opportunity that has arisen since then has been equally missed.

In a democracy, the function of the leadership is to alert the public to the existence of any serious threat, define it, develop a strategy (or alternative strategies) for dealing with it, and seek to mobilize and focus the energies of the people to meet it. One of the principal reasons for America's failure of political will in confronting the competitiveness challenge is that America's leadership has not presented the public with realistic choices, and on occasion has actually created obstacles deflecting the public from working through the issue. The transition obstacles created by the expert-public gap have formed a dense wall of incomprehension, misunderstanding, and confusion.

THE PUBLIC'S PERSPECTIVE

Examining the public's response to the competitiveness issue, one is initially impressed by the high level of consciousness raising reported in opinion poll data. In 1977, a bare majority of the public (53 percent) were aware of the U.S. trade deficit.[1] A decade later, in 1987, 81 percent of the public said they had heard or read "quite a bit" about the problem of U.S. competitiveness.[2] By the mid-1980s, awareness of the trade deficit had reached the 75 percent level,[3] and by the end of the decade awareness was nearly universal (83 percent).[4] Moreover, once people grasp the magnitude of the trade deficit, they say they regard it as a serious problem.[5]

Yet, a nagging doubt persists. Despite these high levels of awareness and concern, something essential is missing in the consciousness raising picture. As the portrait of the public presented below reveals, the preconditions for working through are absent: the public has no genuine understanding of the threat; people have been given no incentive to come to grips with it and to clarify how they feel and where they stand; and no strategies, priorities, or difficult choices and trade-offs have been presented to the public for their deliberation.

One of the biggest disparities between experts and the public concerns how the economy actually works. If one had to abstract the main features of expert thinking on the economy, it would be safe to say that the experts see the workings of the economy in the technical or "hard" factors of capital investment, GNP growth, interest rates, and labor productivity. The expert perspective is that the key to the trade imbalance with Japan lies in correcting yen/dollar exchange rates and in achieving a "level playing field," and the key to America's economic health is greater productivity, which can be enhanced by more investment in technology and in a better educated, trained work force who can skillfully use the new technologies.

The public, on the other hand, sees the economy not in terms of new technology, productivity, and a more technically skilled work force but mainly in terms of consumption and "moral fiber." As Martin Feldstein and others have pointed out, a certain pop Keynesianism has become the "conventional wisdom" of the American public about how the economy works.[6] The public sees the economy as driven by demand and by consumption. Public Agenda studies show, for example, that most people think that more personal savings would be bad for the economy because it takes money out of circulation. If people buy less, others will work less, and then the economy will be in a worse situation. People's concerns about the future are that prices will rise more quickly than wages and that their children will no longer be able to afford housing, education, and a good life. People are also very concerned about how the pie will be divided and that some groups are getting more than others. But there is almost no sense that the economy is driven by production and that a more productive economy will create a bigger pie, regardless of how it is divided.[7]

The public also analyzes the competitiveness issue in moral rather than in technical terms. Both the cause and the cure to America's economic sluggishness are seen to be the same. An increasing number of Americans believe that the country has lost its moral fiber.[8] In government this plays out in corruption and scandal. In the economy, people see the United States as producing shoddy and disposable products that do not match the high quality of Japanese goods. In education, people see permissiveness, drugs, and lack of discipline.[9]

The comparison between today's situation and that after the *Sputnik* launch is instructive. When the Soviets launched *Sputnik* in 1957, Americans immediately interpreted their success as a challenge to America's technical ability, and the solution was obvious and compelling, a greater emphasis on science and math. The response was also highly effective. Today it is hard to imagine that the Soviets could ever have been a technological threat.

In the 1970s and 1980s, the country was faced with an even more dramatic challenge, the triumph of Japanese technology. But the reaction was not the same. There has been little public receptiveness to calls for an increase in scientific and technical training (even though this is precisely what leadership thinks is a main part of the solution).

One reason is that Americans perceive Japanese success as an application of moral rather than technical qualities. There is a feeling that we have more than enough technology, but that we do not have the discipline to take advantage of it. In a Public Agenda study, for example, respondents wrestled with the implications of the competitiveness struggle as it plays out for education. Rather than calling for more computers in the classroom, the respondents were concerned that computers and calculators were making it too easy for students. "They should have to work with slide rules, or do it by pencil, rather than just push a button with these computers," said one focus group participant.[10] The feeling is that we have plenty of educational opportunities, technical skills, and laboratories, but not enough dedicated people to use them. Once the moral fiber is in place, the skills will follow quickly.

All of this creates a miscommunication of massive proportions. The leaders (focusing on production) call for greater savings to stimulate investment. The public (with its focus on consumption) thinks that greater saving will slow the economy and cause America to fall further behind. The leaders see that education is key, and at one level the public agrees. But then leaders are surprised that the public will not support school bonds. This seems like the height of inconsistency—the public agrees that education is all-important but will not pay higher salaries, for example, to attract math teachers. But from the public's perspective this makes perfect sense. When people say that education is the key, they are calling for more discipline and a stronger moral fiber. And the public knows that this cannot be bought with more dollars. The sentiment is that if students did not carry guns in the classroom we would not need to spend more money to hire teachers.

What then is the public's conception of the competitiveness problem? There is no question that the public is jittery about our economic future. In many cases, people perceive themselves as having done well enough, but they feel that the country is skating on thin ice. In particular, they are worried about their children's future. They cannot precisely pinpoint what is going to happen. They take refuge in optimism about the future based on faith that somehow America will find the answer.

When people are asked about the present and the near past, their appraisal is pessimistic. In response to a Gallup question, "In the past ten years, do you think the ability of the United States to compete economically in the world has improved, gotten worse, or hasn't changed much?" by greater than two-to-one margins people say U.S. competitive ability has gotten worse rather than improved (47 percent to 21 percent).[11] When they look to the future, however, the proportions flip-flop: by 46 percent to 17 percent, people believe that in the future the ability of the United States to "compete economically in the world marketplace will improve" rather than worsen.[12] Fewer than one in five (14 percent) see the United States entering a period of long-term economic decline. Half of the public (50 percent) endorse the statement that "We are slipping dangerously but can still turn it around if we act decisively." And the majority think we *will* turn it around.[13] By 53 percent to 41 percent, Americans believe that in the future the United States will move up competitively in the world economy rather than down.[14] It is this faith that permits people to say they take the problem seriously and yet remain complacent and express little urgency about it. The assumption is that the present is bad (through no fault of the public) but will improve in the future almost magically — also without any direct involvement by the public.

Part of the problem is people's confusion about the significance of the trade deficit. Americans know the trade deficit is large and that this is a serious problem. But discussion of the trade deficit in focus groups reveals a great deal of confusion. Many people believe, for example, that we have always had a trade deficit — something like death and taxes or the national debt. The deficit might be larger now but it has always been with us.[15]

The real problem is that although they take it seriously, people do not exactly understand what, if any, negative consequences it has. Other economic terms have a much clearer reference. Average Americans understand what a budget deficit is, because they can see it as analogous to their own personal budgets, and they can see the effects of inflation and unemployment on their daily lives. But the dangers of a trade deficit are harder to see.

Their first guess is that its main impact is the loss of jobs. But as people drive their new Toyotas past miles of stores and restaurants with help wanted signs, it is difficult to make this connection.[16] Failure to link the trade deficit clearly with unemployment or declining wages is an example of mass opinion. Although people say that competition from foreign products is a major cause of unemployment, when they are asked in surveys to rank the five most serious threats to the economy, they rank the threat of unemployment first and the trade deficit last, not making a direct connection between the two.[17]

One of the most commonly mentioned consequences is that the Japanese are buying up American property and businesses. Indeed, less educated respondents often connect the success of Asian countries in world competition with the success of Asians in America. As one respondent put it, "Where I get my hair cut the employees are Americans but the owner is Asian. Pretty soon the president of the country will be Japanese."[18]

THE EXPERT PERSPECTIVE

The community of experts and leaders became aware of the competitiveness problem long before most citizens. By the early 1980s, most business leaders and policy makers had begun to grow alarmed about the problem. By the middle 1980s, an impressive 80 percent of business leaders and economic policy makers had concluded that the United States was losing its competitive edge. A study of leaders conducted for Motorola concluded, "The problem of the Japanese challenge to American industry arouses more concern than any other social or economic issue in the last twenty years."[19]

Despite their concern, the nation's leadership has consistently thrown obstacles in the path of public understanding. Among the most serious are the following four.

Expert "Ownership" of the Issue

One formidable obstacle is the automatic tendency by experts to keep the "ownership" of issues to themselves. This is easily done. All that is required is that the issue be defined in the technical terms of the expert's own discipline. The economists who define the problem in terms of yen/dollar exchange rates are doing two things simultaneously: they are making both an intellectual *and* a turf-related claim. Intellectually, they are stating that the levers of action lie within the economists' specialized domain. They are also communicating both to other experts and to the public that the issue is the property of the economist. "Hands off", they are saying, "this is our game." The businessmen hurt by imports define the problem as one of achieving a more level playing field. Here ownership is being claimed for the domain of trade negotiation while simultaneously making an intellectual statement about the nature of the problem (i.e., that it is essentially a matter of modifying the complex rules of trade). Merger and acquisition experts who state that their purpose is to make American industry more competitive are also, by inference, laying claim to ownership. And so are the various experts who specialize in capital formation, or commercial applications of technology, or industrial policy, and so forth.

About the only thing these experts have in common is their exclusion of the public. With the rare exception of business leaders like Ruben Mettler or MIT economist Lester Thurow, the various experts may sometimes make room for experts in other fields, but they fail to acknowledge either that the public belongs in the dialogue or that the public may have a contribution to make to it. They are encouraged to turn their backs on the public by the enormity of the gap between their understanding of the problem and the public's. They may acknowledge the political power of the public to veto a program they regard as necessary. But it would never occur to them to regard average Americans as intellectual equals who approach the problem from a different perspective just as their fellow experts do.

Akio Morita, the chairman of Sony Corporation, and an almost mythical figure in the international business community because of his leadership in the Japanese electronics industry, told me of a conversation he had with his "good friend, Marty Feldstein," the former chairman of President Reagan's Council of Economic Advisers. Dr. Feldstein, he said, insists that the key to reversing the American trade deficit with Japan is to devalue the dollar further so that American-made products will be more price competitive. "I told him he was wrong," Mr. Morita said. "The secret is not a cheaper dollar, it is more attractive products." In response to my query about what he meant by "attractive products," Morita answered, "Oh, you know what I mean. Products that give consumers the features they want, that are good value for the money, and are nicely designed."[20] This formulation is not only the essence of Sony's success, it is also an apt summary of what the public wants. As a world-class economist, Martin Feldstein engages his friend, the world-class industrialist Mr. Morita, in dialogue, even though he rejects Mr. Morita's views. But he and most other American experts pay scant attention to the public.

The public does not question its exclusion. It is "their problem," that is, a problem for the economists, the businessmen, the government, the bankers, and the unions to solve. Though "they" appear to be screwing up, "they" will recognize what they are doing wrong in the future and do something about it. As long as the public shares the experts' conviction that they, the experts, own the problem, there is little incentive for the public to confront it and work it through.

Different Values

Not only is the public effectively excluded from sharing the problem, the experts who do deal with it hold values different from the public. The Chicago Council on Foreign Relations commissioned the Gallup Organization to conduct a study to compare the attitudes of the general public with those of knowledgeable expert elites. Most of the council's emphasis was on foreign policy, but some of their questions focused on the domestic economy. On attitudes such as the need for protective tariffs and on values such as the desirability of protecting American jobs, the Gallup research shows that the gap between leadership and the public is quite striking. Elites dislike protective tariffs and are not overly concerned about protecting American jobs; the public is keen on protecting jobs, and as we have seen earlier, states that it will support protective tariffs to do so. Specifically, a two-thirds majority of the public thinks tariffs are necessary (66 percent); whereas only three out of ten experts (31 percent) share this conviction. Conversely, fewer than half of the experts think it is "very important" to protect American jobs (44 percent), compared to a whopping 79 percent of the public.[21]

Our system of representative democracy assumes that those who act for the public have superior knowledge but that they share the public's goals and values. But on many issues this assumption is invalid. Leaders and experts seek to advance their own values and interests. This is why so much emphasis is put on public relations. Correcting the public's understanding is rarely the goal of public relations. The usual goal is to make it possible for special interests to achieve objectives and advance values the public does not fully share.

Sometimes differences in values and outlook reflect good faith on both sides. As we saw in the prison overcrowding example, there is no reason to doubt the sincerity of either the experts or the public, even though both sides see the issue in different terms. But other times the conflict of interest between experts and public is sharp and clear.

One example is the frenzied merger-and-acquisition activity of the late 1980s. Many financial leaders opposed changes in the laws governing mergers and acquisitions, especially hostile takeovers. Their argument was that such takeovers keep management on its toes and that without this challenge entrenched management would run their businesses inefficiently and be less competitive in the world marketplace. No more self-serving argument has been made since Nero insisted that the Christians enjoyed being thrown to the lions because it permitted them to become martyrs.

The threat of hostile takeovers is one of the principal reasons American industry has grown so uncompetitive in recent years. To stave off the threat American management has been seriously distracted from the long-term goal of building the business for future generations. Instead of confronting the Japanese on their strongest competitive advantage — their willingness to forego short-term profits for the sake of long-term gains in market share — the threat of hostile takeovers has forced management to burden its balance sheet with debt and to focus on quarter by quarter earnings.

How this threat works in everyday business practice is illustrated by the comments of an executive competing in the tire industry against Bridgestone, the Japanese company that acquired Firestone. In response to a question about the future, the executive said:

> There is no question about it. In the long run, Bridgestone will win. Actually, they are mediocre marketers and that gives us an edge. But they more than make up for it in their investment and production policy. They never let any opportunity slip to improve the product and production efficiencies. Whatever is needed they do regardless of cost. We are just not willing to incur that expense, because of the short-term hit to the bottom line which makes us vulnerable to takeovers. In the long run, Bridgestone's hundreds of tiny improvements will buy them a bigger share of market.[22]

To avert the threat of hostile takeovers, American management has been gradually converted to a short-term, defensive way of thinking. No more important factor accounts for America's loss of competitiveness. It is hard to believe that the financial experts who so fiercely defend the laws supporting hostile takeovers are convinced that they are making America more competitive. Some of America's smartest lawyers and Wall Streeters are being paid massive fees to serve the interests of a handful of entrepreneurs who pursue their own interests and values irrespective of the interests and values of the public.

Conflicting Information

A third elite-created obstacle involves the transmission of confusing and contradictory messages of the public. The subject of savings is an all too clear example. From the expert point of view, our low level of private savings is a prime contributor to the competitiveness problem. Private savings rates in the United States consistently run lower than in Japan; in some years they run at a third or one-half the Japanese savings rate.[23] Private savings are an important source of capital formation for investment in technology, critical to the long-term success of business. But the messages the public receives about the desirability of savings could hardly be more bewildering. One group of economic experts emphasizes the fact that our national savings rates are too low and urges people to save more, while another group warns that avoiding recession depends on the continued vitality of consumer spending and urges people, in effect, to save less. Every holiday season, the public is barraged with economists' fears that "consumer spending may be down." As we have seen, this message reinforces the public's conviction that spending keeps the economy going by circulating money, whereas savings brings it to a halt.

Conflicting messages about savings are not a new phenomenon. In the Carter administration *within the same three-week period* the public was first told to hold down its use of credit cards to avoid fueling inflation and then instructed to use their credit cards more because nonuse was threatening to bring on a recession!

Framework Differences

Overall, the principal obstacle for the public is that the experts bring a different framework and point of departure to the competitiveness problem. As we have seen, for the experts the key factors are the "hard" technical variables (exchange rates, capital formation, production, and the technical skills of the labor force). For the public, the key factors are qualitative, especially the fear that America's moral fiber is deteriorating. American products of poor quality, corporations who take the short-term point of view, Wall Streeters out for a quick buck, corruption in HUD, the savings and loan rip-off, waste in the defense budget, drug use in the schools, the failure of today's students to pay attention at school to acquire the skills they need, doing less than one's best on the job, teachers who care more about their pay and prerogatives than about teaching—these, the public frets, are moral issues, not technical ones.

The experts and the public bring different images to bear on the problem. Economists have an image of equilibrium that dominates their concepts; the public has an image of money circulating and keeping the economy growing. The experts see the importance of technical skills in the workplace; the public sees human strivings and moral virtues (hard work, discipline, concern for quality), or the lack thereof, as central in importance. Communications between groups holding different frameworks is notoriously difficult, especially when each has little interest in understanding the other.

MAKING VALUES CENTRAL

It would be simplistic to imply that the parochialism of the experts is the only reason the United States has yet to confront the competitiveness issue and devise a strategy for dealing with it that the public will support. It will take inspired leadership to fashion a strategy that will counter the threat and win public support, even if pain and sacrifice are involved. (Those experts who doubt the public's willingness to endure sacrifice need only be reminded of the public's patience in the severe recession of 1981–1983, when the public kept faith with Ronald Reagan's highly controversial economic policies even though they caused much economic distress.)

Though parochialism on the expert's part may not be the main cause of the nation's tardy response to the problem, it is an important contributing factor. It discourages economic leadership from formulating strategies and choices the public can debate and work through. Above all, it prevents the underlying value conflicts from being clearly presented. In recent years, America has put consumption ahead of production, spending ahead of saving, immediate gratification ahead of working for the future, the welfare of old people ahead of the interests of the young, greed ahead of sacrifice, self-interest ahead of loyalty, stockholders ahead of employees, short-term profits ahead of long-term growth, expediency ahead of quality, and the needs of the individual ahead of the needs of the society. In the conflict between market values and communal ones, market values have dominated.

To define the issue in these terms is to share the public's framework. It is a framework that the technical experts regard as irrelevant and sentimental. The most fundamental precondition for working through the issue is to resolve this difference between frameworks. Some business leaders understand that the public must be brought into the picture. As Ruben Mettler, former chairman of the influential Business Round Table, observed, "The global competitive battle is no longer just between industry and industry, or company and company, with each seeking competitive advantage on its own, but rather a matter of what the entire society does — government, managers, employees, unions, educational institutions, consumers and taxpayers."[24]

When writing about the competitiveness issue several years ago, my coauthor, Sidney Harman, and I came essentially to the same conclusion as Mettler, that the solution to the competitiveness problem lies in the political will of the many rather than the technical cleverness of the few:

> Unless the American people have the stomach for the competition that lies ahead and are prepared to exert the necessary energy and commitment, there is little the experts can do. Our economic competition with the Japanese is not going to be won or lost by the decision of a few economists, government leaders, and corporate executives. It will ultimately depend on whether average Americans are truly willing to overcome their reluctance to make the sacrifices and the commitment—as workers, as savers, as taxpayers, and as voters—that are necessary for America to compete better. If the energy and commitment are not there, experts cannot compensate for their absence by technical agreements on currency rates, trade practices, or tax policy.[25]

In the time that has elapsed, I have grown even more convinced that the public's frame of reference must be taken into account: if the value issues are resolved correctly, the technical solutions will follow. The alternative—to ignore the moral fiber questions and to focus exclusively on the correct technical policies of exchange rates, trade negotiations, investment in technology, curriculum reform, and so on—is a formula for failure.

The present dominance of the expert point of view means that the working-through the public needs to do is likely to be postponed indefinitely, either until the problem grows more severe or some dramatic event, like the total collapse of a major American company or industry, causes the public to assert some ownership of the issue. Another possibility, and a realistic one, is that some of the more enlightened people and institutions will band together to refocus the nation's attention on strategic choices and value trade-offs that transcend the parochial concerns of the technical experts and special interests. (The Business-Higher Education Forum, for example, is attempting to do precisely this.)

One major piece of consciousness raising must still be put into place. Presently, the key symbol of the competitiveness issue is the trade deficit. From several points of view, it is an ineffective symbol. It is abstract, people do not know what it means, and worst of all, the trade deficit could be reduced without solving the underlying problem and might even aggravate it. The country must come to understand that the true significance of the trade deficit is not that the Japanese are selling us attractive products at attractive prices or buying up our real estate. Rather, the problem is that our faltering competitiveness is undermining the foundation of America's social stability: the ability of the society to offer genuine equality of opportunity through the mechanism of broadly based economic growth.

The connection between the trade deficit and this fundamental value is not clear either to the experts or to the public. It must be made clear to set the stage for wrestling with the hard choices that lie ahead. A brief discussion may clarify the connection.

EQUALITY OF OPPORTUNITY

American society works best when economic and social conditions create opportunities for all strata of the society. One of our most fervent communal values as a society is our belief in equality of opportunity. This is the value we evoke whenever critics confront us with the contradictions between our national ideals of equality and liberty. If equality becomes the nation's exclusive goal, liberty inevitably will suffer. If liberty is the number one priority, equality will suffer, because the freedom to pursue individual goals without constraint results in severe inequities. This is not an easy lesson to learn. Over a twenty-year period from the mid-1960s to the mid-1980s, the nation lived through a wide swing of the pendulum from the programs of the Great Society of the Lyndon Johnson years to the "get-the-government-off-our-back" ideology of the Reagan years.

The cornerstone of the Johnson programs was *entitlements.* The theory of entitlements holds that all citizens have a moral and legal right to enjoy a minimum level of security, health care, education, and civil liberties, with government providing both the resources and the enforcement. In the Johnson years, and well into the Nixon and Carter years, the national priority was equality, even at the expense of certain liberties. Then came the Reagan revolution. Reagan's pet slogan, "Get the government off the backs of people," meant nothing less than a reversal of national priorities. Americans felt the pendulum had swung too far in the direction of equality, and voters wanted a change. Americans had come to believe that the criminal justice system favored the criminal at the expense of the victim and that a morally lax and permissive society tolerated widespread fraud in the welfare system and let students fail to pay back the loans that had permitted them to get college educations. Twice before 1980, Ronald Reagan had failed to impress the mass of voters with his major theme. But by 1980, the voters were prepared to listen and to respond.

In the Reagan presidency, government size did not shrink. It actually grew. But the nation's priorities were turned upside down: now liberty and individualism were top dog, with equality deemphasized. The War on Poverty and the gains of the civil rights movement were stopped in their tracks and in some instances, reversed. When Benjamin Hooks, president of the NAACP, organized a march in Washington in August 1989, he did so to protest the decisions of the Supreme Court and to raise America's consciousness about the sharp reversal in civil rights gains.

In the 1990s, Americans are seeking a new balance between liberty and equality. If class war and race war are to be avoided, the nation will do once again what it has successfully done in the past: it will revitalize its traditional ideal of equality of opportunity. This is the only strategy that has worked in the past to reconcile the conflicting interests of liberty and equality, rich and poor, rural and urban, North and South, East and West, employees and employers, men and women, young and old, Catholics, Protestants and Jews, and above all, the ethnic minorities who form the pluralistic core of American life.

At the start of his brief presidency, Jack Kennedy spoke of his faith in the "rising tide that raises all boats." In the decade that followed, Kennedy's metaphor was proven more than hollow rhetoric. In the 1960s and 1970s, the rising tide did raise many boats. Not surprisingly, young people with college educations were able to improve themselves and make good livings, but so too were young workers *without* college educations. In some instances, as in the highly unionized steel and automotive industries, they were able to make a better living than many of their college-educated peers.

The abundance of opportunity in those years spurred the public to a generous outlook, supporting the thrust toward greater equality throughout the conservative Republican presidency of Richard Nixon as well as through LBJ's era of democratic liberalism. The attitude of the average American was "I'm getting mine, why shouldn't they get theirs?" This outlook began to change in the late 1970s, when many came to fear the constraints of a tightening economy and to become aware of the internal contradictions in the government's entitlement programs. The dominant attitude became "I'm not getting mine because 'they' are being favored at my expense." The ground was prepared for Ronald Reagan.

Genuine equality of opportunity takes the pressure off the society. Everyone wins, including those whose need for remedial help can be met. This happens, however, only when there are sufficient resources and goodwill. And often, as in the 1960s and 1970s, sufficient resources are the key to goodwill. In the 1930s, there was plenty of goodwill among the victims of the depression — a great majority of the citizenry. But there was not much goodwill between the social classes — the minority of wealthy people who still had resources and the majority of sufferers. The class-conscious presidency of Franklin Roosevelt was the result. It took decades of affluence before the bitter climate of class animosity of the 1930s could be dissipated.

The success of the traditional American strategy—advancing equality of opportunity—depends on broad-based economic growth in manufacturing as well as services. Such growth, in turn, depends on the nation's ability to correct the competitive deficiencies that have appeared in recent years. If these deficiencies are not corrected, an economically united European community will add to America's competitive woes.

The social consequences of not coming to grips with the trade deficit are less familiar than the economic ones but far more disturbing. They can be summarized in an all-too-plain formula: in contrast to the "rising tide" of the post-Kennedy years, in today's America it is growing very difficult for those without a college education to make a good living. From the mid-1970s to 1986, the median income of young males without some college education has been slashed by 35 percent (adjusted for inflation). For high school dropouts, median income has dropped an amazing 42 percent![26] And because roughly one-half of all young Americans acquire no college education, a great many young people have been affected.

Approximately 40 million young Americans are age sixteen to twenty-four.[27] The non-college-attending half of this cohort has been aptly dubbed "the forgotten half" in the report of the Grant Commission's three-year study of American youth. This nonpartisan commission, funded by the William T. Grant Foundation and headed by former Commissioner of Education, Harold "Doc" Howe II, concluded that the plight of America's forgotten half is traceable mainly to recent structural changes in the American economy as it has shifted from labor-intensive skilled and semiskilled manufacturing jobs to service jobs and to the practice of exporting manufacturing jobs offshore. If present trends continue, the gap between those with a college education and those without one will grow more severe.

This situation is a formula for social and political instability. The history of this century shows that there is no more potent negative political force than downward mobility. If the American Dream becomes a mockery for tens of millions of vigorous young Americans who, it should be remembered, represent mainstream American youth not just inner city minorities, the nation can expect rising levels of violence, crime, drug addiction, rioting, sabotage, and social instability. The surge of racial tension between young whites and blacks is already an expression of it. We will be lucky if this is the worst of it: history suggests that under such circumstances, demagoguery is almost inevitable.

The stakes for addressing the nation's competitive flaws and working them through are broader than economics. They go to the heart of America's viability as a democratic society.

10

FROM MINUTES TO CENTURIES

Fortunately, not all issues are so totally sucked into the black hole of
the expert-public gap. Many are less complex than competitiveness,
the interests involved less conflict-ridden, and the experts less fragmented. For most issues, the public's choices are more clear, the trade-offs
better understood, and fewer obstacles prevent the public from engaging
the issue.

But the competitiveness issue is far from unique in the difficulties
it presents to working through. Other issues — crime, drugs, race, energy
policy, welfare, and more — are equally encumbered with obstacles. Indeed,
when we examine the range of issues facing the nation from the perspective of successful progress through stage 2, we are struck by the extreme
variability of the time required to complete the working through stage.
It varies from minutes to centuries!

At one extreme where working through takes place swiftly are issues
like the public's stand on the so-called Iran-Contra affair. Here people
quickly made up their minds even though values were in conflict and a
popular president was involved. Opinion polls taken in the mid-1980s
showed that the public was deeply concerned about the American hostages held in Lebanon and anxious to have them returned safely. But when
the public learned that then President Reagan had, in effect, submitted
to blackmail by selling arms to the Iranians in exchange for promises that
they would use their influence to free the hostages, voters quickly resolved
their own conflict between the high value they placed on the lives of the
hostages and the even higher value they placed both on America's honor
and on the long-term dangers of caving in to terrorist demands. America's
honor was not to be besmirched and future hostages jeopardized, even
though lives might be sacrificed. The president was seen to have made a
serious mistake in judgment. The public reached this conclusion swiftly
and without ambivalence. Confidence in Mr. Reagan's presidency plum-

meted; it dropped more swiftly than at any time in the history of opinion polling.[1] In contrast to the many other types of conflict we will be examining in this chapter, the public was able to work through the cross pressures on the Iran-Contra issue without hesitating.

At the other extreme of the time spectrum are issues such as slavery. It took the nations of the Western world centuries to conclude that slavery so violated human rights that it was to be legally banished as well as morally condemned. Economic advantage coupled with attitudes of racial superiority collided head-on with the imperatives of Judeo-Christian ethics. The nations of the West dithered. Cultural mores and life-styles in the southern United States were built around the "peculiar institution," as slavery came to be called. The Civil War resolved the issue legally, but the enduring heritage of racial tensions in the United States shows how obdurate the conflict is. Although racism persists, slavery is no longer an issue. But this change in outlook was not accomplished speedily. Many decades had to pass with much strife and vast amounts of American blood spilled before working through on this issue was completed.

WORKING THROUGH CLOSE UP

From minutes to centuries: What kind of process generates this incredible range of variability? Under what conditions does working through take place expeditiously, as in the Iran-Contra affair? What makes for protracted delays of years and decades? Are there modes of intervention that can speed up the process and make it less strife-ridden?

These questions bear urgently on our theme: improving quality in public opinion by finding better ways to convert mass opinion into public judgment. Admittedly, the slavery issue lies at an extreme pole of the time spectrum. But it is common for issues to remain unresolved for decades. The struggle for women's rights in America has a history almost as long as the debate over slavery and is still going on. The battles over racial discrimination, immigration policy, and urban versus rural interests have deep historical roots. Newer issues like the nuclear arms race, welfare reform, drug abuse, energy policy, and environmental protection have persisted in an unresolved and conflict-ridden state for many years.

It would be an exaggeration to imply that if the public had worked through its ambivalent feelings on these issues, resolution would automatically follow. Having people make up their minds is a necessary condition to resolving most issues legally and politically, but it is rarely a sufficient condition. On some issues, strategically placed special interests thwart the public will. On others, resources may be lacking, or strong leadership, or a basis for compromise. Putting an end to public waffling may not be enough to insure political resolution, but it hastens the process radically. The matter can be stated simply: *without* public judgment, issues fester unresolved virtually without time limit; *with* public judgment, issues can be resolved quickly, saving years of strife, turmoil, waste, and danger.

Unfortunately, the immense effort required to develop public judgment discourages most policy makers, who would rather deal with their fellow elites than with the public. As we inventory the formidable obstacles that interfere with achieving public judgment, those who look for easy solutions will throw their hands up in disgust. So much effort is required that it seems simpler to ignore the public.

Sometimes the strategy of ignoring the public succeeds. Often, the public is so inattentive that much business can be conducted without public involvement. But history shows—a lesson that most public officials have to learn and relearn—that to move ahead on important national issues without public support is to invite being undermined in the long run. Generating consensus, or at least public support, may not be easy to achieve. But in a democracy, it is necessary. Because the United States has been in the democracy business for more than two centuries, Americans know how to accomplish a large part of the process, especially at the beginning stages (consciousness raising) and at the end (compromise, legislative expertise, going along with the majority decision even when one disagrees with it). It is the middle part, the working through, that America does poorly. Partly, this is owing to the complexity of contemporary life. Neighbors getting together around a barn or in a town meeting may have had their disagreements, but they usually understood one another. Getting together around a TV set and having experts explain things is another matter altogether.

Fortunately, analysis of the working-through process leads to many practical methods of improvement. Like most complex subjects, once you untangle them they are less forbidding. In discussing the various forms of working through and the obstacles that beset it, we will have reached the heart of our subject, and, I believe, one of the keys to the successful practice of democracy in the twenty-first century.

MULTIPLE FORMS OF WORKING THROUGH

As stated in chapter 5, the term "working through" derives from psychology (originally from psychoanalysis), where it is used to designate the process whereby an individual adjusts and adapts to a major loss (such as a death, divorce, or adverse change in life-style) or to resolving deep emotional conflicts. In describing the working-through process as a stage of public opinion, I am using the term in a broader, nonclinical sense. I use it to indicate the time and effort required for people to absorb and accept all of the consequences of their own views.

Four types of working through account for most of the variability in the time the process takes. Though they overlap, the four can readily be distinguished from one another. Below is a brief characterization of each, with examples to illustrate how they affect public opinion.

Second Thoughts. The simplest form of working through is one that gives people time to have second thoughts on emotionally packed issues. Typically, the time needed to shift from an impulsive first reaction to more sober and considered second thoughts is brief — days or weeks rather than months or years. President Bush gave a good personal example in a televised interview with David Frost.[2] In the interview, Mr. Bush described his first reaction to seeing the televised body of Colonel Higgins, an American hostage hung by the Hizbullah in Lebanon, as it dangled grotesquely from a rope. His first reaction was fury and a desire for vengeance, an urge to wreak America's military might on the assassins. But eventually prudence prevailed. His thirst for vengeance gave way to concern for the lives of the other hostages, to worry that innocents might be killed, and attention to the larger geopolitical interests of the United States.

The evolution of the president's response accurately mirrors the process the public undergoes in response to events that may initially stimulate rage and the desire for vengeance — not only the hostage incident, but other forms of provocation from Cuba's Castro, Libya's Qadhafi, and Iraq's Saddam Hussein. People need time to cool off, to have second thoughts.

Having second thoughts does not necessarily involve waiting for powerful emotions and impulses to subside. It can be a cooler process. People's first reactions are always colored by their quirks and prejudices; they need time — and reminders — to give their fundamental values a chance to emerge. In studies of public attitudes toward censorship, the Public Agenda has found that as soon as people are reminded of the importance of preserving free speech, their first censorious impulses are softened, especially if children are not involved. When it comes to censoring pornography, for example, the public will be adamant if young children are victimized. But if it concerns adults only, most Americans will curb their initial desire for censorship in favor of free speech once they consider the larger stakes.[3]

Accepting a New Reality. A second form of working through involves accepting new realities. Because reality changes constantly, this process is ongoing. But it is not always accomplished with speed or ease. The energy crunch of the early 1970s affords a typical example of a new reality that people resisted for a long time. After the long lines at the pump brought on by the Arab oil embargo of 1973, the price of gasoline tripled, from about 30 cents per gallon to 90 cents or more. It took people many months and much grumbling and growling before they adjusted to this new reality and accepted it as something other than a vicious conspiracy between the oil companies and the government. It took an even longer time for Americans to acknowledge and to accept the new reality in the 1970s and 1980s that the Soviet Union had achieved parity with the United States in nuclear weapons. (In chap. 11, we will examine public opinion on this issue.)

Opinions, Attitudes, and Values in Conflict. The third and most prevalent form of working through involves coming to grips with ambivalence — divided feelings in one's own opinions, attitudes, and values. Even after consciousness has been raised about an issue, opinion polls frequently find that people's feelings are torn, their attitudes conflict with each other, and on controversial issues their values pull them in opposite directions. Sometimes the conflicts are limited; other times, the mental disarray and confusion are almost total.

A person who says, "I have changed my mind," is using a colloquial expression to indicate an effort to resolve an inner conflict. Consider a simple example. A male college freshman agrees to try marijuana at a party. At first he is uncomfortable because he values obeying the law and he knows that drug use is illegal. He also places a high value on self-control. On the other hand, the experience has proven agreeable. And he is eager for acceptance by peers who believe it is okay to use marijuana under controlled conditions. Asked his opinion about marijuana, he echoes his classmates' view that it is all right to be a casual user.

By the time he is a senior, however, he has dropped the habit. Asked his opinion of casual marijuana use at that later date he states, "I have changed my mind. I don't think you should use an illegal substance, especially something that gives you less control if you happen to be driving or studying for an exam and is also bad for your mind and body." Over a several-year period, our college student has worked through the conflict of peer pressure versus personal conviction and belief. He has brought his opinions and attitudes into better alignment with his values.

Some years ago, psychologist Leon Festinger advanced his theory of "cognitive dissonance." On the basis of experimental evidence, he concluded that people who hold beliefs that are dissonant with each other, as in the example given, experience a tension and discomfort that pushes them toward resolving the dissonance.[4]

Festinger's theory has been subject to various qualifications and criticisms. But the general point that, all things being equal, people strive to resolve conflicting states of mind seems solidly grounded. Certainly, opinion poll results suggest that the process Festinger describes is constantly at work. But opinion polls also suggest that it is a weak force. If obstacles arise, the drive to resolve inner dissonance is easily deflected. And obstacles do arise with great frequency.

By focusing on how people deal with conflicts among their own opinions, attitudes, and values, how they strive to overcome the cognitive dissonance these conflicts create, how obstacles arise to delay or thwart this resolution, and how these obstacles can, themselves, be eliminated or reduced, we have arrived at the real substance of the working-through process. Every day, on dozens of important issues it is the dynamics of this process that occupies people's energies. Here is the key to understanding what makes for good- or poor-quality public opinion. The transmission of information from educators, journalists, and experts is a relatively minor part of this process. The personal struggle of millions of individuals to bring their beliefs into line with their own basic values is the major part of it.

Words like *opinions, attitudes,* and *values* are so familiar that we take their usage and definitions for granted. But each of them harbors some ambiguity. Before plunging into a description of how the public works through conflicts among them, it may be useful to define their meaning.

DEFINITIONS

Following a usage customary in political science, I define "public opinion" as the sum of all of the public's opinions, attitudes, and values. When describing public opinion in this general sense, it is usually not important to distinguish opinions from attitudes and values because they all get thrown into the same pot, like flavors that blend together in a soup.

But as soon as one seeks to learn how people deal with the dissonance created by their own inner conflicts it is illuminating to distinguish opinions and attitudes from values, as long as one does not do so too rigidly. However one differentiates them in theory, in practice opinions, attitudes, and values blur and blend together to such an extent that it is pedantic to force them into mutually exclusive categories. With this caveat in mind, some rough distinctions can be useful.

When we examine the social science literature, we are confronted with a large array of words closely related to opinions, attitudes, and values such as

- norms
- beliefs
- shared meanings
- preferences
- images
- ideas
- expectations
- predispositions
- perceptions
- judgments

- views
- philosophies
- *weltanschauung*
- outlooks
- interests
- ideologies
- credos or faiths
- convictions
- commitments
- hopes and fears

There are several reasons for such a proliferation of terms. One is academic specialization. Each of the various social sciences has its own vocabulary. A sociologist will use the word *norm* to designate almost, but not quite, the same phenomenon as an anthropologist who refers to "shared meanings." Economists favor the word *preferences* for uses that psychologists cover (almost in the same way) with the word *values*. Psychologists think of themselves as studying *attitudes*, whereas policial scientists are more likely to use the word *opinion* to designate the same object of study.

But the main reason for the proliferation of terms is the immense complexity and subtlety of the human mind. People's perceptions and feelings cannot be reduced to a few simple words. To describe public opinion we can concentrate on opinions, attitudes, and values, using some of the other words to clarify their meanings.

In the social science literature, opinions are usually regarded as the most superficial of the three states of mind, attitudes go somewhat deeper, and values deeper still. This concept can be visualized as an inverted pyramid with opinions in the broadest part of the pyramid because they are the most numerous and superficial, attitudes one level deeper than opinions, and values in the deepest, smallest part of the pyramid because a person has fewer values than attitudes and opinions, and they lie deeper within the psyche (see chart 10.1).

Here are a few typical expressions of the "inverted pyramid" theory conveyed in the social science literature.

From a Political Scientist. "Distinctions are often made among *opinions, attitudes* and *values. Opinions* connote less deeply rooted judgments on current policies, leaders and events. . . . Political *attitudes* suggest more fundamental perspectives on enduring social and political questions, such

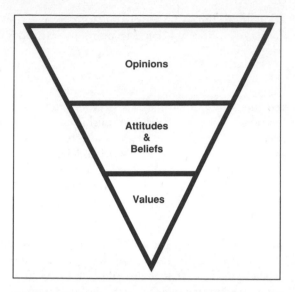

CHART 10.1 Hierarchy of opinions, attitudes, and values.

as attitudes on race relations. *Values* are people's ideals and commitments they make, involving religious beliefs, standards for interpersonal relations, moral and ethical judgments. All three comprise public opinion in the term's broadest sense."[5]

From a Dictionary of the Social Sciences. "An opinion is a judgment, a conviction, a view, or belief held by a person on some issue. . . . It is useful to distinguish [opinions from] broader attitudes and value systems on which they are based. Opinions are generally expressed on fairly narrow and specific points, and a number of expressed opinions may allow us to infer the existence of an underlying, more general, attitude. Thus, while opinions are relatively superficial, changeable, and limited, they often have their roots in attitude systems that are more enduring."[6]

From Social Psychology. "An opinion is tentative in that the subject reserves the right to reverse himself. . . . Opinion is often used . . . synonymously with the term 'attitude.' . . . A *value system* is an individual's overall life aspiration (what he really wants to achieve) . . . an elaboration of attitudes."[7]

In the inverted pyramid theory, opinions are the most unstable, values are the most solid and enduring, and attitudes are in between. Opinions are more specific than attitudes; attitudes are more specific than values. People's attitudes are less likely to change from day to day than their opinions. Values rarely change. Opinions derive from attitudes and attitudes derive from values. The pyramid appears self-contained.

The vast body of public opinion research suggests that some aspects of the inverted pyramid theory are valid, others less so. Aspects of the theory that the data confirm are these:

1. Polls do show that opinions are more numerous and specific than attitudes and values.
2. Opinions are also more susceptible to change than attitudes and values. (But it is a mistake to consider *all* opinions to be fluid; some are remarkably rigid and enduring.)
3. Some opinions do derive from attitudes.
4. Values *are* the most stable, enduring, and fundamental of the three categories.
5. Public opinion, broadly conceived, cannot be reduced to opinions alone but must also include descriptions of relevant attitudes and values.

The changes suggested below are not radical departures from the inverted pyramid theory, but they are necessary qualifications and shifts in emphasis. My analysis of public opinion data shows that

1. Opinions are not necessarily less stable than attitudes and values. They are volatile before working through has taken place. But once public judgment has formed, opinions are often rock-solid in their stability.
2. It is not practical to maintain a hard and fast distinction between opinions and attitudes. For understanding public opinion, opinions and attitudes can be discussed interchangeably, (though the distinction between them may be important in other contexts).
3. Opinions and attitudes, considered together, reflect beliefs about the world that are charged with meaning for the person who holds them. The meaning is usually both cognitive ("In my opinion, communism is finished even in the Soviet Union") and emotional, ("I fervently hope that this is so").
4. Values *should* be distinguished from opinions and attitudes. Values reflect the individual's ideals and goals, expressing either ultimate ideals ("I hold faith with the Golden Rule"), or instrumental ones ("Hard work pays off"), or personal and group interests ("My family means more to me than rising to the top of the company").

5. Most opinions and attitudes do *not* derive from values. People acquire many of their opinions and attitudes from other sources, which is why opinions so often clash with values. (A person with deeply rooted Christian values may hold racial opinions picked up at school or in the workplace.) This point means that the pyramid is not self-enclosed but is, in fact, wide open to the influence of others and to day-to-day experience. Most opinions and attitudes derive from the larger culture, reflecting social norms and information conveyed by the media. People's values also derive from the larger culture but are rooted in early life experience where the culture is mediated through parental and peer influence. People can and do change their values from time to time. But compared to shifts in attitudes and opinions, these are rare occasions.

The most fundamental conflicts are *value versus value* collisions. From our culture we inherit ideals that are shot through with contradiction. The philosopher Alfred North Whitehead once observed that a literal adherence to Christian ethics under the conditions of worldly existence would bring instant death.[8] Our culture teaches honor for equality and freedom, but the imperatives of each collide. Our selfish interests and needs are in constant tension with our ideals, and life is one long balancing act between them. Each of us belongs not only to the larger American culture but also to various subcultures — ethnic, professional, age-related, institution-based, regional, and class-based. To an extraordinary degree, the expectations and demands imposed by the various subcultures collide with the values of the larger culture. The culture of Harvard University and that of South Boston do not mix well. The culture of Wall Street and the inner city are at fierce odds. The corporate culture of the raider and that of the company's employees are even more at odds than their conflict of economic interests. The culture of science and business do not mesh well. The most easily derailed forms of working through are those that require citizens to reconcile inner conflicts in values reflecting the opposing pulls of the various subcultures to which they belong.

Chart 10.2 schematizes the diverse sources of opinion, attitudes, and values.

Whenever we examine public opinion we are holding up to the light the aggregate of people's opinions, attitudes, and values. When the issue is complex, these states of mind rarely form a coherent whole; on the contrary, they are loaded with contradictions and cross pressures. There is, to be sure, a strain toward coherence: cognitive dissonance creates an un-

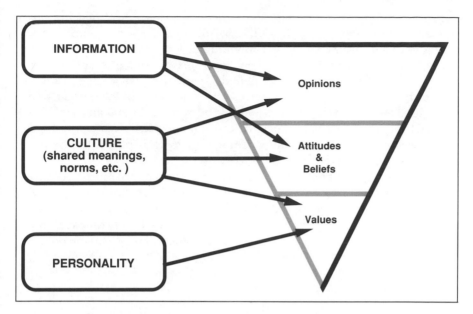

CHART 10.2 Sources of opinions, attitudes, and values.

comfortable tension that the individual seeks to relieve. But it is fatally easy for obstacles to prevail over the discomfort. When this happens, working through is stalled for long periods sometimes for decades or generations.

Finally, there is an ambiguity in how the term "public opinion" is usually used. Sometimes it refers to the totality of opinions, attitudes, and values on an issue and sometimes only to the *opinion* part of the opinion-attitude-value pyramid. The same term "public opinion" is used to designate both the part and the whole. To avoid this confusion, I will, wherever practical, use the term *attitude* to designate the part and reserve the term "public opinion" for the whole.

INTERNAL VALUE CONFLICTS

Americans find themselves in a vortex of conflicting value cross pressures on many issues. Personal needs, reality demands, values derived from parents or absorbed from the larger culture or its many subcultures, lessons learned from living—all pull in different directions. The pop phrase, "getting your act together" is an apt way to refer to an individual's efforts to bring all the diverse influences into some sort of unified response.

In this effort, the public opinion aspect of a person's life has low priority as compared, say, to the conflicting demands of job, family, and personal needs. Developing a responsible position on farm policy, or U.S.-Soviet relations, or airline deregulation, is not exactly an urgent need of people who do not believe that attention is going to be paid to their views anyway—the attitude of most Americans.

Under the circumstances, it is surprising that so much working through on public issues does actually take place. Even though people feel that those in authority are not listening, having a point of view about the life of the nation is important to most Americans, especially on issues that touch their lives directly such as crime, drug abuse, and economic policy.

Examining a few conflicts among opinions, attitudes, and values will illuminate this central core of the working-through process.

THE WOMEN'S MOVEMENT

Few issues exhibit working through as clearly as the response of Americans to the women's movement. Luckily, polling data provides us with an excellent historic record. Almost from the beginning of modern opinion polling in the late 1930s, polling organizations and their sponsors have asked questions about the public's attitudes toward women. In 1937, the Gallup poll asked a national cross section of Americans whether they would vote for a well-qualified woman for president. Two-thirds of the public said no (66 percent).[9] A year later, in 1938, Gallup asked a sample of the public whether they approved or disapproved of "a married woman earning money in business or industry if she has a husband capable of supporting her." The public disapproved by an impressive margin of almost five to one (78 percent to 22 percent).[10]

In future decades, these attitudes were to shift dramatically. Opinion polls in the postwar period report a steady pattern of change in attitudes toward the role of women, especially since the early 1970s when the woman's movement came into its own. A few charts will quickly illustrate the changes.

Chart 10.3 shows the changes in attitudes toward voting for a woman as president. The trend line shows an inexorable erosion of resistance to

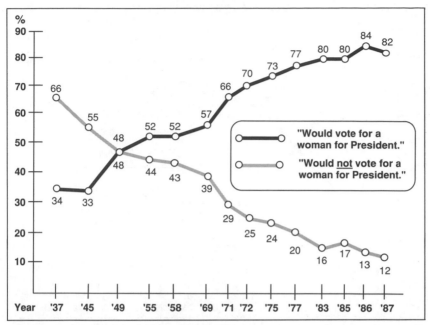

SOURCE: The Gallup Organization with the exception of 1972–1977, (National Opinion Research Center).

CHART 10.3. A woman for president.

the idea — from 66 percent in 1937 to a paltry 12 percent one-half century later in 1987.

Chart 10.4 registers the steady decline in the social norm that married women should not work outside the home if they have a husband capable of supporting them. Few social norms have changed more radically than this once powerful — and almost universally held — attitude. In the fifty years of polling on this question, the pattern of approval and disapproval has been turned upside down. In the late 1930s, the ratio of approval to disapproval was 22 percent to 78 percent; in the late 1980s, it was the reverse (77 percent to 22 percent).

Just two more trend lines will suffice to document the pattern. Over a fifteen-year period there has been a similar public flip-flop in endorsement of the view that men are better suited emotionally to politics than women. By almost two to one margins (62 percent to 32 percent) the public endorsed this stereotype in the early 1970s. By the late 1980s, however, public sentiment had swung in the other direction, with a 60 percent ma-

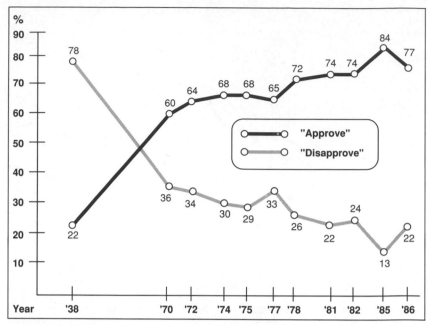

SOURCES: The Gallup Organization, (1938, 1970, and 1975); National Opinion Research Center (1972, 1975, 1978, and 1982–86); and CBS News/*New York Times* (1977 and 1981).

CHART 10.4. Approve or disapprove of a married woman working if she has a husband to support her.

jority rejecting it and a 36 percent minority continuing to endorse it (see Chart 10.5).

Chart 10.6 registers the level of support for strengthening the status of women in our society. In 1970, the balance of sentiment opposed such efforts (by 52 percent to 34 percent). By the mid-1980s, the balance had shifted markedly in the opposite direction, with a healthy 63 percent majority favoring a strengthening of women's status with 25 percent opposed.

It is not at all self-evident why such sweeping shifts in attitudes and norms have taken place. The women's movement gets some of the credit. But the existence of a vigorous women's movement by itself does not explain why Americans were so responsive to changing their point of view in the period extending from the early 1970s to the late mid-1980s.

Economic factors surely played an important role in changing the norms regarding married women working outside the home. By the 1980s, it was clear that most couples could not maintain or improve their stan-

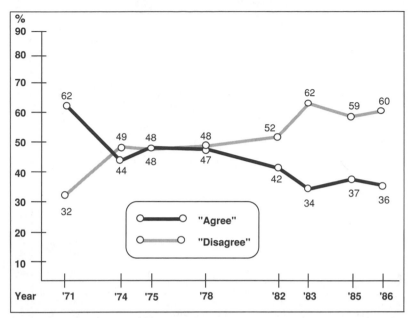

Sources: National Opinion Research Center, with the exception of 1971 (Harris for Virginia Slims).

CHART 10.5. Agree or disagree that men are better suited emotionally for politics than women.

dards of living with only one wage earner. This economic reality is so powerful that in recent years it has come in conflict with the desire of women with children to stay home to care for their children. In fact, almost 90 percent of women (88 percent) agree that "If I could afford it, I would stay home with my children."[11]

I have explored the dynamics of this important social change in other places.[12] The one aspect that is relevant to our concerns here relates to working through. Changes in attitudes toward the role and status of women clearly show how Americans are struggling to assimilate new values with traditional ones. The traditional values relate to home, family, children, fairness, respectability, social status, material security, and ideals of masculinity and femininity. The new values relate to self-expression, self-fulfillment, autonomy, pluralism, expanded choice of life-styles, and other ways of stretching the boundaries of individualism.

These new values exploded on the American scene in the 1960s and

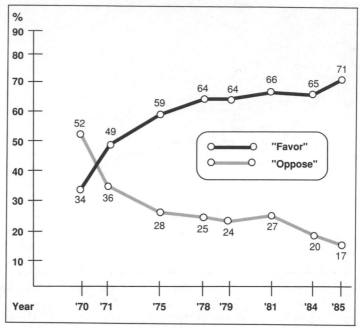

SOURCES: 1970, 1975, and 1978, Harris; 1971, Harris for Virginia Slims; 1979 and 1985, Roper for Virginia Slims; 1981, ABC News/*Washington Post*; and 1984, *Los Angeles Times*.

CHART 10.6. Favor or oppose efforts to strengthen women's status.

1970s, and Americans have been struggling to sort them out ever since. Their potency and the fact that they are not faddish shifts confined to American culture is demonstrated by their spread to Western Europe and Japan where they are creating vast upheavals of social change.

The questions they raise are fundamental. What does it take to live a full and happy life? How well suited are our traditional social arrangements to achieving our most important personal goals? In the American society of the 1950s, conformity to social norms and sacrifice for others (the woman was expected to sacrifice for husband and children; the husband for wife and children) were highly regarded instrumental values. The values revolution of the 1960s and 1970s questioned both on the grounds that conformity to then dominant role expectations for women, ideals of masculinity and femininity, and ideals of sacrifice for others institutionalized a position of inferiority for women. Moreover, the traditional outlook meant that for women more than for men, the new values of autonomy, self-expression, individual life styles, and broadening life choices were being thwarted.

The impact of the new values on traditional values are clearly registered in survey findings. The social norms of the 1930s called for large families with four children or more, rejecting the two-child family as inadequate. Today a majority hold the two-child family to be the ideal.[13] In the mid-1970s, the public was asked which of two forms of marriage — a traditional marriage (with the husband taking responsibility for making a living and the wife for running the home and taking care of the children) or a marriage in which husband and wife share both sets of responsibilities equally — would "give you personally the most satisfying and interesting life." In the seventies, the public was split almost fifty-fifty.[14] A decade later, in response to the same question, the balance had tilted toward the less traditional marriage of sharing responsibilities rather than adhering to the marriage of sharply divided roles.[15]

The very form of the question is striking. People are asked what form of social arrangement would give them the "most satisfying and interesting lives." The question wording reflects the new values. In the 1950s, the emphasis would have been on "the right thing to do," not on personal interest and self-satisfaction.

In the United States, consciousness raising by the woman's movement ensured that women's claims would be raised forcefully. Would such far-reaching changes in attitudes and values have taken place without this prod? There is no sure way to answer this question. My suspicion is that the direction of change would have been the same, but in a slower, more halting fashion — just as in Japan and Western Europe where women's movements have been less activist than in the United States. In present-day America, people are sorting out their feelings about these matters without as much reference to the women's movement as in the recent past. Numerous signs indicate that the direction of change in the 1990s will prove more muddy and inconclusive than in the past, however vigorous the women's movement may be.

On the changing role and status of women, the complexities of working through are well charted. The process begins with the emergence of new values incubated on the nation's campuses in the 1960s. These values spread from campus to the larger society in the 1970s and 1980s, affecting virtually everyone. Contradictions between the new values and the old begin to appear in all walks of life — in work, in play, in religious expression, in art and music, in attitudes toward the self. With respect to women's issues, a powerful and articulate interest group (the women's movement) arises to make sure that the contradictions are interpreted to highlight the plight of women. Not much attention is given to the plight of men — partly because men were so one-sidedly the beneficiaries of the old customs.

Norms that stood in the way of assimilating the new values with the old (e.g., social conformity, premarital virginity, and men as heads of households and exclusive breadwinners) were challenged. The opinions and attitudes these norms reflect began to shift and new norms began to take shape. At the level of individual lives, men and women not only changed their attitudes, but also struggled to find a way to balance the old and the new in their own lives.

The working-through process will continue until the major conflicts and contradictions of women's roles are resolved. They are far from resolved today. In the 1990s, the plight of men under the new social arrangements are claiming more attention — especially because the new life-styles also leave so many women dissatisfied. The life-style of the contemporary woman in the typical dual-earner household is so frenetic that many women are cutting down on their sleep![16] As the 1990s unfold, working through is likely to take place around two questions: Has the thrust toward equality gone far enough? (Men still do not share fifty-fifty in household chores or child care — far from it.)[17] And, are the choices between the sharply differentiated roles of the traditional marriage and the new equal-sharing roles the only or best choices available?

Today's struggle over the role of women shows the working-through process in full bloom. It is far from finished. It concerns society's most fundamental social arrangements, and it expresses itself as an effort to reconcile conflicts raging among opinions, attitudes, and values. On balance, more mass opinion than public judgment still exists on this issue.

This example helps us to see the relatively minor role in shaping public judgment played by experts disseminating factual information, and the central role played by the highly charged encounter between conflicting attitudes and values.

The Conflict with Behavior. The most familiar form of conflict is between people's attitudes and values and their own behavior. Fat people who place a high value on being thin, sedentary people who know that exercise is good for them, rude people who profess a belief in courtesy, people who espouse liberal attitudes but whose behavior reeks with prejudice — this is the stuff of everyday experience.

Most of the disparities between attitudes and behavior lie outside the scope of our inquiry into public opinion. We have defined public opinion as the aggregate of opinions, attitudes, and values on a topic, and deliberately excluded behavior. To include behavior would be to make the study of public opinion virtually synonymous with the study of people.

Such a broadening of scope would vastly complicate an already complex subject. It would stretch the meaning of public opinion beyond reasonable boundaries.

Of course, knowing whether people's behavior is consistent with their attitudes gives perspective to public opinion. One takes opinion more seriously when it is reinforced by behavior. But it is important to recognize that the reasons for gaps between behavior and attitudes are quite varied. In some instances, a gap may reflect the conflict between social norms and people's real opinions. For example, people who profess anti-racist attitudes but who act in a racist manner can be presumed to hold different opinions, attitudes, and values from those who act in keeping with their stated views. Giving lip service to a value one does not truly hold is commonplace because society's norms derive from its culture, not from people's opinions.

Pollers know that to get at people's true attitudes, they have to dig beneath the top layer of socially approved norms. Most people who harbor racist sentiments do not like to admit it because prevailing social norms reject racism. This is one of the reasons why single questions in polls can be so misleading. They tell you what people give lip service to, which is a useful piece of information. But to reveal a person's true values and attitudes, one must ask more probing questions.

Most disparities between attitudes and behavior are not caused by hypocrisy or self-delusion. The field of marketing research focuses sharply on the relationship of attitudes to behavior because the link between them is of such vital importance to marketers. It is common to have consumers express an attitudinal preference for one brand and yet buy another. The reasons are varied. When the consumer is shopping, the preferred brand may not be on the shelves. An eye-catching, point-of-sale display for a competitive brand may momentarily lure the customer away. The consumer may shop for a lower priced brand.

The study of consumer behavior tells us many useful things about the relationship of attitudes to behavior when the intensity of attitudes is low. Consumers may have a favorable attitude toward a brand, but the choice of brand is rarely important to their lives. So they may buy a competitor's brand because of other influences such as good salesmanship or the chance to get a bargain. When the stakes are low, people's attitudes often diverge from their behavior.

Even when the stakes are high, one cannot help but be impressed by the variety of factors that can intervene between attitudes and behavior. Probably the most important factor is people's inability to control their own behavior. The study of smoking affords an illuminating example. A government analysis correctly concludes that "most smokers want to quit, but the task can be so daunting that few try, fewer succeed and even fewer seek any help to stop."[18] Indeed, most smokers intend to stop. Only 5 percent of the almost 50 million adult smokers in the United States intend to smoke five years from now. But there is a high failure rate and a high relapse rate.[19]

Consciousness raising on the dangers of smoking has taken place slowly but steadily over the past few decades. In the early 1950s, only two out of five Americans (41 percent) identified cigarette smoking as a cause of lung cancer.[20] By the late 1980s, however, the number had swelled to an impressive 87 percent of the public.[21] This and other dangers have persuaded most cigarette smokers that they ought to quit. But only a fraction of those who want to quit have done so. Surveys show that in the adult population, the number of smokers declined from 45 percent in 1954 to 30 percent in the late 1980s — a one-third reduction in thirty-five years![22] In a 1957 survey of smokers who had heard about the American Cancer Society study linking cigarette smoking to lung cancer, one out of four said they did not want to quit because they enjoyed it — even though they knew it was bad for them.[23] Many others confess that they are not able to quit because of "lack of will power" or the strength of the addiction.[24]

In brief, then, it is always helpful to know the relationship between public opinion and behavior (to gain insight into the strength of people's views, their sincerity, their control over their own behavior). But owing to the complexity of the relationship, one cannot deduce people's opinions, attitudes, and values from their behavior, or conversely, infer with great confidence what their behavior will be from their opinions, attitudes, and values.

COMMON FEATURES

These four forms of working through share some characteristics. The dimension of *time* is important to all of them. Having second thoughts usually takes the least time, measurable in hours and days. There is no average amount of time for the second form of working through — accepting new realities. It varies both with the temperament of the individual and the nature of the reality. But here, too, it is possible to accomplish working through in a relatively brief time — weeks and months, rather than years and decades. It is when we come to the third and fourth forms of working through — conflicts *among* opinions, attitudes, and values, and *between* these and behavior — that we encounter huge time delays in working through that sometimes go on for years and decades or even longer.

Time can be considered a good measure of the intensity of the underlying conflict and/or the obduracy of the obstacles to working through. If working through is done quickly, this means that the underlying conflicts are not difficult to resolve and the obstacles to resolution are easy to overcome. The converse is true when working through takes a long time to accomplish.

Another feature the various forms of working through share is that they all call for conflict resolution. In coming to second thoughts, one must resolve the conflict between impulse and prudence. Accepting new realities centers on the conflict between the old and the new, between habit and change. People are more or less adept at letting go of the old and accommodating the new. But inertia is always present. There is always stress and conflict in moving from the familiar to new realities.

Conflicts among opinions, attitudes, and values come in many varieties. Opinions based on social norms may collide with a person's underlying attitudes and values. Attitudes grounded in the shared meanings of the larger culture (e.g., what it means to be a man or woman) may clash with values rooted in childhood and personality, and, most difficult of all, deep-seated values may conflict with each other. Often, people's entire system of opinions, attitudes, and values will conflict with their behavior.

The most important common feature is the one mentioned in chapter 5 — all forms of working through are susceptible to obstacles — cognitive, emotional, and moral. Cognitive obstacles are the difficulties associated with perceiving, thinking, judging, connecting, sorting out, and absorbing information. Emotional obstacles involve coping with a wide swathe of feelings and the defenses associated with them: hope, fear, anxiety, idealization, anger, denial, avoidance, resignation, bitterness, self-aggrandizement, self-esteem, and so forth. The moral obstacles involve conflicts between personal desires and commitment to others. They engage the troubled question of when and how much to sacrifice.

In working through to second thoughts, the ferocity of emotions stirred initially by acts of terrorism, brutality against children, or insults to patriotism such as burning the American flag do not lead automatically, even after a cooling down period, to sober and prudent judgment. For this to happen, the cognitive and moral sides of the individual must be engaged. People have to reckon with the likely consequences of acting on their impulses. Some people do this by reasoning with themselves; others need to be aided by respected leaders to whom they turn for guidance. Even after strong emotions subside, cognition and moral concerns play a key role. Lack of information about consequences or poor reasoning ability or bad judgment all constitute obstacles to working through.

The interplay among the cognitive, emotional, and the moral aspects of working through are seen more clearly in the need to accept new realities. On the cognitive side, people have to grasp the new reality, fit it into their existing system of comprehending the world, and see its implications for changing their understanding and their actions. Complex thought processes are involved.

On the moral and emotional side, people have to deal with their own sometimes fierce resistance, especially if the new reality is painful or involves changes in life-styles and sacrifices for others. Resistance usually takes the form of wishful thinking, denial, or avoidance. These are the most frequently encountered defenses against accepting new realities. People are so proficient at procrastination and denial that unless there is some real incentive to face reality, the act of doing so can be postponed for very long periods.

The two other forms of working through fully engage the cognitive, emotional, and moral capacities of people. It takes a high level of cognitive ability to see incompatibilities in one's own system of opinions, attitudes, and values, and to overcome the lazy person's liking for compartmentalized thinking, whereby people store incompatible beliefs in separate mental cubby holes without apprehending — or even caring about — the contradictions among them. It takes a mental openness and judicious turn of mind to entertain a variety of options for resolving inner conflicts. It takes mental energy to absorb the choices and intelligence to see all their ramifications. It takes moral strength to see what is right and commit to it. The lack of any of these abilities retards working through.

It takes both moral and emotional fortitude to confront the familiar defenses of procrastination, denial, and avoidance, as well as other forms of defense well known to psychologists such as projection, scapegoating, and rationalization.

When mistrust of sources of information exists, as it often does, this too constitutes a formidable obstacle to working through. When people encounter demands to change their views of the world, they will sometimes go to great lengths to hold onto their own outlooks even if in the process, they distort reality. (The extreme form of distortion is the denial that historic events such as the Holocaust ever took place.) It requires cognitive, moral, and emotional strength for those with an ideological bent of mind to resolve inner conflicts that threaten their ideology. To preserve it they are tempted either to brush aside all incompatibilities or force them to fit into their ideological preconceptions.

One should not be discouraged by this requirement that people need impressive moral, cognitive, and emotional resources to succeed in working through. The fact is that people do work through their conflicts much of the time and that most of these conflicts can be overcome by a combination of time and focus on them. All individuals have their blind spots, and so do all societies. But in a healthy democratic society, as in a healthy individual, the blind spots are only spots, and there is a depth of moral concern in the public that experts ignore because they do not know what to make of it.

After one more example to illustrate the working through process in full force — in relation to U.S.–Soviet relations — we will be ready to examine the third and final stage of the journey from mass opinion to public judgment (resolution) and how society can help it along.

11

THE END OF THE COLD WAR

W̲e conclude our examination of working through in this chapter and the next with a discussion of the new turn in U.S.–Soviet relations. From the late 1940s for more than two generations, Americans lived with the tensions and preoccupations of the cold war. To a remarkable degree, the United States had persisted with the containment policy developed after World War II by George Kennan, Paul Nitze, and others as the strategy of choice for waging the cold war.

Now, however, the Gorbachev policies of glasnost and perestroika have brought about a major turn in U.S.–Soviet relations. In 1985 and 1986, the early days of his leadership, Gorbachev and his close associates delighted in saying to American visitors: "We are going to present you Americans with a terrible dilemma. We are going to deprive you of an enemy." Initially, Americans were not sure how seriously to take this pronouncement. It was said with irony, but its implications were deadly serious. It suggested that Americans were so wedded to the policies and attitudes of the cold war that we would not know what to do if the Soviet Union abruptly dropped its own cold war policies and attitudes.

In the early 1990s, the American foreign policy elite continues to be divided over what policies toward the Soviets the United States should pursue. Conservative leaders cite the dangers of linking our policies to the actions and words of any one individual. They point out that if we let down our guard and help Mr. Gorbachev succeed, the result might be to strengthen the economic underpinnings of the Soviet Union so that it can at some later date resume its imperialist policies with renewed vigor. They emphasize that Gorbachev is not a Western-style reformer who seeks to democratize the Soviet system because he believes in the principles of democracy, but a tough Communist leader whose every reform is aimed at strengthening the economic base of the Soviet system. They plead with their fellow Americans not to be fools and not to engage in wishful think-ing but to continue with policies that assume the Soviets to be inherently opposed to U.S. interests.

Liberal and moderate members of the foreign policy establishment take a different position. They argue that the old Communist system of Stalin and Brezhnev is dead. Whatever Mr. Gorbachev's motives for in-troducing democratization may have been, a Soviet Union preoccupied with ethnic and nationalist disputes and increasingly characterized by free speech, partially democratic elections, more emphasis on due process under law, and the observance of some market principles in the economy is no longer a Communist state in the old ideological sense.

Not to recognize that our policies have succeeded and that we have won the cold war is the kind of blindness that cannot take yes for an an-swer. Now that Eastern Europe has won a measure of freedom, the Soviet military threat is severely weakened. With the end of the cold war, we are finally free to devote more resources and attention to other problems.

PUBLIC'S RESPONSE

Opinion surveys show how the public is responding to the new situation. The public is much less polarized than the experts. To be sure, extreme views exist at the opposite ends of the political spectrum. But the vast ma-jority of Americans are neither hawks nor doves. They are interested in the new situation but perplexed by it. They are relieved that the threat of an escalating nuclear arms race has receded, hopeful about the spread of free speech and enterprise in the Soviet Union, but at the same time wary because of earlier disappointments.

Though no one has explicitly invited them to do so, Americans are in the process of making up their own minds. They are slowly edging up to the choices of whether to continue some cold war policies and attitudes with their assumption that the Soviets are still the enemy, or whether to regard the Soviets in a more benign post–cold war light and launch a new phase of world history. As the public ponders its choices, opinion polls register a clear pattern of movement away from the attitudes of the past.

In the journey from mass opinion to public judgment, the issue of U.S.–Soviet relations is further along than either competitiveness or the changing role of women. All three issues are broad and sprawling, each one encompasses a complex of subissues and each changes its nature as it evolves. This is why all of these issues are so difficult to resolve.

On U.S.–Soviet relations, it is only in the Gorbachev period that the kinds of clear-cut choices have surfaced that Americans can sink their teeth into. In the past, the public confronted many tactical choices linked with cold war strategy: what weapons systems to support; whether or not to intervene in places like Angola or Nicaragua; how much support to give to CIA-type covert actions, and so on. These questions stirred strong partisan feelings. But they did not generate much public judgment in the sense of stable, settled convictions wherein people accept full responsibility for the consequences of their views.

Before the Gorbachev era, public attitudes toward the Soviet Union had remained remarkably stable over the four decades of the cold war, with one exception. Until the late 1980s, Americans mistrusted Soviet intentions, feared Soviet expansionism, and endorsed most U.S. cold war policies. Negative public attitudes toward the Soviet Union hit a low point in the early years of the Reagan administration (Reagan's "evil empire" period). This decline is shown graphically in chart 11.1.

Throughout this period, the public was eager to control the arms race but also to maintain a high level of military strength. The majority of Americans were convinced that in the past the Soviet Union consistently misinterpreted American conciliation as a sign of weakness and that the "Soviets only respond to military strength" (55 percent in 1988).[1] At times, sentiment favoring relaxation of tensions has been high, at other times the balance of sentiment has favored a hard line. These shifts in mood have been linked to events and to signals from presidential leadership. Beneath the surface, however, overall attitudes remained constant.

The one exception relates to nuclear weapons. In the forties and fifties, the majority of Americans saw nuclear weapons as a "good thing."[2] In those years, America enjoyed unquestioned nuclear superiority, and the public was persuaded that our country would never use its nuclear weapons indiscriminately or destructively. So the possession of nukes was seen as adding to our national security—and everyone else's, too. But once the Soviets caught up to us in nuclear arms and the public realized that we had lost our nuclear superiority, public attitudes shifted radically. Americans changed their minds about nuclear weapons being a good thing.[3] Now the majority came to feel that nuclear weapons were an evil that had to be curbed.[4] By the middle of the 1970s, as a result of this shift in attitudes and the growing fear that the world could be destroyed in a nuclear conflagration,[5] the public had turned against the nuclear arms race.

By the mid-1980s, before the first Reagan-Gorbachev summit, Americans found themselves in a quandary. They were asked to choose between

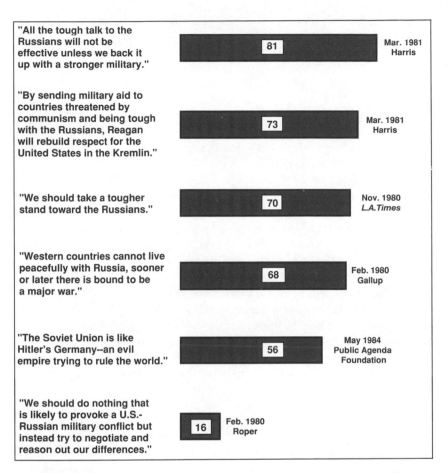

CHART 11.1. Public attitudes in the early Reagan years *(in percentage).*

the dangers of a nuclear stalemate with high levels of nuclear arms on both sides or the dangers inherent in any effort to achieve nuclear superiority, which the majority felt could not succeed. Faced with such unsatisfactory choices, people were unable to work through their feelings. Instead, the public mind was characterized by a vague and unfocused sense of dissatisfaction. Before the election of 1984, President Reagan's handling of the Soviet challenge was the only aspect of his performance (out of seventeen criteria) that the voters ranked as unsatisfactory.[6] After the election, the president who had once pronounced the Soviet Union "an evil empire," became the leading voice for reversing the nuclear arms race — and his approval rating shot up.

CHANGES IN THE GORBACHEV ERA

The public's cold war mind-set began to show sign of thawing only in the 1987–1988 period, several years into the Gorbachev regime. A Gallup poll as late as October 1986 shows the majority of Americans believing that relations between the United States and the Soviets were "getting worse," not better. By March 1988, however, an Americans Talk Security (ATS)[7] survey showed that the tide had turned dramatically, with the majority now believing that relations between the two countries were improving. By mid-summer 1988, by an almost 14 to 1 ratio, Americans had come to believe that our relations were improving (see chart 11.2). And by mid-1989, a two-thirds majority (65 percent) endorsed the view that "we are entering a new era in which relations between the Soviet Union and the United States will be much better than they have been."[8] Large numbers of the public no longer view the Soviet Union as "unfriendly" or as "an enemy." In the short five-year span from 1986 to 1990 the number of Americans who continued to view the Soviets as an enemy dropped from 89 to 49 percent. Correspondingly, those who view the Soviet Union as "friendly" or as "a close ally" shot up from 3 to 47 percent! (See chart 11.3.)

Interestingly, public attitudes toward the Soviet Union have returned to the levels that prevailed just after World War II. In 1945, the public split down the middle in their view of the Soviet Union as either a "peace-loving" or an "aggressive" nation (39 percent and 38 percent, respectively). Just two years later, in 1947, views shifted dramatically with almost seven in ten (68 percent) coming to believe that Russia's ambitions were so strong that it would start a war to get whatever it wanted. This view held constant well into the 1980s (a 1985 survey revealed almost equal levels of mistrust). But by late November 1989, just a week after the collapse of the Berlin Wall, a *New York Times* poll showed public views reverting to 1945 levels.[9] By December 1989, a remarkable 65 percent believed that "the U.S. and the Soviet Union are likely to be allies by the year 2000!"[10]

Nothing has changed America's perceptions more than being a witness to the changes in Eastern Europe. Few symbols of change have been as powerful as the fall of East Germany's infamous Berlin Wall in November 1989. The world watched with astonishment as an arch symbol of Soviet oppression for more than forty-one years was abruptly removed. One survey found almost unanimous public agreement (90 percent) that this

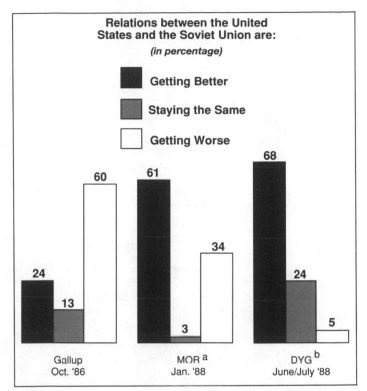

Relations between the United
States and the Soviet Union are:
(in percentage)

■ Getting Better

■ Staying the Same

□ Getting Worse

[a]Market Opinion Research for Americans Talk Security, survey no. 2.
[b]The Daniel Yankelovich Group, Inc., for Americans Talk Security, survey
no. 7.

CHART 11.2. Readiness to open a new phase in U.S.–Soviet relations.

even was "one of the most exciting and encouraging signs of peace in the
world in years."[11] This and other changes (the election of a noncommunist
government in Poland and Hungary, the movement toward a united Germany, and so on) made Americans take notice. Even hard-liners started
to entertain the thought that maybe the Soviets really had changed. Most
Americans (70 percent) concluded that "the changes in Eastern Europe increase the chances of world peace because they reduce the tensions between Communist and non-Communist countries."[12] More than half the
public (52 percent) saw these events as "the beginning of a long-term positive relationship" with the Soviet Union rather than one "temporary and
easily changed" (37 percent).[13]

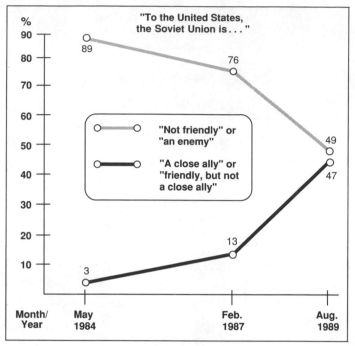

%

"To the United States, the Soviet Union is . . . "

90 — ○ 89

80 — 76

70 —

60 —

| ○ | "Not friendly" or "an enemy" |
| ○ | "A close ally" or "friendly, but not a close ally" |

50 — ○ 49

40 — ○ 47

30 —

20 — 13

10 — 3

Month/Year   May 1984   Feb. 1987   Aug. 1989

SOURCES: The Roper Organization, May 1984; and Louis Harris and Associates, Feb. 1987 and Aug. 1989.

CHART 11.3. Friend or foe?

The key element in American public attitudes is people's perception of Soviet motives. When Americans believe that world domination is the driving force behind Soviet policy, they attribute all manner of aggressive intent to Soviet actions. Conversely, when the public sees protecting their own national security as the Soviet main motive, their actions are perceived in a more benign light. Chart 11.4 depicts a remarkable reversal of American perceptions over the five-year span from 1985–1990.

In the interest of reducing tensions, the public is prepared to endorse a wide range of cooperative efforts. ATS surveys show a majority of the public endorsing cooperation with the Soviets on joint economic ventures, stopping illicit drug traffic, joint environmental projects, fighting terrorism, and even resolving mid-East conflicts (see chart 11.5). Most impressively, a 64 percent majority strongly approved the goal of "moving as quickly as possible to end the cold war between the United States and the Soviet Union." (An additional 24 percent approved with qualifications.)[14]

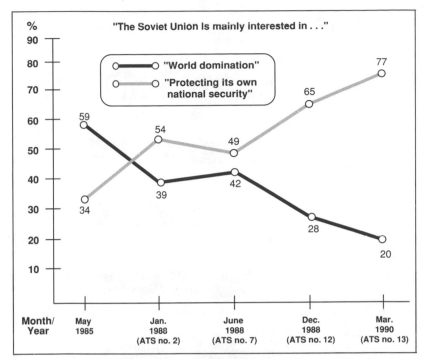

SOURCES: Market Opinion Research, May 1985; all other surveys were conducted by Americans Talk Security.

CHART 11.4. A perceived shift in Soviet motives.

The main reason for the upsurge of hope and optimism has been a positive attitude toward Mr. Gorbachev. Large majorities of the American public hold favorable impressions of him.[15] They believe he is different from past Soviet leaders — one who is more "modern and enlightened,"[16] can be trusted,[17] and is more interested in peaceful relations with the West.[18] He is seen as a Russian leader who recognizes the tremendous danger of nuclear war to both the Soviet Union and the United States and thus welcomes arms control agreements[19] even to the point of making real concessions to the United States.[20] The public also believes that the changes he had introduced to make the Soviet Union and other countries in Eastern Europe more open and democratic societies are significant and lasting.[21] The vast majority are convinced that for world peace and good U.S.–Soviet relations, it is important that Gorbachev remain the leader of the Soviet Union.[22] Solid majorities also feel that Gorbachev's policies stem from a

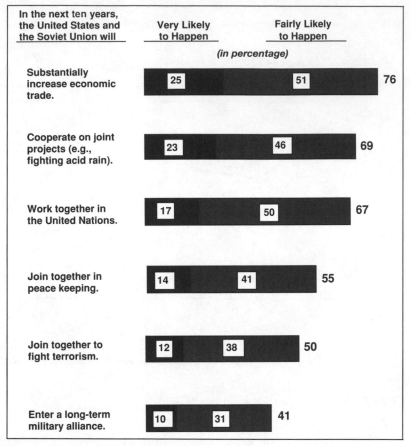

In the next ten years, the United States and the Soviet Union will | Very Likely to Happen | Fairly Likely to Happen

(in percentage)

Substantially increase economic trade. | 25 | 51 | 76

Cooperate on joint projects (e.g., fighting acid rain). | 23 | 46 | 69

Work together in the United Nations. | 17 | 50 | 67

Join together in peace keeping. | 14 | 41 | 55

Join together to fight terrorism. | 12 | 38 | 50

Enter a long-term military alliance. | 10 | 31 | 41

SOURCE: Marttila & Kiley, Inc., for Americans Talk Security, survey no. 4, Mar. 1988.

CHART 11.5. Prospects for cooperation.

belief that the more freedom individuals have, the more productive they will be.[23]

If the desire for improved relations had no other cause than "Gorbymania," one could expect this mood to be as transient and fickle as similar moods in the past, particularly in the heyday of the detente forged in the Nixon-Ford-Kissinger years. But the public opinion data suggests that the public yearns for better relations for other reasons and that the opening provided by Mr. Gorbachev simply creates an opportunity to move in this direction.

Americans had grown weary of the cold war, feeling that it was obsolete and was keeping us from addressing other urgent problems. Americans now see the main threat of nuclear war coming not from the Soviet
side but from terrorists or Third World countries (e.g., Iraq's Saddam
Hussein).[24]

At the same time that the public sees the Soviet threat subsiding,
other threats loom larger. Above all, drugs and drug trafficking have come
to preoccupy the public, not only as domestic issues but also as major
threats to national security.[25] The American public is rethinking the meaning of national security and is defining it more broadly than in the Reagan
years, when it was linked almost exclusively with military strength. Now,
not only are drugs seen to be a national security threat but so also is the
new competitive weakness of the American economy. Majorities see our
trade imbalance as a hazard to national security[26] and believe economic
competitors may pose a graver threat to national security than our military adversaries.[27] The public now feels that we can ill afford all the
money spent on the arms race and on military support of our allies, and
though we must remain strong militarily, voters have concluded that the
levels of expenditure in pursuit of cold war policies have hurt us economically.[28] Americans understand that new threats call for new policies.[29]

If our description of public attitudes ended here, the implication
would be clear: the majority of Americans welcome the end of the cold
war because they think it is obsolete and is deflecting our attention and
resources away from more urgent problems. But such a conclusion is premature and may, in the light of other public opinion data, be misleading. For the public is far from holding these views in a manner sufficiently
firm and stable to warrant calling it public judgment. Large elements of
mass opinion persist. The public is still engaged in the process of working
through.

SIGNS OF MASS OPINION

Americans continue to hold conflicting feelings about the Soviet Union and
the threat it poses, and these conflicts are still deep-seated and unresolved.

Historic events have deposited a residue of fear and mistrust. The
Cuban missile crisis is still part of living memory: the realization that we
were once headed toward nuclear confrontation with the Soviet Union.
The nuclear arms race, which produced fifty thousand nuclear weapons —
more than enough to reduce both nations to rubble — has still barely begun
to reverse itself. In the 1950s McCarthy period, Americans were fearful

that Communist ideology and pro-Soviet feelings were creating internal subversion. The spread of Eurocommunism posed the threat that the Communists might take over our closest European allies.

Even after the fears of the fifties subsided, Communist ideology continued to offend fundamental American values. It was seen as posing a threat to political, religious, and economic freedom. For the entire postwar period, the major challenge to American leadership came from the Communist world and particularly from the Soviet Union. America's most bitter, inconclusive, and divisive war outside its borders, in Southeast Asia, was fought to contain communism.

The threat to national survival, the threat of internal subversion, the threat to our allies, the threat to our own cherished freedoms, the threat to our world leadership position, the threat to peace — it is hard to find a more all-embracing set of concerns. Perhaps some of these threats were exaggerated, but survey data show that they have deep roots in the American consciousness. Such fears do not evaporate overnight, however hopeful people may be, and however promising the prospects of a new relationship.

Without doubting the sincerity of the public's desire to cooperate with the Soviet Union, it is important to emphasize that many of the public's inner conflicts remain unresolved. Just a few bits of evidence will reveal the reality of the inner conflict and ingrained mistrust. The first set of findings summarized below are abstracted from surveys conducted before Eastern Europe's new freedom at the end of 1989. The second set summarizes surveys conducted after the fall of the Berlin Wall.

1. In 1984, two-thirds of Americans (67 percent) expressed the fear that "if we are weak, the Soviet Union at the right moment will attack us or our allies in Europe and Japan."[30] By the end of 1988, this fear that the Soviets would exploit any military weakness we might show had fallen to 55 percent. The reduction is significant, but in late 1988 a majority still expressed this fear.[31]

2. The fear that communism threatens our religious and moral values fell from 74 percent in 1984 to 59 percent in December 1988. Here again, this is a goodly drop but the fear remains widespread.[32]

3. In 1982, two-thirds of Americans (66 percent) felt that the Soviets could not be trusted to keep their part of the bargain in nuclear arms control agreements.[33] Almost seven years later, this critical index of mistrust had fallen to 46 percent. This is substantial progress, but as recently as December 1988 fewer than a majority (44

percent) say they trust the Soviets to keep faith with their nuclear arms agreements.[34]

4. One poll measure of how serious a threat the Soviet Union poses to our national security shows a dramatic drop — from 76 percent who describe the Soviet threat as "very serious" or "serious" in late 1985,[35] to 45 percent three years later.[36] But in the same ATS series of surveys, a question worded in a slightly different manner shows "Soviet aggression around the world" to be regarded as a serious threat to our national security by 69 percent of Americans.[37] (The reader will recall that one of the surest signs of mass opinion is this tendency to respond inconsistently to questions with slightly different wordings.)

5. Another telltale sign of mass opinion is a tendency to say yes to almost every proposal that matches people's values, even when the proposals are incompatible with each other. This happens whenever people embrace two conflicting values without resolving the conflict between them. The persistence of wishful thinking is a sure sign that public judgment has not yet been achieved.

When ATS surveys asked a series of agree/disagree questions on the best ways to strengthen national security, they uncovered these conflicting results: in answer to one question, 59 percent endorsed the view that "we should do everything in our power to achieve military superiority over the Soviet Union";[38] in answer to another question, 70 percent agreed that there is no practical way we can achieve military superiority over the Soviets, so we should, instead, seek a balance of military strength;[39] in response to a third question, 79 percent agreed that the present balance of forces is too dangerous because of the stockpiles of nuclear weapons and that we should, therefore, seek a balance at much lower levels;[40] in response to a fourth question, 70 percent agreed that we should move away from weapons that threaten the other side and shift instead toward weapons designed exclusively for defense.[41] These four opinions are not mutually exclusive. The contradictions among them are not necessarily blatant. But policy makers would (rightly) feel dizzy with confusion if they wished to heed public opinion and it were presented to them in this form.

6. The Public Agenda presented a cross section of the American public with four mutually exclusive policies for future relations with

the Soviet Union, before discussing the pros and cons of each with them. Before the discussion, 32 percent strongly favored the first, 64 percent the second, 77 percent the third one, and 13 percent the fourth one — a total of 186 percent![42]

Significantly, after a three-hour discussion when people were asked to vote on the proposals again, the total vote came, as it should, to 100 percent, indicating that people were taking more realistic and responsible attitudes.[43]

A number of surveys conducted after the collapse of the Berlin Wall show that many people continue to believe that the cold war between the United States and Communist countries is still going on.[44] Although there are signs of rising American trust in the Soviets[45] and a belief that hard-line communism is permanently losing its hold in Eastern Europe,[46] the cold war heritage of mistrust remains powerful. Even after the fall of the Berlin Wall:

1. A clear majority (63 percent) believe that the "Soviet aggression around the world" remains a "serious threat" to U.S. national security interests.[47] More than half (53 percent) continue to believe that the Soviets cannot be "trusted to live up to their arms control agreements."[48]
2. Almost one-half (46 percent) think it is likely that "there will be a backlash and a crackdown by the Soviet Union in Eastern Europe."[49]
3. Almost four out of five (77 percent) oppose allowing "American companies to sell high-technology products to the Soviet Union."[50]
4. A clear majority (54 percent) think it is "not at all likely that "Soviet interference in Central America will end."[51]

We have here a snapshot of the American public at the start of the 1990s struggling with a fateful choice in the throes of working through. People want to embrace "end the cold war," but their views are still laden with mass opinion. The psychological process of working through the choice is also retarded by the uncertain direction of the events themselves, so that many people are taking a "wait and see" attitude. Working through is far from resolution.

12

AN EXPERIMENT IN
WORKING THROUGH

S
o far, I have discussed a number of issues in which the three-step process of coming to public judgment has already occurred or is in the
process of occurring (for example, on women's issues), and I have
also pointed to a number of other issues, such as competitiveness, where
the process has been stalled. But I have not yet directly confronted the
question of whether the movement of mass opinion to public judgment
can be accelerated. In other words, can the lessons learned from observing
public judgment form be translated into techniques to advance public judgment more efficiently?

The advantages of such techniques are obvious. Just as the failure
of the country to move from mass opinion to public judgment has adverse
consequences, techniques for accelerating the formation of public judgment could, under certain conditions, help the country solve the problems
it faces.

Throughout the 1980s, several organizations — the Public Agenda
Foundation, the Charles F. Kettering Foundation, and Brown University's
Center for Foreign Policy Development — have worked together to develop
and test techniques for accelerating the working-through process and reducing the obstacles to reaching public judgment. In this chapter, I want to
describe one series of projects related to the issue of U.S.–Soviet relations.

In 1984, the Public Agenda and Brown's Center for Foreign Policy
Development conducted a study of American attitudes toward the nuclear
arms race.[1] The study revealed that in the 1970s the public had grown dis-
enchanted with the nuclear arms race and was deeply dissatisfied with policies that, in the name of arms control, institutionalized it at unacceptably
high levels of danger. The study showed that the public yearned for an

151

end to the nuclear arms competition; at the same time a majority (56 percent) shared Mr. Reagan's characterization of the Soviet Union as an "evil empire."[2] Unable to reconcile these conflicting pulls, public opinion in the 1980s turned volatile and frustrated.

In the late 1980s, with the support of a number of leading foundations,[3] Brown's center and Public Agenda launched an experiment to stimulate the working-through process on the public's stand about future American policies toward the Soviet Union. The purpose of the project, conducted before the Berlin Wall came down, was to gain insight into the direction of the public's thinking and to determine how the American public in the Gorbachev era might in the future resolve its ambivalence toward U.S.-Soviet relations.

The first task of the project was to develop choices for the public to wrestle with. After extensive discussions with experts and focus group research with the public, the project team developed four long-term policy choices, called "futures." For probing public attitudes, these futures had to be simple enough to be intelligible to the public. Yet, at the same time, they could not be so simplistic as to be irrelevant and meaningless to foreign policy experts and leaders. Fulfilling these dual criteria was difficult because the gap between the experts and public understanding on nuclear arms is particularly wide. For the average citizen, the technical terminology used in expert debate on arms control is impenetrable.

Once the four futures were developed, the Brown–Public Agenda study team convened cross sections of the public in cities across the country for intensive three-hour workshops. In these workshops, the futures were presented and discussed in detail. Before each discussion began, participants were invited to assess the four futures, which were presented to them as follows:

> People have different ideas about what our relationship with the Soviet Union should be like in the year 2010. Keeping in mind what you think is possible along with what you'd like the country to do, consider these four alternative visions of what the United States should try to achieve by the year 2010. Indicate how you feel about each of them.
>
> *Future 1. The U.S. Gains the Upper Hand.* Regain clear superiority over the Soviets in military matters and world affairs.
>
> *Future 2. Eliminate the Nuclear Threat; Compete Otherwise.* Reach agreements with the Soviets to end the arms race and prevent local conflicts, such as those in the Middle East, from posing a nuclear threat; at the same time, fight Communist expansion in the Third World.
>
> *Future 3. Cooperative Problem Solving.* Make agreements with the Soviets on problems facing both nations, such as threats to the environ-

ment and the spread of nuclear weapons to nations around the world.

Future 4. Defend Only North America. Bring our troops home, gradually ending our treaty commitments and letting our allies take care of themselves.[4]

After people rated the four futures, a half-hour video was presented with printed materials prepared by the Public Agenda and the Brown Center specifically for this project. In the video the salient features of each of the four futures and the costs, risks, and trade-offs associated with it (pros and cons) were explained and reiterated. The Public Agenda recruited university professors from outside the foreign policy field as moderators for the lively discussion that followed each video presentation. Only professors with a reputation as outstanding teachers were selected, and all of the moderators were given intensive training so that all of the group discussions would be conducted in a parallel manner. (Foreign policy experts were not used, on the premise that they might unintentionally introduce their own biases or terminology.)

In the final half-hour of each session, participants answered an extensive battery of questions about their opinions of the four futures and evaluated them for a second time. Although the wording of the futures was identical in both pre- and postratings, the posttest evaluation also asked participants to keep in mind the pros and cons of each future and the arguments and counterarguments that had been the main focus of the three-hour interventions. A cross section of 963 citizens participated in these sessions, which were held in Baltimore, Nashville, Seattle, San Antonio, and Chicago.

Differences and similarities between the "before" and "after" parts of the public's ratings tell us some useful things about the working-through process.

"BEFORE" AND "AFTER" DIFFERENCES

Because the project was done before the Berlin Wall was dismantled and before non-Communist governments were installed in Eastern Europe, our interest is less with the project's substantive findings than with process and technique. We want to learn how working through advances toward resolution under carefully controlled conditions. The key question is whether a three-hour intervention designed to assist working through actually did so. To what extent, if any, did it help participants to resolve their inner conflicts and to clarify their thinking? If it did help, how did the process work and is it applicable under "real world" conditions?

A cautionary note: In reviewing the results below, readers with a scientific background should keep in mind that the Brown–Public Agenda project was not designed as a controlled experiment. Its purpose was not the scientific objective of testing a research method, but the practical one of learning more about how people would react if they had an opportunity to confront, under ideal conditions, choices on U.S.–Soviet relations they had not considered before. Though the results are provocative, they require testing with controls before they can be considered "proven" in a scientific sense.

With this caveat in mind, we can summarize what happened as a result of the intervention.

Initial Public Reaction to the Futures Betrays Many Signs of Mass Opinion

The public's evaluation of the four futures before the three-hour intervention shows that participants did not recognize the tensions and contradictions among the futures. Their responses failed to discriminate between competing alternatives. A clear indication of this is shown in table 12.1.

The majority of participants (63 percent) said they "strongly favored" two or more futures simultaneously (table 12.1). At this prediscussion stage, the participants' first reaction was to combine the futures or gloss over the incompatibilities between them. Many wanted, for example, to engage in "cooperative problem solving" with the Soviets on medical research while aggressively pursuing dominance in military power. Only after the moderators pointed out the tensions between these sentiments did participants begin to sort out their feelings. When participants, at the suggestion of the moderators, put themselves in the Soviets' shoes, they started to see how hard it would be for the USSR to work cooperatively with another country that was simultaneously seeking "to gain an upper hand" militarily.

Attitudes measured in the pretest also show signs of wishful thinking and a desire to have it all — the "say-yes-to-everything" phenomenon. In prediscussion interviews, even small changes in question wording caused large changes in response — a sure sign of mass opinion. People's initial top-of-the-head responses were volatile, unrealistic, and inconsistent. People wanted something different, but they had not yet taken into account the

TABLE 12.1

COMPARISON OF PRETEST AND POSTTEST RESPONSES
TO THE FOUR FUTURES
(in percentage)

| FUTURE | STRONGLY FAVOR | | |
	Pretest	Posttest	Change
1. The United States gains the upper hand	32	26	− 6
2. Eliminate the nuclear threat	64	21	−43
3. Cooperative problem solving	77	39	−38
4. Defend only North America	13	14	+ 1
Total	186	100	−86

consequences of what they wanted. The public at this stage is like the person who says yes to the question "Do you want an apple or an orange?"

Changes in the Posttest

During the intervention, participants engaged in extended discussions of each of the four futures. They were also exposed to a variety of pro and con arguments for each. Afterwards, their attitudes toward three of the four futures changed dramatically. By contrast, the public's response to future 4 — Defend Only North America — remained remarkably constant throughout the process.

Both the changes and nonchange are revealing. After the discussions, favorable ratings for the three most popular futures plummeted! Why did this happen? In the discussions, participants began to face reality and to think through the implications of what they truly wanted the long-term picture to look like. They grew less prone to endorse incompatible futures and more likely to select realistically among them. Having wrestled with the pros and cons of each future, they began to see that they could not have it all. As Villanova Professor John Immerwahr, who helped train the moderators, observed, "After hearing the pros and cons and after being given the time and opportunity to work through the choices, we found people moving toward a more responsible and consistent view about where they want the country to move in the long run.[5] (See table 12.1 for the differences between the pre- and postratings.)

The shifts in people's preferences at the end of the three-hour intervention do not mean that the participants' thinking had become completely consistent or realistic. The posttest reveals many areas where participants have not yet worked through fundamental contradictions. Even in posttest, nearly one-third (29 percent) of those who support future 2, which calls for extensive arms control treaties, also say that "because the Soviets will not keep their end of the bargain, we should not sign any agreements with them limiting nuclear arms."[6]

Interestingly, the largest drop in public support occurred in relation to future 2—the policy of cooperating with the Soviets to eliminate the nuclear threat while continuing to treat them as adversaries in all other arenas. The 64 percent who "strongly approved" this policy before discussing it in detail dropped to 21 percent—a startling and dramatic shift! Part of the explanation is that participants see future 2 as more complex than the others. The idea of cooperating in one arena while competing vigorously in all others is confusing and counterintuitive for many people. There is also reason to believe that some people may not have understood all of the ramifications of this future in the pretest and became less enchanted by it when they understood it better.[7]

At least part of the drop is owing to people having second thoughts about future 2. Future 2, with its emphasis on arms control and more limited competition, became people's favorite *second* choice. When in the posttest, participants were asked to make a first and second choice among the four futures, 28 percent ranked future 2 as their first choice, but 46 percent selected it as their second choice. Joint problem solving (future 3) was the first choice of 46 percent and the second choice of 30 percent. Gaining the upper hand (future 1) won a 24 percent first choice and 15 percent second choice, and "defend only North America" (future 4) received a paltry 4 percent first-choice vote and an additional 8 percent second choice vote.

Some Questions Showed Little Change Between Pretest and Posttest

Attitudes that show little change can be as revealing as those in which change is dramatic. In a three-hour intervention, there should be little or no change on topics where people have already worked through their attitudes to a more thoughtful and stable level of opinion. And, indeed, several important topics showed virtually no change between the pretests and posttests. Responses to future 4 (defend only North America), for example, showed no change. The support for this future was low in the pretest (13 percent) and hardly changed as a result of the intervention (14 percent) despite arguments pointing to the advantages of this "isolationist" future. The reason is that participants have already thought about isolationism and have rejected it. It is true that at one level people do resonate with isolationist thinking. Many feel that America is overextended, that we have more urgent problems here at home, and that our allies are, in some sense, "ripping us off." But these sentiments do not translate into support for isolationist policies. In the discussions, participants spontaneously said that in today's interdependent world, the United States cannot afford to turn its back on the rest of the globe. In preliminary research, this was the only one of the four futures that had low volatility; people from all demographic groupings opposed it no matter how the wording was phrased. People are firm on this point and not likely to change.

In both the pretests and posttests, participants were asked a battery of questions about their overall views of the Soviet Union and about the threats to America's national security. These questions focused not on policies, but on the nature of the Soviets and our own national security. The public has thought long and hard about the Soviet Union and is aware of some of the changes that are taking place. People are cautiously adjusting their attitudes to accommodate these changes. Public judgment does not mean rigidity; people will change their judgments about the Soviets in response to new events, but they are not easily swayed to change a judgment that has been formed over a period of years. On a number of these questions, little change was registered between pretest and posttest, as can be seen in table 12.2.

Overall, the findings point to an interesting distinction between how people feel about the Soviet Union and what they want U.S.–Soviet policy to look like. Over the years, people have thought quite a bit about the Soviet Union. They are now incorporating the fast-breaking changes of the last few years into their overall world view. But the habit of thinking about the long-term future of U.S.–Soviet relations is not as familiar to them. Public thinking in this regard is still larded with large chunks of mass opinion. The outline of an acceptable long-term future emerges only after people have had a chance to think about, discuss, and work through some of the choices and conflicts.

TABLE 12.2

COMPARISON OF ATTITUDES: Pretest and Posttest
(in percentage)

	AGREE	
	Pretest	Posttest
"The Soviets are constantly testing us, probing for weakness, and they're quick to take advantage whenever they find any."	68	71
"We should live and let live; let the Communists have their system and we have ours; there's room in the world for both."	50	49
"We may damage our economy by spending too much money to defend other countries."	73	74
"We may neglect problems in the United States because of arms race spending."	70	72
"Soviets will increase their support of terrorists and countries like Libya."	67	69
"Soviets will launch an all out nuclear attack on the United States."	27	20

SUMMARY

This project gives a number of hints about how working through toward resolution takes place:

1. Even on as difficult and complex a subject as U.S.–Soviet relations, working through can, under ideal conditions, be advanced significantly in a short period.
2. The form working through takes is not that people shift their basic positions, especially on a subject which has engaged their deepest convictions for many years! In three hours of objective and

balanced discussions, hawks were not transformed into doves, nor doves into hawks. On the other hand, there is evidence that many second thoughts in the direction of greater realism were stimulated. People who initially favored cooperating with the Soviets only on nuclear arms reduction while vigorously competing with them in the Third World, came to believe that this policy had more drawbacks than they had initially assumed. There is evidence that in the course of the three-hour intervention participants achieved a much higher level of realistic and consistent thought. Wishful thinking was diminished. Participants were enticed away from their initial "say-yes-to-everything" response. The kind of compartmentalized thinking that permits people to hold onto incompatible ideas was broken through and a higher level of integration reached.

3. Though invited to make clear-cut choices, participants retained their ambivalent feelings toward the Soviets. It will probably take a decade or more of good relations between the United States and the Soviet Union to dissipate the heritage of mistrust built up over the past forty years. But significantly, that ambivalence does not prevent people from opting for more cooperative relationships, without letting down our guard.

4. The principal form taken by working through in this project was to reduce people's enthusiasm for all three credible futures. (From the outset, there was little credibility for the fourth.) Once the pros and cons of each choice were clearly set forth, their drawbacks stood out and people's attitudes became more sober.

5. It always helps when people are motivated to do the hard work that working through entails. In this instance, participants were highly motivated: the subject is of supreme importance; there is dissatisfaction with the status quo, participants enjoyed being invited to participate and were greatly stimulated by the discussion.

13

TEN RULES FOR RESOLUTION

W e turn now to the third stage of the public judgment process — resolution. How does the public complete working through and come to form stable, coherent, and responsible judgments on issues? I present ten rules for resolution. Each one identifies the obstacles standing in the way of resolution and offers suggestions for overcoming them.

The ten rules are formulated as guides for those leaders who desire to engage the public in the kind of dialogue that develops public judgment and enhances the quality of public opinion. (In the book's final chapter [chap. 19], I sketch the outlines of a plan of action for improving public judgment in America, that incorporates these ten rules into a larger strategy.)

RULE ONE: On any given issue, it is usually safe to assume that the public and the experts will be out of phase. To bridge the gap leaders must learn what the public's starting point is and how to address it.

Most of the time on most issues, experts and the public start from different positions. If experts have been thinking about a subject for years (such as the federal budget deficit) but the public has not, leaders need to take this factor into account, and if they want to communicate effectively with the public, they need to learn to start where the public starts. Unfortunately, most experts address issues without even knowing what the public's starting position is. Examples are not difficult to unearth.

1. Rising health care costs: Experts start with such factors as the high cost of new medical technology and the aging of the population. But, as Jean Johnson of Public Agenda explains, the public sees

the high cost of health care differently. People see it primarily as an insurance problem. They say, "If I am fully insured and every-one else is fully insured, health costs will not be a problem." Johnson adds that people grossly underestimate (by thousands of dollars) how much their employers must pay for health insurance coverage. They also exaggerate how much doctors earn, greatly overestimate the extent to which doctors' fees contribute to the high cost of health care (surprisingly little), and turn doctors into scapegoats in the process.[1]

2. Social security: Most Americans believe it is a savings plan that physically holds their money for them until they reach age sixty-five. Any reduction in benefits is, therefore, seen as theft: the gov-ernment is robbing them of money they saved over a lifetime. Younger Americans fear that when their turn comes, the till will be empty.[2]

3. The crisis in education: Experts and leaders stress the need for young people to acquire the technical skills needed in our high-tech world; citizens see the problem largely in ethical terms. Citizens stress the need for schools to impart moral virtues, such as good study and work habits and a high level of motivation, on the premise that if students make the effort they will acquire the skills they need without requiring special skill training.[3]

4. Immunizing children in the Third World: Americans have an image of Third World people living in remote villages where they never see a doctor. They assume that it is just about impossible to immunize the children. They have no concept of the commitment and progress that has already been made on universal immunization. When leaders fail to take this awareness-lag into account, they find themselves talking past people, failing to communicate.[4]

5. Campaign finance reform: The public is most concerned with the consequences of excess expenditures in creating "negative" or "distorted campaigns." Most people do not understand how abuses affect them personally, or how they undermine the public interest. Moreover, even after learning more about it, most people give campaign finance reform a very low priority compared to other issues. The experts give campaign finance reform much more importance because they claim current regulation is undermining the democratic process. Their central concern revolves around the growing influence of political action committees (PACs) in the legislative process. As one participant at a conference on this topic stated, "The question is whether Congress is going to represent

> average people as a whole, or the group of interests that are increasingly funding them."[5]

These examples can be multiplied almost endlessly. It is not an exaggeration that on virtually every public policy issue, experts and public do not share the same point of departure. Experts have little concept of where the public starts and how this differs from their own point of departure or how to bridge the gap.

RULE TWO: Do not depend on experts to present issues.

As specialization has grown, so has the use of jargon and technical terms. These semiprivate languages serve many purposes; a principal one is a gatekeeper function. No force is more powerful in maintaining the distinction between insiders and outsiders: if you do not speak the lingo, you are automatically an outsider, which thereby safeguards the subculture from invasion by outsiders and preserves it for insiders.

So deeply rooted is this tendency and so unconscious, that even when experts genuinely wish to include the public, their language, tone of voice, and distinctive framework distance them from the mass of people. For example, in the interests of public education, television has presented many programs featuring discussions among experts in the arms control and foreign policy fields. Often, these programs have the opposite effect of what was intended. Instead of making people feel that they understand the issues better, the talk about MIRVing and MARVing missiles, throw weights, and Stealth bombers confirm in viewers their assumption that the discussion could not conceivably be aimed at them. Even experts sincerely committed to bringing the public into policy discussions will sometimes impede the process by insisting on correct terminology as the "price" of the public's participation. For example, experts concerned about prison overcrowding may feel that the first order of business is to teach citizens the distinction between prison and jail. Although teaching people this distinction satisfies experts, it does little to help citizens resolve their conflicting desires to keep criminals off the street *and* at the same time avoid the tax increases needed to build new prisons. Instead the precious resource of limited public attention is spent on details that are irrelevant to advancing resolution of the issue at hand.

The problem is exacerbated by the fact that many words that do not sound technical have, for the experts, technical meanings that run counter to the assumptions of the public. For more than two decades, expert discussions of arms control agreements have meant something different than the public thought. By arms control, experts meant achieving a *balance* of arms, usually at a high and escalating level. By arms control the public assumed that experts meant not arms balance but arms *reductions*. It was not until the Strategic Arms Reduction Treaty (START) talks initiated in the Reagan years that arms control began to mean what the public thought it meant.

RULE THREE: Learn what the public's pet preoccupation is and address it before discussing any other facet of the issue.

Everyone has had the experience of discussing a subject with people who simply will not pay attention because they are so busy with what they themselves want to say. With ill-concealed impatience they wait until you have finished so they can speak their own piece. So it is with public issues. On every issue that stirs strong feelings, the majority of people invariably bring with them a pet theory or preoccupation, an *idee fixe*. If you address this preoccupation, they will listen to what you have to say. If you do not address it, they will not listen. It is almost as if people have grown so obsessed with their own theories bursting within them that they cannot pay attention until these have been addressed. Nor is this idiosyncrasy confined to the public; it characterizes experts and leaders as well.

One reason former President Reagan was so persuasive to the public on issues such as welfare was that he homed in on people's pet convictions. His picture of the "welfare queen" collecting multiple welfare checks and riding around town in a Cadillac tapped the worst fears—and convictions—of hard-pressed taxpayers. Reagan's great skill as a communicator was his uncanny feel for people's pet preoccupations, such as the public's convictions that "waste, fraud, and abuse" in government spending underlies the federal budget deficit.

The fact that many of the public's preoccupations may be tinged with irrationality does not make them any weaker. In fact, it makes them all the stronger. One sees nonrational influences in many issues. If someone threatens to take even a nickel away from government programs for older Americans, they respond as if this would leave them destitute. (Actually, most older Americans are not opposed to compromises in principle, if they could be convinced that these were not the first step to the poorhouse.) As we have seen, the public takes a hard line on prison overcrowding because, all evidence to the contrary, people are convinced that prisoners have it soft and that the criminal justice system is coddling criminals at the expense of victims. Some people also resist higher pay for school teachers out of a residual idealism that somehow teaching is like a religious calling and that when teachers strike for higher pay they are violating a sacred social ethic.

Often the public's preoccupations are serious concerns that have, at least in the public's mind, gotten too little attention from leadership. In the Public Agenda study of the prison problem, the public's overriding concern was for public safety. Prison officials might be rightly troubled about overcrowding and prison safety, but the public was concerned about the *public's* safety. Moreover, many citizens were angry that so many criminal justice professionals seemed to dismiss the legitimacy of the public's fears out of hand. (Republican campaign strategist Roger Ailes tapped into this reservoir of public concern and anger in his famed "Willie Horton" TV spot for then Vice-president Bush.) In the Public Agenda study, support for alternative sentencing programs was widespread as long as they were seen as rehabilitative programs for *nonviolent* criminals. But expanding these programs to include criminals with violent histories was unacceptable to most of the study's participants. As the report states: "Public support for alternatives is not open-ended. Alternatives are for offenders who pose little risk of violence to the community. If people think that violent offenders are being allowed in their communities, or that alternatives are . . . 'revolving doors' for career criminals, public support for them will evaporate."[6]

The principle here is fundamental. If one is interested in advancing the working-through process for the public, one must acknowledge and directly address the public's preoccupations, whether they are rational or irrational, serious or trivial. Merely acknowledging them is often enough. People want to know that someone knows what is on their minds and that someone has taken it into account. It is acceptable to disagree with people; they expect this. It is not acceptable to fail to acknowledge their concerns, however irrational or stereotypic.

RULE FOUR: Give the public the incentive of knowing that someone is listening . . . and cares.

The public also needs to know that their deliberations will be taken into account by leaders. Sorting through and weighing choices is hard work, and people will typically resist the task unless they have some reason to bother. One powerful way to motivate people to work through public policy choices is to convince them that their leaders want to know and will actually listen to what they say. In a presidential election a debate on foreign policy will draw seventy to eighty million viewers. This same debate, in a nonelection context, will draw only two to three million viewers. The main reason people follow debates in presidential elections more closely than debates at other times is that an election offers them an incentive: at some future date they will vote, and their vote may make a difference.

In conducting focus group interviews among average citizens, something revealing happens in the first few minutes of each session. If the discussion is on a complex issue, like the nuclear arms race or the trade deficit, invariably the participants will be embarrassed. Often someone will say, "You really don't want my opinion. I don't know much about the subject." This participant is implying that he or she was invited to the focus group under false pretenses and is now embarrassed to be put on the spot. When the group is reassured that no mistake has been made and that their views and reactions are valued, the transformation is dramatic. Within fifteen to twenty minutes, participants plunge enthusiastically into the fray of the discussion. And they enjoy it hugely. Sometimes they even listen to what others are saying but only if they have had a chance to express their own views.

This reaction is hardly surprising. Everyone wants attention. Everyone wants his or her views attended with respect and understanding. Of all the obstacles to working through, apathy is the easiest to dispel. As soon as the public comes to feel that the leadership is genuinely interested in what they have to say, the apathy disappears as if by magic.

RULE FIVE: Limit the number of issues to which people must attend at any one time to two or three at most.

We live in an era of information overload. Too many issues clamor for people's attention. It is a truism of the public opinion field that the public can give full attention to only two and one-half issues at any one time. The formulation is, of course, a pedantic joke. But like many jokes, it contains much truth. The public's attention span *is* limited. And, at any one time, the limits are severe.

Awareness of this constraint is one reason why there has been so much public support for ending the cold war: it takes up too much space in the national attention span. Politically shrewd leaders of the past like Ronald Reagan understood this principle and limited their priorities. Less shrewd leaders like Jimmy Carter — a man of otherwise outstanding intelligence — did not understand it. The danger in seeking to address too many issues is that one can end up empty-handed. If more than two or three issues *must* be addressed, they should be paced and timed.

How to focus the public's attention on the two or three top priority issues is a subject of some complexity. Partly, it depends on the priorities of leadership, partly on the media. But to a considerable degree the attention arises spontaneously from the public itself. The Bush administration decided to give the war on drugs top priority after public opinion polls showed that the public cited drugs as their number one domestic concern and also the number one threat to national security.

RULE SIX: Working through is best accomplished when people have choices to consider.

Most Americans are only partly attentive to the issues and highly selective in what information they absorb. When they discuss issues, they generally do so with like-minded friends and family members. When they listen to leadership — the president of the United States, the governor of their state, or the mayor, or prestigious community leaders, or activist organizations, or the editorial comment conveyed by their favorite newspapers — they are rarely exposed to balanced choices but instead to preferred solutions or partisan stands. The conventional method is for the leader to urge a course of action and to present arguments in support of it. The public rarely hears alternative choices argued with equal authority and persuasiveness.

In authoritarian countries, leaders do not even permit their subjects to weigh and balance choices. Instead, they demand obedience, and they use the power and authority of the state to secure it. In such societies there is no need to learn how to deal with choices because there are few choices to worry about. But, as the Soviet Union and other Communist states are learning, this kind of authoritarian leadership undermines initiative and breeds rigidity and corruption in the leadership itself. Today, the entire world is moving toward greater democratic participation because the democratic way matches the imperatives of our high-tech world better than politics based on centralized authority.

People can follow orders without considering choices. They can go along passively; they can waffle, or drift, or mindlessly agree. But without choices they cannot work through to public judgment.

Choices are so necessary to working through that in many contexts the process does not begin until the choices become real. For example, several years after the death of a beloved wife a friend may say to the grieving widower, "You can go on mourning her, living in the past, keeping her clothes in the closet as if it were a shrine, cutting yourself off from new experience, or you can resume living." Only when the widower internalizes the choices can the grief process be worked through.

Another example: parents initially resist making choices when it comes to their children's schooling. They want the schools to do every-thing: teach the basics, prepare young people for jobs, help them be good citizens, impart moral values to them, introduce them to the arts, make them good drivers, teach them to be computer literate, engage them in sports, and help them cope with emotional difficulties. Our schools are in crisis today partly because people have refused to work through the hard choices.

The environmental issue faces the same dilemma. Americans grow ever more anxious about dangers to the environment. But the issue has only partly been translated into choices people can grapple with. It is still largely in the stage of consciousness raising — pointing with alarm and clar-ifying the problem. Working through to public judgment will not take place until formulation of specific choices with all their painful trade-offs spelled out are formulated and confronted.

In no respect is the art of leadership more demanding than in the need to grasp the available choices. Of course, leaders must urge the choice they prefer, but must do so in the larger context of knowing what the alter-natives for the citizenry are. At a certain point, leaders must let go. For democracy to work, the leader's arguments and persuasion and arm twist-ing must come to an end, and the work of the citizens begin. That work consists of weighing the leaders' recommendations against alternative choices. One of the critical stages in democracy comes when the "choice work" is transferred from leader to public.

RULE SEVEN: Leaders must take the initiative in highlighting the value components of choices.

Thus far in the text, I have blurred the distinction between leaders and experts, grouping them together under the single rubric of elites. I have done so because, except for elected officials, leaders in the civil society are often experts of one sort or another, and their roles as experts or leaders are blurred. But in rule 7, the distinction between the role of the leader and the role of the expert must be kept clearly in mind.

Rule 7 proposes that it is possible, and desirable, as a service to the public to sort out the technical and the value components of each issue. On the arms race issue, for example, whether to seek an overall balance of arms, a competitive edge, or mutual reductions is a question of goals and values. *How* to achieve any one of these results when there is asym-metry on both sides is a technical question. On the tax policy issue, whether or not to raise the rate of taxation of the nation's wealthiest people is a question of values; how to do it to maximize tax revenue is a technical matter. In the earlier example of the expert on bridges, the value of maintaining safety is taken for granted, but the questions of how safe the bridge is and what it would take to make it safer are technical.

When experts analyze issues, they highlight the technical side. They do so automatically because that is what they are trained to do, paid to do, and can do better than nonexperts. Automatically and unthinkingly, experts play down the value side of issues because from their point of view it muddies the issue and removes it from their fields of competence.

To the extent that leaders are dependent on experts — and increasingly they are — they are likely to accept the expert's point of view in the form in which it is presented. Leaders may request, or even insist, that technical language be minimized and the issue be presented in clear English that a layperson can understand. They may seek the opinions of other experts. The others may agree or disagree, but it is likely that they too will focus on the technical side of the issue and scant the value side. A conscientious expert may note the value side but is unlikely to develop it with the same skill and completeness as the technical side.

Leaders must reverse the process. They must turn the expert's analysis on its head: uncover the value components, make them explicit to reveal them, and tease out their pros and cons. When the issue is presented to the public, it is the value side that must be accentuated and the technical side deemphasized, with the understanding that once the value questions are settled the issue can be safely returned to the experts. In this respect, the leaders' and the experts' approaches to issues are radically different.

The failure to differentiate the roles of leaders from experts in presenting issues to the public is responsible for many miscarriages of the democratic process. Unfortunately, once they get hold of an issue, experts do not like to let its ownership slip out of their hands — to leaders or to the public. Deliberately or unconsciously, it hardly matters, the experts play up the technical aspects and play down the value ones. Being human, they either fail to recognize their own value bias, or they assume that others share it, or on ideologically charged issues they may be so emotionally involved that they cannot help but advance their own value agenda. They do so not openly or explicitly but by the cunning device of cloaking the issue in technical language so that its value elements are masked.

An example may help to make this point concrete. I recall the experience in the 1970s and early 1980s of a small group of influential Americans who had come to the conclusion that the nuclear arms race in which the United States and the Soviets were engaged was a form of madness. This group included Thomas Watson, former head of IBM and former ambassador to the Soviet Union; Robert J. McNamara, former secretary of defense; George Ball, former undersecretary of state; Jerome Wiesner, former president of MIT; Sovietologist and historian George Kennan; historian Barbara Tuchman, and a number of other equally distinguished Americans, all of whom enjoyed impeccable credentials as elites and experts. As elites they were accustomed to talking mostly with other elites who were also experts. Each one had, however, independently come to the horrified conclusion that their appeals to their fellow experts were falling on deaf ears. They could not persuade them that a continued buildup of nuclear overkill was an act of supreme folly, endangering life on earth.

Reluctantly, they concluded that they must "go public" with their concerns. Tirelessly, they addressed audiences of average citizens, assuring people that the issue was not too complicated for nonexperts to understand and that it was too important to be left to the experts because it involved fundamental moral values. Their own moral conviction had spurred them to break out of their normal practice. In going public, they assumed the responsibilities of leaders, not experts. As leaders, they proved successful in bridging the gap and in engaging the public in thoughtful and mutually enlightening dialogue.

As long as the nuclear arms race was couched in forbidding technical jargon, the public was intimidated from engaging it on the grounds that it was a complex, technical problem that belonged to the experts. It took a heroic effort on the part of those who were not bamboozled to question the legitimacy of this technicalizing process and to unmask the issue as essentially a matter of political values to be judged by the citizenry not the arms control community. Anyone who has talked with experts even in nontechnical fields such as education will recognize their automatic tendency to slip into a specialized language. It is an effective method for keeping outsiders (e.g., the public) at arm's length so that the issue can be discussed and decided among a small group of professional "educators."

Dialogue can be established across the elite-public divide provided that the leadership function of elites prevails over the expert function when the two roles collide. But it takes an extraordinary provocation to force the leadership function to assert itself.

RULE EIGHT: To move beyond the "say-yes-to-everything" form of procrastination, the public needs help.

Denial, avoidance, procrastination, wishful thinking, mental laziness — these are the most common forms of resistance to working through to resolution. There is nothing strange or pathological about them. We encounter them every day in every conceivable context. They are not special to public opinion. They are aspects of normal behavior in all spheres of life. They are universal traits of humankind.

In opinion polling, one constantly encounters the say-yes-to-every-thing phenomenon when people are asked whether they agree or disagree with various proposals. If the proposals sound appealing, people will say that they agree with them, even though they may be incompatible with other proposals that people also agree with.

We have already reviewed various examples. People say they agree with protectionist legislation because it helps to preserve American jobs. But they also agree with antiprotectionist proposals because these appeal to their consumer values. People eagerly agree with proposals not to raise taxes. But they also agree with proposals to balance the budget and even proposals to pay higher taxes to fight drugs, strengthen education, take better care of the homeless, address the needs of children, and other specific objectives that they value.

Leaders seeking to encourage the public to work through their views and make hard choices must have a sound understanding of the dynamics of compartmentalized thinking and to what extent it prevents people from understanding the practical consequences of issues. People cannot take responsibility for their opinions if they are not alert to their consequences.

Sometimes it is easy for the public to take the consequences of their own views into account. The simple leadership act of clarifying what these consequences are is often sufficient. But when wishful thinking dominates, clarification of consequences is not enough. When people persist in being unrealistic, quite often they know it, at a certain level of consciousness. In the Reagan years after the severe recession from 1981 to 1983, Americans went on a prolonged mental holiday. They were encouraged to do so by Mr. Reagan's own wishful thinking, which seemed to bring good times to the country. Opinion polls showed that once one got beyond the first superficial questions, people realized it was not possible to lower taxes, vastly increase defense expenditures, and balance the budget all at the same time. But Ronald Reagan was president. He accepted the responsibility. He said what people desperately wanted to hear after so many years of increased taxes, stagflation, divisiveness over the war in Vietnam, and social policies that deeply troubled average Americans. When in the 1980 campaign candidate Walter Mondale spoiled the fun by stating that, as president, he would raise taxes because it was the only realistic thing to do, he violated the national mood and threw away whatever chances he had of being elected.

Sometimes getting people to abandon easy answers and wishful thinking requires no more than reminding them of what they already know.

In the Public Agenda series of public education campaigns on health care costs, persuading people to take the problem seriously meant getting them to abandon their initial superficial reaction: "My employer gives me health insurance. Therefore, it's free."

This task was surprisingly straightforward. People were reminded in a series of TV spots that health benefits cost their employers money and that this money spent on insurance was not available for salaries and was added to the cost of products. The TV tag line, "After all, nothing's free," merely reiterated what people knew already. They easily accepted this commonsense fact of life when reminded of it.

Logic and rationality and clarity and realism may be admirable virtues. But they are not what political leadership is all about. The poet T. S. Eliot observed that people's capacity for reality is limited. There are demagogues who pander to the public's propensity for wishful thinking and there are leaders who lecture and scold and moralize and try to push reality down people's throats. Most successful leaders fall between these extremes. They know they cannot get too far ahead of their constituents — one or two baby steps, not much more. But on most issues, one or two steps is enough. The public is not passive. Rarely does it need to be pushed. Often a mere nudge in the right direction will add the needed momentum, leading people gently and gradually toward accepting enough reality to advance working through and move toward resolution.

No cookbook formula can teach leaders the subtleties of the art of timing. That political skill is bred in the bone. The point of rule 8 is that, in a democracy, leaders must make it their business to know when the say-yes-to-everything form of mass opinion is operating and to what extent. If it is, leaders must also know whether it can be overcome simply by articulating the realistic consequences of the public's views, or whether people must be forced to confront realism, at least in small doses. Good public opinion research can help leaders to make this judgment.

RULE NINE: *When two conflicting values are both important to the public, resolution should be sought by tinkering to preserve some element of each.*

This rule is second nature to skilled political leaders. They know that inspired tinkering is always to be preferred over bureaucratic neatness or ideological purity. But outside the political domain, this rule is not generally well understood.

There are many creative tensions in American life. They are formed by values Americans wish to uphold that conflict with one another. Earlier we discussed the cross pressures created by the conflict between freedom and equality. The battles in recent decades between political liberals and conservatives revolve around the discovery in the years following Lyndon Johnson's Great Society programs that policies that give people what they "need" and policies that give them what they "deserve" are in greater conflict with one another than policy makers in the 1960s and 1970s realized.

The two values collide in many different ways. Older jobholders resent affirmative action programs designed to push women and minorities ahead in a fashion that violates their hard-earned seniority rights. Parents who sacrifice and save for their children's college educations resent that their neighbors who have not sacrificed or saved can get college aid for their children whereas they cannot. Ronald Reagan became president of the United States partly by capitalizing on this resentment. He made the need-based entitlement programs of the Great Society (e.g., demands for "welfare rights") the symbol of middle America's resentment that people less deserving than themselves were being given priority over them simply because of their neediness.

Perhaps the most widespread cross pressures in American life come from the conflict between *market* values and *communal* values. We discussed this theme earlier (in chap. 8) in relation to the water shortage in the Western states. In another work, I defined the difference between market and communal values as follows:

> Market values are those associated with the workings of market forces in a free enterprise system. The use of competition to bring consumers the products and services that give the best value for the money is a market value. Communal . . . values are those that people regard as so important that they wish to preserve them even when they run counter to market forces. On the communal side, Americans do not want market forces to prevail irrespective of consequences when it comes to such matters as health care for the elderly and the indigent, education for young people who are willing to work hard and sacrifice, help for the small farmer, the crippled, the blind, the mentally ill and all Americans who cannot help themselves. . . . Americans do not want to be ripped off by business, either as consumers or as employees; they do not want their jobs to be victimized by market forces; and they want to win the economic struggle at the personal as well as the national level.[7]

The Reagan era was based on the premise that the liberal social welfare policies of the 1960s and 1970s had pushed the pendulum too far toward the communal side of the value conflict. By the time the Reagan years ended, the public was eager to nudge the pendulum back to the pragmatic center with its emphasis on compromise solutions. In American politics, the public's position resembles a Chinese menu (one dish from column A, another from column B) more closely than it does a coherent ideological program, liberal or conservative. The public favors solutions that are the result of tinkering so that some elements of competing values can be preserved.

An excellent example of rule 9 can be seen in the long-standing debates over farm policy that exemplify the conflict between communal and market values. An exclusive reliance on market values would lead to the elimination of farm subsidies and, in practice, to the demise of most small farmers and the consolidation of farming in giant farm enterprises. The trend has moved in this direction for many years because market values have consistently proven stronger than communal values. But communal values still have a lot of kick in them. Americans retain positive attitudes toward farmers that trace back to colonial days. Majorities of Americans believe that "farmers have closer ties to their families than most Americans" (67 percent), that they are more hardworking (64 percent), and that "life on a farm is more honest and moral than life in the rest of the country" (58 percent).[8] A whopping 85 percent agree that farming is a good way of life.[9]

In particular, Americans are sentimental about those small farmers whom they see as symbolizing traditional American values. Three out of four people believe that small farmers are so important to this country that special programs must be devised to ensure their survival (78 percent),[10] and that if small farmers were to lose their farms it would have a major negative effect (73 percent),[11] even though they also believe that large farms are more efficient.[12] A majority (52 percent) endorse the view that small farmers should get special treatment and not be treated in the same fashion as other small businesses.[13]

When the farm issue was addressed in the National Issues Forums, the clash of communal versus market values dominated the early discussions. Participants endorsed the principle of a free market economy that would gradually eliminate all government subsidies to farmers (a market value). But they also expressed their deeply felt conviction that small family-owned farms must be protected and preserved (a communal value). As the discussion evolved, participants gradually moved toward a compromise position that would preserve elements of each value.[14]

By the end of the discussions majorities had reached the following conclusions:

1. Farming is different and special and deserves some form of government help.[15]

2. More help should be given to the small and medium-sized farmer than to the large, profitable farms.[16]
3. Subsidies that encourage overproduction should be reduced all along the line.[17]
4. Special incentives should be given to those who use environmentally sound methods of farming.[18]

National surveys by the Roper organization suggest similar forms of resolution. Only 15 percent of the public opt for the uncompromising market value that there should be no price supports whatever and that farmers should succeed or fail like any other business. Another minority (28 percent) takes the opposite communal view that the government should guarantee farmers a reasonable income even in poor years. In the middle, a 47 percent plurality endorses the view that there should be a free market for farm products but with a safety net in case of crop failure or a sharp drop in prices.[19] Put another way, the majority of Americans (62 percent) lean toward a market-values position (the 15 percent who do so uncompromisingly plus the 47 percent who do so with concessions) but want to see it cushioned with a communal safety net. (This value orientation is not confined to farms; it is the dominant American ethos.) To assist small farmers, two-thirds of all Americans (66 percent) say they would pay a little more for their bread if the government devised a program that gave economic security to the hardworking small farmer without subsidizing either those who do not really try or big farmers who do not need the subsidy.[20]

RULE TEN: Use the time factor as a key part of the communication strategy.

A brief word is enough to elaborate rule 10. In working through, timing is of the essence. It takes an irreducible minimum amount of time to accomplish any difficult form of working through, especially if emotions are involved. Even when an issue does not stir emotional conflict, it takes time to grasp all of its choice ramifications and to accept them.

The time factor is particularly important when leaders are out of phase with the public. I know of situations in which leaders took several years to understand the full impact of an issue, such as the environmental crisis, or the decline of America's energy independence or the importance of the trade deficit, under conditions in which they had access to the best experts and information. These leaders became impatient with the public because people did not respond overnight when the issue was explained to them. Leaders should allow a generous time for the public to accomplish working through — and then double or quadruple it!

Time is the best ally the leader has. Even when the resolution of an issue is bogged down by obstacles, a surprising number of these will begin to erode as time elapses. All studies of working through suggest there is a dynamic momentum to the process that moves it forward, however slow the pace may be, even when not assisted by outside forces. This is particularly fortunate when the outside forces are weak. When leaders fail to lead, when experts fail to translate their thinking into the public's own framework (rule 1), when events that would hasten working through refuse to cooperate, then the passage of time is the *only* force moving the public forward on its arduous journey from mass opinion to public judgment.

SUMMARY

When the experience of working through is reduced to this handful of rules, the effect may be too much compression. Each one of these rules expresses in shorthand a vastly complex set of processes and experiences. The compression, however, serves the useful purpose of showing that it is possible to codify techniques and theories for advancing the process.

At least two institutional methods are available for elaborating, correcting, refining, and adding to these rules. One is to regard them as seedbeds for curriculum materials designed for the nation's schools of management and journalism. Presently, even though these schools are supposed to educate and train leaders, they are actually educating and training specialists. That is the main thrust of their curriculum which, unfortunately, widens the gap between experts and the public, rather than narrowing it. In part 3 that follows this chapter, I will argue that the present direction of American culture, as represented by the tendency to technicalize the professional graduate schools, makes these institutions part of the problem rather than part of the solution. What these ten rules suggest is that it is as feasible to teach methods for improving leadership dialogue with the public as it is to teach finance or marketing or organizational development.

The second area in which these ten rules can be applied is that informal but powerful institution some people call "the invisible university." This university is the vast network of corporate seminars, think tanks, leadership meetings, conferences, and workshops that take place every day in hotels and conference centers around the country. Although it has no formal status or recognition, it can properly be regarded as America's school for leadership. At great expense, experts from the think tanks, academia, law, foreign policy, demography, economics, and the worlds of science and social thought are brought together with leaders from government, business, and local communities to discuss the important issues and to point the direction of the future. Invited speakers are paid generous honorariums, which give them incentives to invest time and energy to prepare and organize their presentations skillfully. Here is where much of the leadership learning and dialogue takes place. This "invisible university" is a highly effective institution for which, unfortunately, there is no counterpart to serve the general public.

In these meetings, great attention is paid to the technical analysis of issues. At almost all of them, the need for public education, consciousness raising, and consensus building is acknowledged because not much that is of fundamental importance in America can be accomplished without it. But the level of discourse on these subjects is amateurish, as compared to the sophistication with which the technical side of policy issues are discussed. Conceivably, these ten rules could become the primer for bringing the task of wooing the public's consent and elevating the quality of the public's opinions to the same level of sophistication as the expert-driven technical analyses.

Unlike the schools of management, which do not even recognize the need for such a strategy, most of those people who attend the invisible university understand the urgency of the need. What they do not understand is how to meet it.

Part Three

UNRAVELING THE MYSTERY

14

EPISTEMOLOGICAL ANXIETY

At the beginning of chapter 1, I referred to a mystery. The mystery concerned the status of concepts described in subsequent chapters. These include: missing standards of quality for public opinion, the peculiar coexistence in the public mind of strands of poor-quality opinion alongside strands of good-quality opinion, the lack of accepted methods for distinguishing one from the other, the complexity of the three-stage process of moving from mass opinion to public judgment, the many potholes that make that road a bumpy one, the inadvertent obstacles thrown up by the mass media as they single-mindedly pursue their task of consciousness raising, the various principles that can, if applied skillfully and in good faith, elevate the quality of public opinion in America, and so on. Why are concepts such as these not a familiar and staple feature of American public life?

For years I have been bewildered about why these ideas are not part of the core vocabulary of democracy along with freedom of opportunity, one person/one vote, the separation of powers, due process, equality before the law, a government of laws not persons, freedom of expression for unpopular ideas, and the other familiar concepts that are the building blocks of our American democracy. Why is there no felt need for such ideas? Why are so few institutions skilled in techniques for enhancing the quality of public opinion and dedicated to doing so? Surely such institutions are as indispensable to the practice of democracy as lawyers and courts and journalists and public interest groups.

These concepts are not particularly subtle or elusive. Indeed, they are as plain as the need for giving greater attention to protecting the environment or taking better care of our nation's children. Why they are neglected and ignored poses a genuine mystery.

When I first began to present these ideas in the mid-1970s, I did so with a mounting sense of discovery, expecting them to be received with enthusiasm and relief. Why enthusiasm? Because theorists of democracy have always recognized that people are not born with a fully developed capacity for self-governance. It is not like walking. It is a high-order skill that must be developed with much nurturing, training, and practice. Many civilizations never develop these skills. Even in our own times, a great civilization like that of China, so gifted in other ways, shows itself pathetically awkward in moving toward genuine democratic institutions. I expected that practitioners like myself who were exploring new ways to enhance public opinion and the capacity for self-governance would be greeted warmly, as bearers of good news. In some circles, that surmise has proven true. There are citizen groups dedicated to enhancing the practice of democracy, as distinct from peddling their pet nostrums to their fellow citizens, and they welcome new approaches.

But not the mainstream. I have learned that the majority of institutions, citizen groups, experts, and political leaders react as the editors of *Time* did to the volatility index (see chap. 2). In the abstract, they approve. They see the theoretical point of it. But in the end it turns out to be an unwelcome distraction. They do not know what to do with it. Their heads are somewhere else. Impatiently, they turn back to their own projects and preoccupations.

I had expected these concepts to be welcome news to journalists, academics, and educators who deplore the ignorance of the American public. As Everett Ladd learned from Gallup poll data, the factual ignorance of the public and its fickleness is often counterbalanced by a remarkable stability and sureness of judgment in applying basic values. My own public opinion surveys also show that Americans can form sound judgments on issues without requiring the kind of factual mastery scholars assume to be necessary. It is true that the majority is ignorant of many things. *And* fickle. *And* often inattentive. What a relief, then, to learn that the public has developed compensatory skills that permit people, under proper conditions, to form the kinds of judgments necessary for self-governance.

Here, too, I proved naïve. The optimistic conclusions that Everett Ladd, myself, and other practitioners of public opinion have reached after years of immersion in public opinion surveys make little impression on those who insist on the public's invincible ignorance. Far from being relieved by our conclusions, the journalistic and academic mainstream seem to delight in the idea that the public is ignorant and fickle. They do not want to hear otherwise. They seem committed to the notion that there is only one way to arrive at sound judgments — by experts piling up masses of information — their way. To suggest that the public has another path to sound judgment smacks of sentimentality, mysticism, or just plain non-sense. They will have none of it. Far from being relieved, they are irritated, annoyed. And because they are the gatekeepers of communication, their point of view prevails.

It would be disingenuous to give the impression that I was an innocent and naïve youngster who expected gratitude for goring the experts' oxen. Anyone whose profession consists of conveying bad news much of the time is quickly disabused of naïveté. These days they no longer shoot the messengers bearing the bad news, but neither do they treat them with tender loving care. Many years ago I had ceased to be a stranger to the phenomenon of people's resistance to facts. I had learned that the facts do *not* speak for themselves. If the facts happen to run counter to people's deeply ingrained prejudices or interests or emotional commitments, then so much the worse for the facts.

Even with this experience, I was unprepared for the depth of the resistance. What can be so threatening about the idea that the public reaches judgment through the three-stage process described in the preceding chapters? Why is the idea of public opinion quality based on criteria other than being well informed so strange and unacceptable? Why do journalists lament the ignorance of the public with such satisfaction and turn a deaf ear to the evidence that the public has other ways of reaching sound conclusions? It is these questions that made me feel that something beyond ordinary resistance might be at issue, and that a mystery needed to be dispelled.

SOURCES OF RESISTANCE

As I examined the sources of resistance, I was startled to find so many. Some are obvious, others subtle. Some are ordinary, others are special. In recounting them, I will mention most in passing in the interest of focusing on one particular form of resistance.

A quite understandable source of resistance is the tendency of successful, busy people to be impatient with other people's preoccupations. I recall the answer a chief executive of a major corporation gave me when I was haranguing him about his failure to make his convictions on the harmful effects of hostile takeovers felt in Washington. He said, "You have to remember that we are like jockeys in a horse race. While the race is on, we simply cannot permit ourselves to get distracted by long-term issues. These days the only thing that counts is short-term earnings."

Many successful executives in today's America feel like jockeys in a horse race. They feel they cannot afford to be distracted by other people's projects, especially if doing so requires time and effort and if unfamiliar ideas are involved. What one person may regard as a mission, another sees as crankiness. We have broad tolerance for our own pet projects, but little tolerance for those of others. The field of journalism, for example, is full of crochets and rituals and idiosyncrasies. It has its own standards of quality that it fusses over to the point of obsession. But it does not give a hoot about anyone else's standards of quality and is prepared to override them without a moment's hesitation.

A less obvious source of resistance, but still quite "ordinary," is the threat to the status of experts posed by these ideas about the quality of public opinion. The threat is subtle but real. Typically, fields such as public policy, law, medicine, journalism, science, economics, and foreign policy require a long period of training and accreditation. Much of it takes place in institutions that convey a flattering subtext alongside their specialized training. The subtext is "You are special. You are privileged. Your education and training at this institution makes you so." In the elite Ivy League universities, the spin on the message is "You are more intelligent, more knowledgeable, more cultured than the great mass. Your education here guarantees you a place of honor among the elite." At other institutions, such as the better schools of journalism, the spin on the message is, "You have a special mission. It will depend on you to inform the public, to safeguard the First Amendment, to protect and preserve the integrity of our freedom against all those ignoramuses and special interests who threaten it."

All cultures support and promote a status system. That is a universal characteristic of humankind. The positions of honor and status go to those who are most skillful and vigorous in advancing the main thrust of the culture, and in our culture that thrust is related to the ability to control the forces that impinge on our lives.

Those whose training and skills give them mastery over the economy and over fields like medicine and the media enjoy a high status in our culture and the privileges that go with it. One of those privileges is constant reinforcement of a self-congratulatory self-image. "I am successful. I am well-to-do. I am well informed. I enjoy a position of influence in the society. I am (in author Tom Wolfe's telling phrase) a 'master of the Universe.'" This is a comforting, and deeply satisfying message. It makes one feel special.

Being special means being different from the mass, a cut above. For some, it is wealth that confirms their special status. But the bulk of influential gatekeepers of the society — journalists and technologists and professors and writers and executives and specialists — are not usually persons of wealth. Their status derives from their expertise. It is their prize possession, the source not only of their livelihood but their status and self-image. It distinguishes them from the majority of Americans by giving them a privileged vantage point, as befitting people who are "special." They naturally resist when someone comes along and says to them, in effect, "You are less special than you think. The expertise you possess does not make you superior to the public simply because you are better informed." Better informed turns out to be not all that important.

This latter consideration brings me to the form of resistance I wish to emphasize. It is not at all ordinary; it is subtle and extraordinary. It has little to do with diverting the attention of busy people or diminishing their status. It is, I believe, the most important — and the most obdurate — form of resistance. Elites of goodwill who are too self-confident and generous-minded to have their status threatened by giving more power to the people and who truly desire to elevate the quality of public opinion in America are still caught up in it. It is the form of resistance that creates *epistemological anxiety.*

As children grow up in any culture they acquire modes of knowing favored by that culture. These modes of knowing are deeply embedded in the language structures of the culture. They form an important part of the knowledge base needed to survive that is passed down from one generation to the next. As cultures have evolved from the hunter-gatherer world of primitive times to the modern era, the knowledge base has been progressively formalized and systematized. It has grown immensely complex. Arguably, for the individual it represents the culture's most valuable heritage.

To understand the strength of the epistemological anxiety people feel when they stray too far from the culture's approved modes of knowing, it is necessary to elaborate the brief reference I made in the introduction to the dynamism of that aspect of Western civilization I called the Culture of Technical Control.

The concept of culture is one of the most powerful in the arsenal of social science. As defined by anthropologists, culture has a quasi-biological mission. We know that one of the principal reasons the human species has been so successful, compared with other species, is its amazing flexibility. Other animals are more limited by their specialized instincts. In humans, biological instincts are more generalized, more flexible, more adaptable. If the environment changes, humans have the wired-in capability of adapting themselves to the new conditions. The mechanism that permits that flexibility is human culture — the world of shared meanings, values, frameworks, history, tradition, and experience that we inhabit together. Isolated from culture, a person can hardly be considered human. It takes the interaction of genetic endowment with culture to form the human person. Every culture, and every society and individual within culture, is unique and must be understood in its full particularity. Culture is evolution by nonbiological means: humanity completes itself in culture.

Powerful cultures always breed a specific outlook, a world view, a general philosophy—what the French call *mentalité* and Germans call *Weltanschauung*. Commonly, scholars refer to the dominant world view of the West since the eighteenth century as *modernism*. Among modernism's principal features are its emphasis on market values and other manifestations of individual choice, secularism, a concept of instrumental rationality, democracy as a political system, and a culture characterized by individualism, diversity, and pluralism in values and forms of cultural expression.

Modernism has wonderful achievements to its credit: it has generated political freedom and opportunities for the individual; it has reduced the ravages of child mortality, malnutrition, many forms of illness, illiteracy, and poverty; and it has given us the wonders of science and technology. Not surprisingly, the idea of progress is synonymous with the culture of modernism.

But increasingly, there is a sense that modernism as a philosophy of life suffers from serious flaws. One such flaw is a certain spiritual thinness. People find it difficult to live by modernism as an ethic. And modernism has a tendency to be relentlessly destructive of values that conflict with its imperatives, particularly traditional values of community (what I've called communal values).

A closely related flaw is the elevation—almost worship—of science, technology, and expertise at the expense of other values. It is this side of modernism that I have called the Culture of Technical Control. It has gained a dominant position in modernism because it has proven so efficacious in permitting those who master its modes of knowing to exercise a great deal of control over the human environment. This capability has given humanity more control than it has ever had in human history over the ancient challenges to the human habitat—reliable sources of food, shelter, clothing, a stable environment in which to raise children, warmth, light, comfort, entertainment, health care, security against enemies, longevity, a fixed social order, and, when basic needs have been satisfied, the indulgences of individualism.

With such stunning accomplishments to its credit, it is hardly surprising that the Culture of Technical Control is pursued so relentlessly and one-sidedly that other values and modes of knowing get shoved into the background. Although it may not be surprising, it is—as many social thinkers have come to understand—a serious failing, so serious that, if left unchecked, it could prove fatal. Throughout the latter part of the nineteenth century and the whole of the twentieth century, a debate has raged among social thinkers on the nature of this destructiveness and its sources.

The social thinker who has looked into this distorting tendency of modernism with the greatest prescience is the German social scientist and philosopher Max Weber who did his great work in the early part of this century. Weber was particularly concerned with modifying the work of Karl Marx, who, Weber believed, had gotten some of the fundamentals wrong. For Weber, the most destructive element in modernism is not its economic power relationships but its tendency to give "instrumental rationality" precedence over all other forms of thinking, feeling, and valuing.

Instrumental rationality is the systematizing, objectifying, and technicalizing mentality that dominates industrial culture. Weber saw the growth of instrumental rationality as the master key to modern history, and he did not like it. His fear was that the dynamism of this world view would ultimately destroy quality of life in Western civilization. At one point in his writings he describes this effect as "an icy-cold, polar night." He predicted that it would shape the social character of humanity so adversely that the typical individual would become a "heartless expert, a spineless pleasure seeker."[1]

In his most familiar metaphor, Weber described the effects of instrumental rationality as an "iron cage" that imprisons the human spirit and cuts us off from the deepest sources of our being. Through the unfolding of instrumental rationality, Weber discerned an ultimate despair as it stripped life of mystery and charm, destroying what the English philosopher Edmund Burke had called "the inns and resting places of the human spirit." Weber says, "With the progress of science and technology, reality has become dreary, flat, and utilitarian, leaving a great void in the souls of men which they seek to fill by curious activity and through various devices and substitutes."[2]

Instrumental rationality is a mode of abstracting from experience and arranging reality in a hierarchy of importance—systematizing knowledge about it, breaking it down into components that are suitable to the management of experts and specialists, reducing each component to its most readily measurable and manipulable aspects. These forms of rationalization do not concern themselves with ultimate goals or values; they are merely instrumental and administered by experts and specialists.

Weber warned against tendencies that lead to the elevation of the technical expert armed with superior information at the expense of the citizen, armed not with information but with certain key values that include a sense of the sacred and communal that instrumental rationality tends to brush aside. One can readily see that the dominance of instrumental rationality as a world view is ill-suited to the domain of human concerns — the everyday world of human bonds, beliefs, and feelings, in which love, loyalty, politics, family relations, and friendship shape a moral life. That is the domain of public judgment, the domain of values.

In the years that have passed since Weber wrote his prophesies, some of these concerns have proven groundless, or at least not as destructive as he had feared; others, unfortunately, are working themselves out much as Weber predicted.

The essence of the Culture of Technical Control is instrumental rationality and the modes of knowing associated with it. More than any other factor, these modes of knowing account for the spectacular success of our uniquely Western form of civilization. Even in the present era, we see many societies that despise and resent most aspects of our culture — for example, the Moslem world — who nevertheless lust after our technology. And what is our technology but a highly formalized version of our peculiarly Western modes of knowing, with its roots in Aristotelian logic and Galilean-Newtonian-Einsteinian science.

As children grow up in the United States and France and Germany and Sweden they learn a uniquely Western way of thinking about the world and apprehending reality. These modes of learning are powerful, and they stay with us as adults, marking us as the products of Western civilization. Some people become thinkers of breadth, blending gifts for rote learning with high levels of logical analysis, measurement, synthesis, technical skills, intuitive insight, empathetic understanding, and articulateness. Most of us stumble along, lucky if we become proficient in just one or two of these modes of knowing and expressing knowledge.

People are subject to anxiety when the styles of knowing that have become second nature to them are questioned. Our cognitive styles (modes of knowing) are part of our basic equipment for coping with the world and controlling the environment. Anything that threatens loss of control creates anxiety. I mean by epistemological anxiety the feeling that your special way of making sense of the world is being threatened. Inevitably, one's first impulse is to protect against such anxiety. If logical people are told that their logic is irrelevant *in situations where logic has always worked for them before,* they will understandably resist, unless they are given powerful reasons for thinking otherwise. And these powerful reasons would probably have to be couched in logical terms to be persuasive to them. If factually minded people are told that the facts do not count — once again in situations where the facts have always counted, they will naturally resist. If such people encounter situations where logic or factuality does not seem to work, it is hardly surprising that anxiety is aroused.

The instrumental rationality associated with the Culture of Technical Control — logical, factual, analytic, focusing on how and why things work, time and space bound, valuing clarity and order and narrative — generates a set of matching values. I remember my surprise, as a philosophy major in college, to learn how influential the value of certainty was in the history of philosophy. So many of the questions we studied as students revolved around the question, "How can you be *sure* you know x, y, or z?" More than three hundred years of modern European and American philosophy exhibit a clear preference for knowledge that is certain (even if trivial) over knowledge that is less certain, even if important to living. Philosopher John Dewey wrote an influential book, *The Quest for Certainty*, explaining powerful trends in philosophy in terms of this quest. When immersed in this literature, I first became aware that lack of certainty causes many people to feel uncomfortable and anxious.[3]

In later years, I was to stumble upon this phenomenon again and again. In graduate school, as a student of behaviorism, it became clear that this school of thought was more than a set of empirical observations about how to study human behavior. It was an ideology held with almost religious fervor. Those most wedded to behavioristic approaches seemed to need to believe that human behavior could *only* be studied by observing and measuring its tangible, overt forms. The idea that the interior life of the individual could be a proper subject for study, even if it could not be measured in the same precise fashion, was rejected not only on methodological grounds but also was treated with emotional disdain. Oddly (to me, anyway), studying the interior life of the individual seemed profoundly offensive to the behaviorists' "scientific" approach. For a period, I thought that behaviorism might have merit on methodological grounds, but I was never able to fathom the almost religious zeal with which this doctrine was held. I later realized that alternative approaches, because they dealt with intangibles and uncertainties, caused confirmed behaviorists serious epistemological anxiety. In questioning their preferred mode of knowing, one was also raising doubts about their style of controlling their environment.

I recall an attack of epistemological anxiety that I personally experienced. As a college student I developed an awed respect for the power of logic, feeling that logic was the royal road to truth. Therefore, even though in graduate school I had shifted my major from philosophy to social science, I continued to take graduate courses in logic in the philosophy department. In that period just after World War II, an outstanding group of logicians dominated Harvard's philosophy department. I was particularly impressed with one professor and took every course in logic he gave. At that time, Professor Willard Van Orman Quine was not yet the world-famous logician he was to become later. But his subsequent fame did not surprise me, because Quine had by far the most impressively logical mind I had ever encountered.

Following the development of his thought up through Mathematical Logic 19B, in which I was the only native American (in a class of eight persons), was an intellectual adventure of unique interest. In an intellectual tour de force, Quine was able to demonstrate persuasively the poverty of logic as a mode of knowing. This conclusion caused me much anxiety. Logic, my preferred mode of knowing, so vaunted in the history of philosophy, turned out to be a narrow set of techniques grounded in convention and allied to arithmetic—a boon to subsequent generations of computer programmers but almost irrelevant to the great questions posed by philosophy of life. Shortly thereafter, I left the university, never to return, even though I had previously assumed that my life would be spent as a professor of philosophy.

From my professional work later, I discovered that certain clients in the corporate world are subject to a related form of epistemological anxiety. They can accept as genuine knowledge only those data that can be quantified. Some business clients, if an insight cannot be expressed in the form of a statistic, cannot deal with it. They are just plain uncomfortable with qualitative insights. Even when these express an important truth and the statistics are superficial, they prefer the statistics. The quantitative approach to knowledge seems more scientific to them, and it promises greater objectivity and control. The qualitative approach undermines their feeling of mastery and control; it makes them anxious.

The key to the mystery of why there is so much resistance to the concept of public judgment lies, I believe, in its tendency to create epistemological anxiety. It suggests that the dominant modes of knowing associated with the Culture of Technical Control may not be as powerful or inclusive as its devotees have believed and that for some important purposes other modes of knowing, including public judgment, may be superior.

SUMMARY

The combined impact of these varied forms of resistance exerts a powerful force. The experts who hold positions of influence in the society are, characteristically, too preoccupied with their own concerns to give much attention to a set of ideas that does not fit well with their predispositions and frameworks. The fact that such alien ideas also diminish the status of their own expertise hardly enhances its attractiveness to them. If, superimposed on these ordinary sources of resistance, the ideas also cause them a twinge (or more than a twinge) of epistemological anxiety because they run counter to modes of knowing that enable the experts to maintain a high degree of control over their work, then it is only realistic to expect a barrier — a glass ceiling — to block the serious consideration of public judgment and its attendant ideas.

If the strongest resistance comes from the epistemological anxiety caused by proposing a mode of knowing that goes against the grain of the Culture of Technical Control, then sound strategies are available for dealing with it. There are many ways to reduce anxiety. With healthy, well-functioning people, the best way is to confront the anxiety by making its sources conscious and explicit so that one can deal with them on their merits. Some experiences *should* make us anxious. But many sources of anxiety, such as this one, are dysfunctional: they get in the way of coping effectively with the complex realities of the world.

In the chapters that follow I sketch the broad outlines of a strategy for breaking through the barriers of resistance by making the sources of our culture's epistemological anxiety explicit. The Culture of Technical Control favors modes of knowing that are objective, scientific, quantitative, systematic, empirical, information-rich, and technologically manipulable. It is this kind of knowledge that has proven so wonderfully useful to our mastery of the environment. So influential are these modes of knowing that others seem weak by comparison, including public judgment. By dipping into the reflections of a handful of leading twentieth-century philosophers, I hope to show that the claims of our culture's favorite type of knowledge, for all its power, are grossly overstated. By forcing all other forms of knowledge into the shadows, we are destroying some of the fine balances our society needs to realize fully the Dream of Self-governance.

15

DEFINING OBJECTIVISM

Controlling the environment and enjoying the fruits of modern technology are not the sole purposes of life on earth. There are other purposes, other values, other goals. In our Culture of Technical Control these are scanted, forging the iron cage that Weber saw as the inevitable outcome of our love affair with a single mode of knowing (instrumental reason). I want to provide the reader with a brief summary of the critique modern philosophy has developed of this dominant mode of knowing and the dark side of the culture to which it gives rise. Taking the reader on a side trip through the landscape of modern philosophy is not a diversion from the thesis of this book. It is a direct realization of the purpose that animates it: to give legitimacy to the concept of public judgment as a genuine mode of knowing, equal or superior in power for the purposes of self-governance to the knowledge gained by instrumental reason.

Thomas Kuhn points out in his seminal book, *The Structure of Scientific Revolutions*, that resistance greets all theories that do not fit comfortably into existing paradigms. Kuhn used the word "paradigm" to designate those cognitive maps of reality dominant in every era that serve as explanatory frameworks for scientific theories. Though often criticized, the central idea of Kuhn's book has become a familiar part of our intellectual vocabulary. Thanks to his insight we are alert to the fact that theories which fit comfortably with existing paradigms are assimilated with ease into the common stock of knowledge, whereas theories that do not quite fit are brushed aside with indifference or angrily rejected, even to the point of abuse and contempt.[1]

In brief, challenges to prevailing paradigms are disturbing cognitively and evoke inappropriate emotional responses. What makes the resistance to public judgment intriguing is that on the surface it does not appear to pose a fundamental challenge to existing paradigms. But on closer inspection it does just that: to consider public judgment as a legitimate form of knowing is to cast doubt on the driving assumptions of the Culture of Technical Control.

JUDGMENT AND INFORMATION

Among these driving assumptions, three are particularly relevant. The first is that information is a form of knowledge and opinion is not. The second is that judgment is a form of opinion. The third assumption is that in decision making, information (genuine knowledge) is to be preferred over judgment (opinion). The assumption here is that when it comes to making important decisions, good information is assumed to be the key ingredient. If you have good information, then sound policies follow. From a practical standpoint, because good information is often lacking, it may sometimes be necessary to substitute judgment for the missing information, but that is clearly a second-best compromise.

These assumptions are so deeply ingrained in our culture that they are enshrined in our dictionary definitions. In *Webster's Third New International Dictionary*, some of the meanings of judgment are defined as follows:

> **judgment.**
> 1. The pronouncing of an opinion or decision of a formal or authoritative nature; also, the opinion or decision given; censure; criticism. . . .
> 7. The power of arriving at a wise decision or conclusion on the basis of indications and probabilities when the facts are not clearly ascertained; as to use your best judgment; discretion; discernment; as, a man of sound judgment.

In meaning number 7, the dictionary definition makes clear that in decision making, judgment serves as a substitute for missing factual information. It states explicitly that judgment permits people to arrive at "wise decisions or conclusions" even when all of the facts are not available. The implication is that having the facts is the surer, safer way to reach decisions, but, if the facts are lacking, judgment may substitute for them.

Henry Kissinger implies a similar assumption when he observes that when one's latitude for action in foreign policy is greatest, adequate information is usually lacking. As more information piles up, the options for action diminish. The implication is that the more facts you have, the better your decision will be. When the facts are missing and there is need to act, judgment, unfortunately, has to fill the vacuum.[2]

I want to argue that this assumption reflects an outmoded epistemology and that contrary to the views of many of the gatekeepers of knowledge in our society, judgment is not a substitute for information but a separate and independent variable playing a different role in the decision-making process than information does. (By gatekeepers of knowledge, I refer to those people in our universities and professions who define and protect the canons of knowledge — scientists [natural and social], philosophers, policy experts, journalists, lawyers and judges, medical researchers, and so forth. These are the people who safeguard the standards of what knowledge is in their various fields of expertise, distinguishing genuine knowledge from mere opinion, belief, hearsay, rumor, prejudice, emotional conviction, and unproven assertion.)

For many of these gatekeepers, journalists in particular, it is an article of faith that the more facts you have the less you need to depend on judgment and the sounder your decisions will be. I want to show that this article of faith is based on a deep misunderstanding of the relationship of information to judgment and that when decisions concern matters of policy, good judgment is as important, if not more important, than good information and different from it.

By definition, policy decisions concern broad, nontechnical matters that involve goals and values and strategies as well as tactics. All large policy decisions contain both factual and judgmental elements. The judgmental elements are not substitutes for missing facts. Facts and judgments are not reducible to one another, and they are not fungible. No amount of good information can compensate for bad judgment. The widely held assumption that good information leads to sound policy decisions is almost deliberately wrong-headed.

If pressed, people will acknowledge this point because the weight of evidence makes it so unmistakably clear. History abounds in examples of knowledgeable, well-informed people making stupid, vile, atrocious policy decisions. Neville Chamberlain's policy of appeasing Hitler at Munich was not a mistake of information, it was bad judgment. Pol Pot's policy of forced countrification resulting in the death of several million Cambodians was owing to bad judgment, not faulty information. It is a sad fact, known to every thoughtful person, that well-informed, well-intentioned people sometimes make mistakes in judgment that result in bad policies. That point was the central message of David Halberstam's book *The Best and the Brightest*.[3] The title says it all: the people who made the worst policy decisions about involving America in the quagmire of Vietnam were among the best and the brightest our society produces, certainly in the sense of being among the best informed and most knowledgeable. Their superior information did not, however, prevent them from making policy mistakes — not from faulty information but from faulty judgment.

The reason for haranguing the reader on this embarrassingly obvious point is that it is so widely ignored in practice. When Henry Kissinger observes that the facts are most scant when the latitude for policy is greatest, he is focusing on the missing factual information and is taking for granted the presence of good judgment (his own). But good judgment cannot be taken for granted. In today's society it is in far shorter supply than factual information. Our culture is heavily biased toward information; good judgment is almost a forgotten afterthought.

If in the introduction to this book I had said, "My thesis is that an informed public is indispensable to the proper functioning of democracy," the declaration would have been met with a yawn. Far from being controversial, my words would have been regarded as a tired truism — a preachy statement of the kind that civics teachers and journalists like to make on ceremonial occasions. The truth of the statement would not have been doubted, only its lack of originality. The desirability of giving the public more *information* is never questioned. Improving the *judgment* of the public is, however, an unfamiliar and alien concept.

I am not implying that being well informed is a negligible asset. We could not survive in our complex world without specialized information; information is indispensable for what experts do. But what experts do and what the public does is not at all the same. Experts seek answers to technical questions. The public makes judgments that go beyond technical matters. As we have seen in one example after another in earlier chapters of this book, factual information plays a narrower role in helping people to arrive at their judgments than is commonly presupposed.

Our social system does recognize the distinction between information and judgment and does institutionalize it in various ways. In our judicial system, for example, juries are charged with sorting the facts; making judgments is the prerogative of the judge. The most revealing form of institutionalization is implicit, to be seen in the relationship of boards of directors to operating management in large corporations. Every business corporation has a dual structure of leadership: a board of directors who represent the owners and a group of managers who operate the company. The board of directors has "sovereignty" in the political sense. It has the power, in law and in practice, to remove and replace the management of the company.

There are rules, many of them informal and unwritten, for boards of directors, just as there are rules for managers. In an insightful study of these rules, Professor Thomas Whisler observes that most boards of directors do not and should not manage the company or even set strategy for it. He points to the obvious fact that "a group of individuals who get together every month or two cannot be seriously regarded as managing the company." He concludes: "We (the board) govern; the executives manage." The distinction Whisler makes between governance and management is dictated by the need to distinguish between information and judgment.[4]

One of the board of directors' major governance responsibilities, says Whisler, is to set corporate policy. This is done in conjunction with management, but the ultimate responsibility is that of the board. Sometimes boards and managers collide on policy. To be sure, this does not happen often — for a special reason. It is so embarrassing to management when directors veto a management initiative that managers are extremely careful to avoid overt conflict at board meetings. But in the give-and-take that precedes formal board meetings discussion aimed at reconciling conflicting points of view is considerable. These discussions rarely involve matters of information. They almost always involve matters of judgment.

Several examples will be helpful. A New Jersey–based corporation had for many years been disposing of its chemical wastes in a manner that kept it within the confines of the law but contributed to ocean pollution. Everyone in the company, including the directors, had been aware of the practice (they all shared roughly the same information); they felt defensive about it, but they persisted anyway because the alternative would have reduced profits for shareholders. In the fall of 1988, however, after a number of New Jersey's beaches had been closed during record-breaking days of summer heat, several of the directors proposed that the company stop the dumping even if it meant "taking a hit" to the bottom line. Their grounds were their concern that the political climate might turn punitive and also their realization that though the dumping practice was legal, it did not meet the high ethical standards the directors felt the company ought to observe. Management was reluctant to make the change, but the directors insisted, and management finally agreed.

A second example: the directors of a Chicago-based corporation considered a management recommendation that the company acquire a business for sale in another industry. Management presented information on the growth potential of the company to be acquired and on its current condition of robust economic health. The information clearly justified the price the company was being asked to pay. Moreover, there were significant tax advantages to the deal. The directors discussed management's proposal but after considerable debate rejected it. Their grounds were that managing a new company in an unfamiliar industry was likely to be too much of a diversion that would deflect management attention away from the main business of the corporation.

In this example as in the first, the information available to both management and directors was the same. But their judgment differed, because factors in addition to information were at work. What were those other factors? They included: varying interpretations of the long-term interests of the corporation; differing time perspectives; differing interpretations of the political climate; the articulation and reinforcement of institutional values. (These examples do not imply that the board's judgment is always correct. Sometimes the judgment is bad. The point here is that managing and governing call upon different thought processes.)

The distinction between managing and governing accentuates the distinction between information and judgment. Managing and governing both require good information *and* good judgment. But in managing, the information component is larger both in scope and depth of detail. Judgment is surely needed: a manager with bad judgment is a destructive loose canon. But in day-to-day operations, judgment relates more to tactical concerns, less to policy matters.

The board of directors needs far less information than management, particularly information about operating details unless these are directly germane to a policy decision. The structure of the board is organized less as an information-processing body than as a judgment-forming body. To the extent possible, information is dispensed in advance so that board meetings can be devoted to their major function: formal discussion and deliberation of policy issues with a view to bringing collective judgment to bear. Sometimes the discussion focuses on clarification of factual matters. Mostly, however, it centers on goals and values and how well designed proposed policies are to meet them.

In the past when many large corporations were privately owned (few are today), boards of directors were typically filled by the owners themselves or their bankers and lawyers. For these boards the economic interests of the owners were unmistakably clear, sometimes crassly so. Today's directors of publicly owned large corporations still represent the economic interests of the owners, but these are interpreted broadly. Boards of directors are political bodies, structured to make judgments that include but are not confined to economic interests.

The importance of judgment can be justified on practical grounds; it need not be regarded as genuine knowledge in a theoretical sense to be respected and useful. Whatever one's theories, as a practical matter society *must* rely on judgment whether it wants to or not. But it makes the case for judgment immensely more potent if one can demonstrate, as I hope to do, that judgment is not only a separate and distinct variable in decision making (alongside information) but also in its own right is a legitimate form of knowledge — different to be sure, from information or scientific theory or purely logical (analytic) truths (the accepted forms of knowledge), but nonetheless valid knowledge.

OBJECTIVISM

The assumption that factual information is real knowledge whereas judgment is not, is rooted in a philosophical doctrine that can be regarded as the "official" epistemology of the Culture of Technical Control. It is a doctrine that philosopher Richard Bernstein calls *objectivism*. Objectivism, says Bernstein, is the belief that "in the final analysis there is a realm of basic uninterpreted hard facts that serve as the foundation for all empirical knowledge."[5] The proper apprehension of this factual core is the only genuine mode of knowing. The realm of "hard facts" excludes values and norms and opinions and judgments because these express subjective preferences that cannot be scientifically verified in the way that factual assertions can. Facts represent those aspects of reality that can be ascertained through objective methods whereas judgment is rooted in the emotions and values that are the hallmarks of subjectivity.[6]

From an objectivist point of view, any discipline that seeks knowledge about the world must guard against the danger of passing off mere judgments as if they were facts. The goal of giving an objective and value-neutral description of the facts is the ideal of science. This ideal reflects "the conviction that science alone is the measure of reality and the standard for assessing legitimate knowledge of what human beings are."[7] Only by strict observation of the canons of verifiability and testability can we achieve valid empirical knowledge of human reality.[8]

On the face of it, objectivism seems nothing more than formalized common sense. Everyone knows the difference between fact and judgment based on opinion and what a relief it is to extricate oneself from the morass of opinion to reach the solid ground of fact. Is the patient's tumor malignant or not? Do the voters support proposition 101 or do they oppose it? Is the old bridge safe for heavy truck traffic or is it unsafe?

On matters such as these we want solid facts and not subjective judgments. We want experts and all of their technical paraphernalia — C-T scans and X rays and computers and voter surveys and tests for metal fatigue.

We want our experts to put aside their own biases and emotions. Our advanced industrial culture is firmly grounded on the belief that the most valuable form of knowledge is factual information arrived at through objective means. Beside this type of information, other forms of knowing seem second-rate.

Objectivism has many sources of support in our society. It fits neatly into an economic system based on specialization, expertise, and division of labor; it supports and is supported by the technology-driven aspects of American culture; it fits the ideological predilections of our journalism, especially TV news with its focus on the sound-bite, the headline, the isolated fact (which permits TV news to present itself as objective); and it matches the preferences of the more *macho* elements of our society who find themselves more comfortable with the "facts" than with abstractions, emotions, and opinions. Somehow, attention to the facts suggests realism, pragmatism, down-to-earthness. And, in addition to all of these powerful cultural and social supports, objectivism presents itself as a self-evident form of knowledge based on scientific methods. No wonder, with so much going for it, it appears impervious to criticism or challenge.

The quest for knowledge enjoys enormous prestige in our society and scientific technical-factual information has hegemony over other modes of seeking knowledge. Those who possess it — the experts — lord it over those who do not. Experts play a dominant role in public life because they are presumed to have the knowledge that ordinary folk lack. Nor is our culture likely to diminish its high regard for experts in the future because their type of knowledge has contributed so much to our national successes in extending longevity, creating affluence, and using technology to make life more comfortable, convenient, and stimulating. The trend is to entrust the experts with ever more power and influence.

From this vantage point, Professor Bernstein's deeply felt conclusion may come as a shock. He believes that the objectivist theory of knowledge is harmful and destructive. It is not, he says, "an innocent epistemological doctrine. It has dangerous consequences."[9] The message Professor Bernstein urges on us is this: In our reliance on objectivism, we are unleashing a destructive force that distorts reality and undermines wisdom and good sense. Unless it is moderated, it will destroy all that our society deems precious: freedom, democracy, cohesion and stability, and perhaps even life on earth.

The dangerous consequences to which Bernstein refers are all too familiar to readers of twentieth-century social thought. This century's most creative sociologists, such as Max Weber and Emile Durkheim, the critical theorists of the Frankfurt school (to be discussed later), existentialist phi-

losophers, and many artists, novelists, journalists, and others have all elo-
quently voiced their fears about the dark side of the Culture of Technical
Control. One of the most stunning insights of twentieth-century philosophy has been its gradually developing understanding that so many of the
abuses and dangers of our lopsided culture are directly traceable to the
seemingly innocuous doctrine of objectivism. We have here a striking paradox: *the type of knowledge* on which all of us rely for our health, safety,
and material well being is, at the same time, denounced as dangerous because it will subvert our civilization and, perhaps, destroy it when it is
relied upon as the sole, legitimate mode of knowing. This is a paradox
we must confront head-on because the distinction between judgment and
information lies at the heart of it.

The lesson the history of philosophy in this century teaches is that
the powerful hold objectivism has on Western culture, and in particular
on American culture, is not grounded in sound epistemology. Considered
from a philosophical point of view, objectivism is a piece of metaphysics
that reflects a set of arbitrary biases.

This conclusion flies in the face of the conventional wisdom that the
success of science — perhaps the greatest of all achievements of Western
culture — resides in its adherence to objectivism. According to conventional
wisdom, the test of time has proven the objectivist theory of knowledge
to be superior to all others.

But the conventional wisdom does not stand up to careful scrutiny.
The claim that objectivism works better than any alternative is a purely
pragmatic argument. It seems persuasive because it shrouds itself in the
prestigious mantle of science. On closer inspection, however, it falters. If
it can be demonstrated that its identification with science is misleading,
if the dangerous consequences associated with the Culture of Technical Control can be directly traceable to it, and above all, if its imperialist preten-
sions to be the only form of valid knowledge are shown to be ill-founded,
then serious doubt is cast on its claim to pragmatic success as well as on
its claim to reputable philosophical status.

Most intelligent people seem well aware of how one-sided our culture is but believe that ugly phenomena such as the nuclear arms race,
the pollution of the planet, the narrow specialization of our professions
and experts, the widespread alienation, the spiritual superficiality, and the
failure of community are the necessary price we must pay for our technological progress and its undoubted benefits. Most Americans — and other
Westerners — are willing to pay that price. There is a pervasive sense of
fatalism about this ugly side, a suspicion that it is a necessary trade-off.

There does not seem to be any alternative; to achieve the benefits of modern technology without its negative side effects seems a hopelessly idealist dream.

But probing the underpinnings of objectivism shows that such fatalism is not justified. To be sure, there will always be trade-offs and drawbacks. But the barbaric element in the Culture of Technical Control — and that is not too strong a term for its dark side — is unnecessary. The barbarism can be tempered and the excesses of the Culture of Technical Control moderated if a way can be found to replace objectivism with a less dogmatic and more pluralistic concept of knowledge.

The heart of philosophy's quarrel with objectivism is its claim that it is the only valid form of knowledge, and that there are no others. Where objectivism goes most seriously awry is in taking the step from the proposition "factual information is a valid mode of knowledge" to the conclusion that "there are no other valid forms of knowledge, certainly not those based on judgment." Culturally and practically, this is a momentous leap in the wrong direction. In examining it we find ourselves face to face with one of the most deeply ingrained prejudices of our culture. We should not fool ourselves about how stubborn and immovable it is.

Logically, we can respect the search for the unadorned facts without leaping to the conclusion that this is the only legitimate method of seeking knowledge and without brushing aside forms of knowing based on judgments, values, insights, and norms. In the practical world of business and private life and in the domains of art, religion, and morality we pursue many paths to knowledge without formalizing any of them. But in those parts of the society where the objectivist philosophy holds sway — the world of the technical expert — the methods for gaining knowledge *are* formalized and the status of genuine knowledge is reserved almost exclusively for factual information and the theories that support it. This is the point of view that needs to be dislodged from the center of our culture.

It is in the light of the insights of twentieth-century philosophy (summarized in the next two chapters) that the doctrine of objectivism becomes less persuasive, its dangerous consequences more self-evident, and above all for our purposes in this book, room is made for serious consideration of other modes of knowing, including public judgment. The most seductive aspect of objectivism is its appearance of being a commonsense, down-to-earth, practical, successful "scientific" approach to which there is no obvious alternative. In what follows I want to draw on the lessons of twentieth-century philosophy to show how wrong this view of objectivism is and what alternative would better serve our culture.

16

DECONSTRUCTING OBJECTIVISM

I n the advanced industrial democracies the tempo of change advances inexorably, year by year, decade by decade. All of us are stretched to the limits of our adaptive powers to keep pace with it. Clearly, we need a mental strategy for dealing with all the disruptive changes and the cascade of information that pours down on us. Objectivism is an appealing mental strategy. It says, in effect, "Ignore everything but the facts; check them carefully to sort conflicting claims on your attention; push away the opinions, the idiosyncratic feelings, the grandiose theories, the hunches, and assorted guesses. In dealing with complexity, specialize to avoid the trap of the amateur in trying to be all things to all people. Adopt this rational and logical approach, and you should be able to cope without being overwhelmed."

Up to a point this is sound advice. It is a way to avoid epistemological anxiety. And it is not a bad method for coping with small problems. But it is a disastrous strategy for coping with big ones. What at first seems down-to-earth common sense — stay with the facts; do not bite off more than you can chew — turns out on closer inspection to be unnecessarily narrow and exclusionary. A mental strategy originally adopted for pragmatic purposes ("the only way I can cope with so much complexity is to get the facts and stick with them") is transposed into blindsided dogma.

One of the great intellectual accomplishments of twentieth-century philosophy is its insight into these limitations of the objectivist world view. The most cogent critics of objectivism are, by profession, professors of philosophy in the great universities of America and Europe. Unfortunately, our era is not one that pays much heed to philosophy — partly because objectivism devalues the kind of reflection and search for understanding associated with philosophy and partly because the objectivist point of view has itself cannibalized large parts of philosophy. Many philosophers, like so many others, have succumbed to the temptations of specialization and technical expertise, the hallmarks of objectivism. Like other experts, they communicate largely with each other and not with the general public. Their language and the issues to which they are responsive are ingrown. They write for each other. They hold conferences with each other. They do not reach out.

Inside the field of philosophy, the case against objectivism is multi-faceted. It comes from Anglo-American philosophy, from Continental philosophy, and from philosophically minded historians, sociologists, and other leading thinkers. The critique from Anglo-American philosophy is the most systematic—not surprisingly, because objectivism has had its greatest influence on Anglo-American academic circles and on the American social system overall. Though cogent and precise in expression, the Anglo-American critique is probably the most difficult for those who are not professional philosophers to grasp fully and absorb into their own world view. This is not because the writing is inaccessible: indeed, the quality of the writing, especially by the British philosophers, is exceptional (at least by academic standards). The difficulty lies in the lack of context in the Anglo-American critique.

This lack and the stylistic mannerisms of Anglo-American philosophy make it almost impossible for the general reader to see the point of the argument. "I understand what you are asserting," the reader might say, "but I don't see why you are saying it. What larger point are you making that is relevant to me and my life?" When people fail to see the connection between their own concerns and someone's work, they pay scant attention to the work, however brilliant it may be. This failure to connect the arguments against objectivism to the larger concerns of the society is one of the principal reasons the Anglo-American critique against objectivism, for all its power, has had so little impact.

It would take us too far from our main theme to describe the historical and cultural context in which objectivism came to exercise its great power. But one contextual element cannot be excluded; if it were, the evolution of objectivism would be inexplicable. I refer, of course, to the role and influence of science, especially nineteenth- and twentieth-century physics. Objectivism draws much of its prestige from the successes of science. In all human history few enterprises have enjoyed the immense success the natural sciences have achieved. It has been spectacular and sustained and international in scope. If science is based on objectivism, then pragmatically speaking, there is no way its hold on the culture can be reduced—or perhaps even should be. But philosophy and science itself teach us that the image of science as an objectivist discipline is badly distorted. Of course, facts and the theories that generate them are important to science. But they are not the only modes of knowing what science embraces. The "official" picture of how scientists work and the reality diverge sharply from one another. The great scientists are not advocates of so-called scientism, or objectivism, nor do they practice it.

The influence of the image of science on the mind-set of our civilization can hardly be exaggerated. It has inspired professionals from every discipline, especially social scientists, to force their disciplines to adhere, to the extent possible, to the model of science as it is popularly imagined. In view of science's all-encompassing influence, I want to focus my summary of the Anglo-American critique of objectivism on certain philosophers who have had a particular interest in science and how it works. To keep the discussion limited, I will look only at a single episode from the prehistory of modern linguistic philosophy — the encounter in Cambridge, England, of Bertrand Russell with Alfred North Whitehead and Ludwig Wittgenstein.

In later years, post-Wittgensteinian philosophy was to become immensely subtle in the writings of Louch, Rorty, Ryle, Sellars, Strawson, Charles Taylor, Winch, and others. But never were the basic themes as clear as they were when, in the early years of the century, these three very different men struggled with the issue of what kind of truths logic and science were conveying and how they were doing so.

WHITEHEAD

Whitehead wrote his slim volume, *Science and the Modern World*, to make explicit the philosophy that underlay the physical science of his time. He wrote it in 1925 before the application of modern physics to the development of nuclear weapons. He was a great admirer of scientific achievement, which he saw as one of the glories of our civilization. But he was troubled by the philosophy on which the science of his era was based. His comments on this philosophy contain the essence of the critique of objectivism that others were to develop more systematically in later years. Whitehead's thesis in *Science and the Modern World* is that the growth of science has "recolored our mentality" and that this new mentality is "more important even than the new science and the new technology."[1] The shift in mentality represented by the modern scientific outlook is, in Whitehead's view, one of the most momentous changes in all human history. Referring to Galileo's persecution, which can be taken as one of the symbolic acts associated with the founding of modern science, Whitehead states, "Since a babe was born in a manger, it may be doubted whether so great a thing has happened with so little stir."[2]

I emphasize Whitehead's reverence for science in order to put into perspective his critique of its underlying philosophical assumptions. So sharp is the critique that one might think it came from an enemy of the scientific outlook rather than from one of science's most ardent admirers. In another context, Whitehead observed that "great ideas often enter reality in strange guises and with disgusting alliances."[3] He leaves no doubt that he regards the advent of the scientific outlook as one of the greatest of all ideas. But he is also mindful that ideas, as they evolve, undergo a process of clarification and purification to divest themselves of the "strange guises" with which they first appear.

One of philosophy's main tasks is to advance this process of clarification. Reviewing the history of thought, it is evident that no thinkers, however towering, ever entirely escape the parochialism of their time. We are all time-bound and culture-bound, even Plato and Kant and Einstein. The diamonds of original thought are always rough, and the act of polishing them is indispensable to showing them in their true color. So it is with science. To describe the "true color" of the scientific mentality, Whitehead quotes William James, who, as he was completing his treatise on *The Principles of Psychology*,[4] wrote to his brother Henry that he was forced "to forge every sentence in the teeth of irreducible and stubborn facts." Whitehead comments that the new scientific mentality resides precisely in this "vehement and passionate interest in the relationship of general principles to irreducible and stubborn facts."[5]

The objectionable feature of objectivism is not its unwavering focus on the facts and the theories that account for them. That is its strength. Almost four hundred years of modern science have taught us how to wed theories to facts in a stunningly successful manner. The crippling weakness in objectivism is that, in modeling itself on science, it has also adopted some of science's most questionable metaphysics — a metaphysics that science itself has mostly jettisoned in its evolution while the wider culture has continued to be burdened by it.

It is these metaphysical presuppositions made in the early years of scientific discovery that Whitehead has pinpointed and challenged:

> There persists throughout the whole period the fixed scientific cosmology which presupposes the ultimate fact of an irreducible brute matter, or material, spread throughout space in a flux of configurations. In itself such a material is senseless, valueless, purposeless. It just does what it

does do, following a fixed routine imposed by external relations which do not spring from the nature of its being. It is this assumption that I call "scientific materialism." Also it is an assumption that I shall challenge as being entirely unsuited to the scientific situation at which we have now arrived.[6]

Scientific materialism, Whitehead notes, did not arise in response to "the stubborn, irreducible facts." It was excess baggage that scientists brought with them from the larger culture in which they were immersed. Whitehead's objection to scientific materialism is not that it is false. As he states, its flaw is that it focuses too exclusively on a severely limited aspect of reality. It is not a faithful and full description of the stubborn irreducible facts as they occur in experience but a narrow abstraction often systematically misapplied by those who use it.

Whitehead concludes that its application to science suffers from two serious fallacies. The first he calls the "fallacy of misplaced concreteness."[7] This is the tendency to mistake an abstraction for a concrete reality without realizing that it is an abstraction. The other fallacy Whitehead calls the "fallacy of simple location."[8] This is the mistake of assuming that whatever is real must occupy a specific location in time-space. We come here to the fundamental metaphysical assumption of materialism: the view that the only true reality is that which has the property of simple location. This is a literal application of the "body" half of the Cartesian mind-body dichotomy. The body is *rēs extēnsa*, that which occupies a spatial location. In the materialist view, the mind and its mental activity have no independent reality apart from the physical substrate, the electrical/chemical processes of the brain, because the brain can be described in terms of simple location, whereas ideas and concepts cannot.

Scientific materialism thus is a complex of abstractions that should be confined to appropriate limited applications and only to those applications. Whitehead makes this point cogently. "The truth is that science started its modern career by taking over ideas derived from the weakest side of Aristotle's successors. In some respects it was a happy choice. It enabled the knowledge of the seventeenth century to be formularized as far as physics and chemistry were concerned, with a completeness that has lasted to the present time. But the progress of biology and psychology has probably been checked by the uncritical assumption of half-truths."[9]

Abstractions are, by definition, half-truths, or more precisely, one-tenth truths, or one-hundreth truths, or one-thousandth truths. They single out and call attention to one tiny aspect of reality, ignoring all the others. Perhaps they are best thought of as specialized searchlights. They illuminate some aspects of reality while plunging others into darkness. Scientific materialism is a searchlight with a narrow but sharp focus that served a historically valuable purpose: "If we confine ourselves to certain types of facts . . . the materialistic assumption expresses these facts to perfection," Whitehead writes. "But when we pass beyond the abstraction . . . the scheme breaks down at once. The narrow efficiency of the scheme was the very cause of its supreme methodological success."[10]

When one employs a set of abstractions for purposes for which it is unsuitable, trouble comes fast. In our book *Ego and Instinct*, philosopher William Barrett and I showed how badly Sigmund Freud was handicapped by being saddled with the scientific materialism he had absorbed in his graduate training in physiology. In later years when Freud was making his great discoveries and forging his theories in the teeth of the stubborn, irreducible facts of his patients' suffering he was fearful that his case history reports were not "scientific" enough. Therefore, he went to enormous pains to translate his discoveries from the ordinary language of the case histories, which express them clearly and cogently, to the "more scientific" language of his "metapsychology," which only succeeded in obscuring their meaning because it was steeped in the inappropriate — and irrelevant — abstractions of scientific materialism. Laboriously, Freud translated the anguish and confusion and rich experience of his patients into the dead language of seventeenth-century metaphysics. He was inordinately proud of this "achievement," which, ironically, has almost destroyed psychoanalysis.

Until very recently, most psychoanalysts have followed Freud's lead in translating clear clinical insights into murky and obscure metapsychological language and have derived a sense of accomplishment from doing so because it is hard work, however zany it may be. As a result, psychoanalysts have been virtually unable to communicate with each other, let alone with the general public. No other obstacle has retarded the development of their field as severely.

There is, perhaps, no better illustration of Whitehead's point about the heuristic character of framework assumptions. The abstractions of scientific materialism illuminated one aspect of physical reality that helped seventeenth-century physics to fructify. But when we come to the truths of human experience, these abstractions are utterly inappropriate. Even when we approach, for example, the quantum mechanics of twentieth-century physics, these same abstractions prove a hindrance. They have proved more than a hindrance to the human and social sciences. They have been a total disaster in the scientific study of mental and social processes.

The Whitehead analysis contains the seeds of the extensive critique of objectivism that was to follow in later years. All of the elements are present: adopting the weakest side of science (its secondhand a priori metaphysics); mistaking abstractions for brute facts and then reifying these abstractions; applying an inappropriate test of "truth" to these abstractions rather than regarding them as heuristic—to be used if applicable to the subject matter and casually discarded if they do not; adopting a hierarchy of reality that identifies the "facts" with knowledge of those aspects of reality that enjoy simple location while dismissing modes of knowing appropriate to other aspects of reality as inferior or even as not representing knowledge at all, and attempting to reduce all aspects of experience to its material substrate.

WITTGENSTEIN

Bertrand Russell was the link between Whitehead and Wittgenstein. Russell exercised a great influence on both men, one older, the other much younger. Whitehead and Russell had collaborated for years on their path-breaking work, *Principia Mathematica*, which explores the nature of mathematics and logic and attempts to reduce arithmetic to logic.[11] (Whitehead even worked with Russell in his jail cell in London when Russell was incarcerated for his civic disturbances at the start of World War I.) Wittgenstein was Russell's favorite student—and disciple—at Cambridge. Wittgenstein was only twenty-two when he met Russell (who was at that time almost twice his age). But Russell's respect for the younger man was unbounded. Barrett quotes Russell as writing, "Getting to know Wittgenstein was one of the most exciting adventures of my life."[12]

Wittgenstein, a man of much intensity of emotion, rarely did anything halfway. In his early work, he had translated Russell's methodological procedures into a more extreme statement of the relation between logic and reality. He did this in a work that became one of the seminal books in philosophy in the early part of the century, the *Tractatus Logico-Philosophicus*.[13]

In some circles the *Tractatus* grew into a virtual cult book. Philosophers recognized Wittgenstein's genius, and the cryptic, aphoristic style of the book was made to order for cultlike awe. The work exercised a degree of influence that, in retrospect, is astonishing—and unwarranted by any inherent merit. It takes nothing away from Wittgenstein's genius to recognize that the book was based on a preposterous premise, however brilliantly the logical implications of that premise were elaborated.

Wittgenstein was a very young man when he wrote the *Tractatus*. He was an engineer by training, so he brought to philosophy a mind that had not spent years struggling with old philosophical puzzles and the agonized thinking of the great philosophers of the past, who in their own struggles with these puzzles had achieved a sense of their complexity that Wittgenstein did not share. At that stage of his life, what he knew of philosophy came mainly from Bertrand Russell, who was brilliant, idiosyncratic, and more superficial than either Wittgenstein or Whitehead.

Not surprisingly, the maturing Wittgenstein later repudiated his earlier thought (and with it the philosophy of Bertrand Russell) so thoroughly that it is customary to refer to Wittgenstein I and Wittgenstein II to mark the change. Wittgenstein is hardly the first philosopher to have changed his mind, but there are no other thinkers of stature for whom the discontinuity between their earlier and later works is so sharp that they are treated almost as if they were separate people, each opposed to the other.

What is the underlying premise of the *Tractatus*, and why is it preposterous? Please remember that I am saying it is preposterous only in retrospect. In the climate of opinion that prevailed at the time, it did not seem odd at all.

The gifted student of Bertrand Russell had swallowed whole Russell's doctrine of logical atomist — and carried it a step further even than Russell had. Barrett quotes Russell in 1920, "Logic is concerned with the real world just as truly as zoology, though with its more abstract features."[14] Where Russell assumed for methodological purposes that the structure of logic reflected abstract aspects of reality, the young Wittgenstein took the more extreme position that the structure of logic was a literal, if a priori, reflection of the empirical world. He held that the structure of logic mirrors the structure of reality, at least in certain abstract respects. The two features that reality and logic share in common, he believed at that time, are atomicity and disconnectedness. Logic deals with atomistic and disconnected units and classes of units and seeks to draw inferences from their external relations to one another. (It is indifferent to the nature of these units.) Empirical reality is like logic, Wittgenstein believed, in that it is also reducible to unrelated atomistic units. Reality equals the totality of all of the disconnected facts in the world, facts that have no more inherent relation to each other than one grain of sand has to any other or to an abandoned child's shovel that happens to be lying on the beach.

This bleak metaphysics mirrors precisely the doctrine of scientific materialism — not by coincidence; scientific materialism was the dominant doctrine of the times. Wittgenstein's philosophical method is the familiar one of "starting all over again." Because philosophy deals with ultimate things, with basics, there is a tendency among the most ambitious philosophical thinkers to pose to themselves the question, "What is the best starting point for recreating reality? Where shall I begin?" How this question is answered probably shapes a thinker's philosophy more than any other influence. The young Wittgenstein begins with logic — having made the Russell-inspired leap that logic mirrors reality. He proceeds on the premise that reality is merely the sum of all of the "facts" in the world, in imitation of the premise of scientific materialism that reality is the sum of all the bits of matter in the universe.

In Wittgenstein I, language mirrors reality only when we polish and clarify it until its logical structure shines forth. When we impose this severe discipline on language, we begin to see that the ancient puzzles of philosophy are merely the dirt and grime that have built up on the mirror. By cleaning away the grime — reducing the sloppiness of everyday language to the neat precision of logic — we have the key to reality and to the puzzles of the past.

Though he was later to repudiate this doctrine utterly, Wittgenstein II did not abandon the strategy of starting all over again. But in his second pass at describing reality, he concluded that logic was not a suitable starting point because he had come to realize that logic does not mirror reality after all. Always the extremist, Wittgenstein II came to characterize logic as one vast tautology, which, in effect, reveals nothing whatever about the nature of reality. On the relationship of logic to reality, Wittgenstein swings from one extreme to the other: from exalting it as the royal road to reality to confining it to the narrowest of technical tasks.

The only possible starting point for philosophic inquiry into reality, he concludes, is not logic but "forms of life" — the variegated expressions of everyday experience as reflected in our ordinary language. The philosophic enterprise is no longer a matter of arguing and proving through logic but a way of seeing and showing forms of life. What was once to be discarded as the dirt and grime covering the mirror is now seen to be the mirror itself — discourse about everyday forms of life.

It is fascinating to look back on the intellectual adventures of these three towering figures of twentieth-century thought as, like Moses in the desert, they search for the promised land, both together and separately. In a sense, Russell mistook the desert itself (the dry world of logical abstractions and vast piles of unrelated atoms of matter) for the promised land — or at least a platonic abstract image of it. Whitehead, recognizing that there was something beyond the desert, developed his own "philosophy of organism" to reflect his faith in the inherent relatedness of all things under the sun. Whitehead sensed the mystery of life. He once observed that scientists frequently mistook the merely unmeasured for the unknown. What is unknown, he said, is "truly unknown." But Wittgenstein was both the most logically consistent of the three and the most mystical. He had a deep and profound sense of the mysterious that haunted him and that he was never able to incorporate into his formal thought.

The logic of his thought led him to conclude that however much one plays the "language games" he was so ingenious in inventing, one cannot use language to express any reality lying beneath or beyond ordinary experience. He, therefore, concluded that the most profound and important side of life, which extended beyond ordinary experience, was inexpressible through language. Perhaps his most famous dictum is "Whereof one cannot speak, thereof one must be silent."[15] Wittgenstein's way of life expressed the conviction that there was something beyond the desert, but he never found the language to express it, nor did he believe that language could be used to do so.

If the example of Wittgenstein seems too remote from our American experience, let us glance at an example closer to home. I first met Robert McNamara when he was president of the Ford Motor Company. He had been one of the pentagon "whiz kids" in World War II and had developed great confidence in techniques for separating fact from opinion and judgment. He was like the young Wittgenstein in his faith in the measurable facts, and he indoctrinated those around him with this same point of view to such an extent that it sometimes seemed at the Ford Motor Company that if something was not measurable and expressible in the form of statistics, it did not exist. During his stint as secretary of defense in the Kennedy and Johnson years, McNamara applied this same mental strategy to the task of defining and protecting national security and running the Pentagon.

Then came the war in Vietnam and the agony it created for McNamara and other men and women of conscience, intelligence, and sensibility. The objectivist strategy utterly failed to give those responsible for our nation's policies a proper sense of the issues and how to deal with them. It more than failed the test of adequacy. It led to distortions and grotesque parodies of rationality, such as the body count and the village pacification program.

After the war in Southeast Asia and particularly after the death of his beloved wife, Margaret, McNamara became less fact-driven, more compassionate, more intuitive. He threw himself with total commitment into a crusade based on his judgment that the folly of the nuclear arms race must end. Those who knew him best observed that the change did not represent a basic change of personality: he had always been a caring and committed person. Rather the change was in his mental strategy—his cognitive approach to coping with problems, policies, and issues. He forsook the narrow objectivist strategy that had led him and so many others to develop massive blind spots to areas of life where an exclusive preoccupation with the measurable facts distorted reality and twisted judgment. He did not become a mystic or an irrationalist: his respect for the facts remained intact. But now he had opened his mind to additional forms of knowing. He had not abandoned the discipline of wedding general principles to the irreducible and stubborn facts. But he had abandoned objectivism with its imperialist and arrogant claim to be the only valid form of knowing.

A similar observation could be made about Wittgenstein. His personality did not change. The young Wittgenstein was just as brooding and as much a loner as the mature man. But the older Wittgenstein changed his mental strategy once he recognized that objectivism, and the tool of logic that accompanied it, was too simpleminded, too narrow, too limited for the larger meanings of life.

Wittgenstein's change of mind illustrates that objectivism is not a narrow technical assumption; it is a world view, a mentality deeply entrenched in our culture that, if left unchecked, shapes itself into the iron cage that Max Weber so rightly feared imprisons the heart and soul of our civilization.

17

SEARCHING FOR PUBLIC JUDGMENT

ollowing Wittgenstein, many illuminating papers and books were devoted to the critique of objectivism. Summarizing them would take
us too far afield of our main theme. So, with regret, I make the leap
from Whitehead, Russell, and Wittgenstein to Jürgen Habermas, a contemporary German philosopher still in his peak productive years.

Such a leap would seem to exclude much of the richness and subtlety
of post-Wittgensteinian philosophy. Despite the isolation of philosophy from
the cultural mainstream, this century has produced a number of seminal
philosophers. But for our purposes, focusing on a single philosopher, Habermas, has several advantages. A systematic thinker, Habermas has built
his philosophy not only on his own great German tradition, which extends from Kant through Marx, Hegel, and Nietzsche to Heidegger, Max
Weber, Freud, Dilthey, Schultz, Gadamer, Apel, and the thinkers associated
with the Frankfurt school. He has also immersed himself in the writings
of the American pragmatists and the Anglo-American school of analytic
philosophy. This is not a philosophy book, so there is no opportunity to
cite the many contributions of these schools of thought. But I take comfort in the fact that Habermas has made a conscientious effort to do so
(although many philosophers, a critical lot, are not in full agreement with
how well he has done).

Another reason for focusing on Habermas is his civility. By and large,
the tone of twentieth-century philosophy has not been civil. The heritage
of the Anglo-American analytic style of argument has been confrontational,
even vicious. It has been the custom to attack the weaknesses of one's adversaries, often with clever malice. The British do this sort of thing with
panache, the Americans more heavy-handedly. But its effect is to suggest,
in trial-lawyer fashion, that one's opponents' arguments are absurd, whereas
one's own shine forth bathed in purest truth. Thinkers like Habermas, al-

211

though occasionally slipping, seek consciously to keep faith with the Socratic tradition of listening carefully, assuming that one's partner in dialogue has a useful point to make, and showing it in the best possible light. Gadamer sums up this style of civility when he says that in such philosophical dialogue "one does not seek to score a point but to strengthen the other's argument".[1]

This constructive style suits our purpose here, which is not to attack the tradition that gave rise to the Culture of Technical Control on the grounds that it is steeped in error and must be extirpated root and branch. Quite the contrary, our purpose is to conserve the tradition, while seeking at the margins to curb its excesses and one-sidedness.

What recommends Habermas above all is the depth of his commitment to democratic practice, a commitment with deep roots in his life experience. In an insightful essay, Richard Bernstein recounts an incident when Habermas was seventeen years old that had an enduring influence on his life and work. One of Habermas's most disturbing experiences as an adolescent was listening to the radio coverage of the Nuremberg trials with his family and being stunned to realize that his parents were more concerned with the procedural legalities of the trial than with the horror of the Nazi atrocities it revealed.[2] Habermas felt suddenly estranged from his parents as he confronted the full horror of what happened when democracy in Germany collapsed and nazism took its place. Suddenly, in a flash, the young Habermas realized how strong the resistance was even in his own family to facing up to the painful truth of the German experience with nazism.

That episode launched Habermas on a lifelong quest for ways to strengthen democratic practice despite all obstacles. A glance at the evolution of his thought will complete our critique of objectivism.

THREE FORMS OF KNOWING

In an early work, *Knowledge and Human Interests*, published in 1968, Habermas made one of his most original contributions to modern philosophy.[3] He argued that knowledge conceived as a body of facts and truths existing apart from human purpose is a myth. He developed his thesis that knowledge is *always* linked to purpose and is never properly conceived as a stand-alone body of information and theory. Habermas's concept of knowledge extends Kant's stunning insight that we never escape our human limitations and that we always construct reality within certain inherent structures of the mind.

In his 1968 book, Habermas described three categories of knowledge, the human purpose each serves, and the procedures we use in each for distinguishing between valid and invalid modes of knowing.[4] Empirical-analytic science, as pursued in the natural sciences, is the first type of knowledge. This form of knowing works best when we describe and explain spatio-temporal events and engage in causal analysis of objectified data. Its main purpose is to exercise control over nature, so as to accommodate it to human uses. It is closely linked to learning by trial, error, and experimentation. Its claim to represent valid forms of knowledge is tied to well-accepted procedures for confirming and falsifying hypotheses and theories, always remaining open to the possibility of discovering new hypotheses.

The second category is closely related to a form of knowing that Dilthey called *Verstehen* and Habermas refers to as "intersubjective understanding." It is this type of knowing that we associate with insight into people's motives, character, values, and world views. To refer to this form of knowing in the American vernacular, we would probably use terms such as "intuitive understanding" or "interpretive insight." It is associated with the humanities and their truths and with aspects of the human sciences (e.g., psychology, sociology, social anthropology, and linguistics).

The purpose associated with this form of knowing is to enhance human understanding and communication. Its methods are based on insightful interpretation of texts, narratives, myths, interviews, therapies, cultures, languages, conversations, observations, and so on. About this form of knowing based on intuitive understanding, Habermas's contemporary, Karl-Otto Apel, observes, "I cannot imagine that this function of the humanities could ever be replaced by reducing understanding and interpretation to the method of objectifying science."[5]

Habermas's third category is knowledge having an emancipatory purpose — to make people free, to emancipate them mentally from false forms of consciousness, ideology, prejudice, and mental coercion.

Throughout Habermas's work we find constant reference to forms of coercion, distortion, and domination. For someone haunted by the experience of nazism, the cause of this concern is not difficult to find. Nazism was not only a virulent form of physical coercion, its ideology of fascism intimidated millions. To be sure, many Germans embraced the doctrine of fascism warmly, but millions more accepted it passively and unthinkingly out of the habit of obedience to and respect for authority and power — forms of domination, in Habermas's terms.

The purpose of the emancipatory form of knowledge is to empower people through self-reflection to recognize when they are entrapped in harmful ideologies. This meaning of knowledge harkens back to the ancient

Greek dictum that "the truth shall make you free." More immediately, it builds on the Frankfurt school's concept of critical theory. The term "Frankfurt school" is the name given to a brilliant and temperamental group of German social thinkers affiliated with the Institute for Social Research, founded in the 1920s, interrupted by World War II (when it was partially reconstructed in the United States), and then reconstructed after the war, once again in Frankfurt. The guiding spirits of the institute were its director, Max Horkheimer, along with Theodor Adorno, Herbert Marcuse, Erich Fromm, Leo Lowenthal and others, and after the war, Jürgen Habermas.

This group of seminal thinkers drew upon the insights of Kant, Hegel, Marx, Lukacs, and Freud for their social theory. From Kant and earlier thinkers they used the concept of critique to indicate rational analysis as opposed to religious revelation. Following Hegel they added the connotation that critique should concern itself with a broader set of constraints than those relating solely to knowledge. They also incorporated Marx's concept of critique as reflected in his *Critique of Political Economy*. In this work, Marx focused on unmasking the constraints imposed by class relations and elaborated his theory that much of the ideological thinking of his era mirrored the special interests of the dominant social classes.[6] Freud's insights made the Frankfurt theorists realize that Marx's orientation was overly restrictive. Freud convinced them that the critique of ideology should also examine unconscious motivations unrelated to the clashing economic interests of the social classes.

Gradually, the thinkers of the Frankfurt school divested the idea of critique from its specific Marxist and Kantian constraints. In their hands it became a general method to liberate people from the stranglehold of all obsolete or tainted ideologies. Horkheimer describes critical theory as guided by an interest in the future achievement of a truly rational society in which "men will make their own history with will and consciousness."[7]

Clearly, Habermas has these various applications of critical theory in mind when he refers to the emancipatory mode of knowing as different in purpose and nature either from scientific knowledge or intuitive understanding.

Even though Habermas was later to modify his views in response to the critics of *Knowledge and Human Interests*, the boldness and simplicity of its main thesis gives this early work, as Anthony Giddens points out, its special distinctiveness.[8] Its utility for our purposes here is decisive. To Habermas and like-minded philosophers goes the credit for demonstrating that scientific knowledge is not the only genuine and legitimate form of knowing, but only one mode among many. For some purposes, it is vastly superior to other modes of knowing. For others, it is badly wanting. Once we accept the conclusion that there is no such thing as knowledge per se, but only knowledge to serve a particular purpose or interest, we have begun to pry open the iron cage that objectivism has imposed on our Western culture.

Habermas shows that although the objectivist approach may be superior to other modes of knowing for purposes of exercising technical control over nature, it utterly fails to address other human purposes such as the great philosophical questions of how to live, what values to pursue, what meaning to give to life, how to achieve a just and free society, and how to be a fully realized and free human being.

THE MEANING OF REASON

In addition to his insistence on the pluralism of modes of knowing, Habermas developed a second concept later in his work that supports the argument that judgment is a genuine mode of knowing. Habermas redefines the concept of human reason, deemphasizing its identification with logic and analysis and emphasizing instead its biological rootedness in the universal human ability to communicate across barriers of language and culture. It is this concept of reason that is reflected in public judgment.

In his historical studies, Habermas deplored the fate of reason as it has evolved since the eighteenth century. For the thinkers of the Enlightenment, reason was synonymous with liberation and emancipation. It was reason that would sweep aside ignorance and injustice and superstition and special privilege, paving the way for democratic society. In the two centuries of modernism following the Enlightenment, the concept of reason has, however, gradually narrowed, losing its normative force and its exhilarating sense of breaking out of darkness into light. Progressively, reason has been reduced to technological perspectives.

Habermas is eager to recapture some of the old meaning of reason. He believes that the gift of reason is wired into our genes but not merely in the sense of formal reasoning ability. Habermas believes that people are endowed by nature as an inherent part of the human condition with a larger form of reason. This larger form is a gift that enables people to communicate with each other across national, linguistic, and ideological boundaries in ways that can lead to a shared concept of what is true and what is false.

This genetic endowment does not find expression under any and all conditions. It is not as robust, say, as the ability to walk upright or to express anger or sexual desire. It is intimately linked to speech and language but speech and language expressed under special conditions. For reason in this sense to prevail there must (1) be dialogue rather than monologue (i.e., people must be talking *to* and *with* each other, not *at* each other), and (2) the dialogue must be free from domination and distortion.

This subtle capability to achieve mutual understanding through language and speech when coercion is absent is a concept of human reason that differs markedly from traditional definitions equating reason either with logic or with objectivist forms of knowing. Its survival value is that in enhancing people's ability to understand each other, it permits them to take concerted action when necessary.

One way to grasp what Habermas has in mind is to apply his concept of reason to the American scene. One of former President Lyndon Johnson's favorite phrases was "Let us reason together." Johnson would often make this appeal when confronted with opposition to his point of view. We know from many anecdotes of the Johnson era that in these sessions of "reasoning together" LBJ was not talking about formal logical reasoning or scientific empirical inquiry any more than Habermas is. Johnson never hesitated to use the power at the command of a forceful president of the United States to "communicate" his point of view. For Habermas on the other hand, the use of power, coercion, or manipulation undermines the possibility of genuine communication. And yet, despite this profound difference, one senses that the two men, the earthy Texas wheeler-dealer president and the highly theoretical German philosopher, at some deep level, shared the same faith — that people can, through dialogue and discussion, reach mutual understanding even when their interests and points of view collide, and that this capability is, in some sense, a process of "reasoning together."

Habermas is quite insistent, however, that genuine communication in a democracy can take place only when all forms of domination — overt and hidden — have been removed. His emphasis on hidden and indirect forms of domination means that he is not confining his caveat to the obvious forms of power — either of the brutal Nazi variety or the mild arm-twisting LBJ variety. He encompasses the many subtle, indirect forms of distortion. In the American context, examples might include experts who "educate" the public by imposing their points of view on them (especially when they use technical jargon); political candidates who tailor their images manipulatively in political advertising to match public opinion poll results; and even the new forms of information overload that blunt people's abilities to keep issues in perspective.

When coercion is hidden, people may think they are participating when they are really being manipulated or intimidated or largely ignored by those who possess real power, for example, those companies that observe the outward forms of participation without their substance. ("Call me Jim," says the boss, who adds, "Before making a major decision I always consult my people.") The phrase "my people" is a giveaway: it suggests ownership, condescension, attitudes of superiority. It expresses the attitude of those who feel that in some sense they "own" those who work for them. Invariably, in these settings people are very careful when their views are sought not to say anything that will rub the boss the wrong way. Forms of hidden domination such as these erode genuine communication.

To replace these power-contaminated forms of communication, Habermas is groping to describe a different type of communication based on reason. This new form of communication is developed in his most ambitious work, his two-volume *Theory of Communicative Action*, which, I believe, harbors a profound insight.[9] His doctrine of communicative action is based on his concept of rationality defined as the ability of people to reach mutual understanding even when interests, cultural frameworks, and languages conflict. The goals of communicative action are to permit us to comprehend each other well enough so that common goals and understandings are possible. In Habermas's view, communicative action is the key to building democratic consensus.

Communicative action, he urges, is a form of reason just as compelling as those embedded in our technology and objectivist modes of knowing. In Habermas's own words, part of our natural endowment is "a gentle but obstinate, a never silent although seldom redeemed claim to reason, a claim that must be recognized whenever and wherever there is to be consensual action."[10] It is this "claim to reason" that can eventually lead to the kind of open dialogue among public, experts, and leaders in which there is give-and-take, two-way communication rather than monologue and the genuine encounter between leaders and citizens on which true democracy depends.

Only through mutual understanding created by such a process can citizens participate in the decisions that shape our common destiny as a nation and a community. Throughout the history of Western civilization, from the *Polis* in ancient Greece through the ideals of the Enlightenment of the eighteenth century to the revolutions of the twentieth century, thinkers have searched for the conditions within which human community and freedom can thrive. Habermas, working in this tradition, has attempted in his theory of communicative action to sketch what might be called a "dialogue of democracy"—the unique and difficult form of communication between public and leaders that genuine democracy requires.

In his *Theory of Communicative Action*, Habermas's thinking has evolved considerably from his early analysis that linked forms of knowledge with purpose. In this later work, he builds on the "linguistic turn" introduced by Wittgenstein as a way to finesse the complexities of traditional epistemology rooted in the Cartesian subject-object and mind-body dichotomies. Instead of the starting point being the solitary individual imprisoned in his own interior subjectivity and searching for reliable ways to have knowledge of the outside world, the starting point is the social act of language, the dialogue of people attempting through language to communicate with one another to achieve mutual understanding.

This new perspective led Habermas to reduce the three forms of knowing he proposed earlier to two: "instrumental rationality" and "communicative action." Instrumental rationality enlarges objective scientific knowledge to include some forms of understanding Habermas had earlier subsumed under the historical and hermeneutical disciplines, and communicative action includes what had previously been the emancipatory mode of knowing as well as the more intuitive aspects of the historical and psychological modes of knowing.

Knowledge remains tied to purpose. When our purpose is control over nature, objectivist knowledge is appropriate, involving instrumental reason. When our purpose is mutual understanding to realize common goals and values, another type of knowledge — and another facet of human reason — is more appropriate. Here we want communicative action, with public judgment as an important aspect of it.

Our Western culture is strong in skills and institutions associated with instrumental rationality. It is the basis for all of our technology and specialized expertise. What we are lacking is equal strength in skills and institutions devoted to effective communicative action and public judgment.

SUMMARY

One can look at Habermas's dialogue of democracy either as a philosopher's utopian ideal that is largely irrelevant to the power-driven, money-driven world in which we live or as a practical and realistic way to accomplish national goals we believe are important. Habermas himself always stressed his practical intent. Indeed, one of his harshest criticisms of German philosophy was that it had become so disconnected from the everyday life of the nation that an ugly Nazified culture could coexist side by side with professors mouthing the most lofty and noble sentiments and not be aware of their bad faith in doing so.

With some qualifications, I find the "practical intent" of Habermas's theory of communicative action credible. Transferred from the German to the American scene, a few modifications are in order. But overall, from my perspective as a practitioner who has long been engaged in objectivist research on social-political processes, I believe Habermas and like-minded philosophers have successfully reconnected theoretical philosophy to the practical goals of Western democratic society.

Unfortunately, however, the insularity of modern philosophy may, in practice, mean simply that objectivism has lost influence in academic philosophy while retaining it everywhere else. There is evidence that this may be so. Objectivism has been under a cloud in philosophy for three decades or more without having much effect on the world outside of academia, especially in the United States. But climates of opinion do eventually change. Concern about the excesses of the Culture of Technical Control is widespread. Unhappily, the objectivist outlook—its dogmatic narrowness, its equation of reality with the measurable and quantifiable, its dedication to specialization and expertise, its contempt for modes of knowing that are not information driven—is still in its virulent phase of ascendancy in the United States, and no amount of philosophical analysis can stop it. But it may be possible to win some minor skirmishes along its extended front.

18

YOU *CAN* ARGUE WITH EINSTEIN

The startling conclusion we draw from Habermas is that there are potentially as many varieties of knowing as there are human purposes and interests. The idea of varieties of knowledge linked to purpose is radical and unfamiliar. It has many implications. It means that there are modes of knowing not yet discovered or codified. It means that in the rush over the past two centuries to acquire scientific knowledge as rapidly as we can, we may have mindlessly shoved aside older authentic modes of knowing, thereby losing access to important truths. It means that we cannot judge one mode of knowing by the rules that apply to another. We cannot assume, for example, that scientific knowledge is canonical and that all other forms of knowledge are to be evaluated by whether they meet the standards of "scientific proof," as science defines it.

In this light, we are ready to examine the claim that public judgment is a genuine form of knowledge. In practice, what does this claim mean? It is a radical claim and one should be fully aware of how far-reaching its implications are. It means, in practice, that for certain purposes, public judgment should carry more weight than expert opinion — and not simply because the majority may have more political power than the individual expert but because the public's claim to *know* is actually stronger than the experts'. It means that the judgment of the general public can, under some conditions, be equal or superior in quality to the judgment of experts and elites who possess far more information, education, and ability to articulate their views.

To put the point simply, when Albert Einstein was alive he held a number of political and social attitudes that were at variance with the views of the public. Albert Einstein was an authentic genius, one of the most intellectually gifted men who ever lived. But Habermas helps us to understand that his genius was limited to certain modes of knowing. On relativity theory, the public could not argue with him. But on issues such as the goals of public education and the role of government in the welfare state the public could argue, and in many instances the chances are that the public had the better case.

Several years ago a series of articles discussed the late scholar, Joseph Campbell, whom Bill Moyers had featured in a popular series of television broadcasts on the role of myth. I recall watching these broadcasts with fascination. Campbell had a wonderful presence, a gift for bringing the difficult subject of myth making to life. He conveyed not only scholarly knowledge but also insight and compassion for people's aspirations and longings. I felt distressed — and somehow cheated — when it was revealed that Campbell was a rather extreme bigot, bristling with anti-Semitic, antiblack, antiwomen attitudes. I felt the same way in earlier years upon learning that creative thinkers of the stature of Martin Heidegger and Ezra Pound had similar propensities, including for Heidegger a period of sympathy with Nazi fascism.[1]

Do such beliefs compromise the scholarship of Campbell, the poetry of Pound, the analyses of Martin Heidegger? I do not believe they do. They may diminish our admiration for these outstanding thinkers as human beings. They may cause us to question the extent of their *wisdom* — a characteristic that transcends knowledge. But, for better or worse, they do not take away anything essential from their claims of knowledge.

What these examples do is help us realize how severely limited any one form of knowledge is. We have come to learn that experts, however impressive, do not have a good grasp of all modes of knowing.

We may know this bit of common sense from experience, but it is excluded from our culture's formal concepts of knowledge. Habermas's contribution (building on the insights of many others) permits us to amend and broaden our formal concepts of knowledge, (thereby gratifying our intuitive conviction that there is more to knowledge and truth than is revealed through formal scientific discoveries). This is what I mean when I say that Habermas has pried open the bars of the iron cage. Because the tyranny of objectivism insists that there is only one form of genuine knowledge, the claims made by religious truths, the insights of art and literature, the truths of history, the judgments of the public, and the truths of psychological insight and intuitive understanding get lumped together with the claims of astrology, people who see flying saucers with extraterrestrial beings on them, those convinced that they have knowledge of previous incarnations, and all are held suspect as knowledge claims.

From the standpoint of objectivism, all of these nonscientific modes of knowing have the status of nonknowledge. We may be more attracted to some than to others, and we may find some useful in practical day-to-day life, but presumably none can challenge the monopoly of objective, empirically based scientific knowledge. This is the imperialist claim that Habermas and so many other twentieth-century philosophers have undermined so thoroughly that sooner or later it will be rooted out of the larger culture, just as it has been (mainly) rooted out of academic philosophy. In its place, a pluralism of modes of knowing is likely to arise as older disciplines in the humanities, philosophy, religion, and ethical conduct and the newer disciplines of therapy, human resources, and communication arts are encouraged to codify and strengthen their own unique address to truth and knowledge. In this sense, the Habermas insight may prove both wonderfully liberating but also confusing.

A pluralism of modes of knowledge has its dangers, as all who live in the era of New Age philosophy should be well aware. How in the new flowering of modes of knowing are we to distinguish between false claims and the real thing, between genuine and fake knowledge, between strong claims and weak ones? These questions are germane to public judgment's claim to status as genuine knowledge. How strong or weak is its claim?

I believe public judgment's claim to be quite strong, once we approach it with a better understanding of what knowledge is and what hurdles and tests any claimant to knowledge must pass. We can distill the testimony of the philosophers we have been considering into a condensed definition of knowledge, as follows: *Knowledge consists of truths, interpreted within a framework of purpose, which enjoy strong validity claims.* If we take seriously philosophy's critique of objectivism, the claim that public judgment is a valid form of knowing depends on its ability to pass three tests implicit in this definition. Is it responsive to some large human purpose or interest? Does it reveal some important aspect of truth and reality? Is there a method for distinguishing false judgment from the real thing? The three key words are *purpose, truth,* and *proof.* These are the requirements any genuine mode of knowing must meet, the hurdles it must surmount.

PURPOSE

The first test is the easiest, but it is far from self-evident. The purpose of public judgment is to achieve knowledge of how people can practice self-governance in a fragmented and unruly world. Today's world is organized mainly along lines of the nation-state. Within their national borders, some nations have learned valuable lessons about democracy and self-governance.

Other nations are beginning to learn. But the disparity between what needs to be known and what is known is vast.

Some of the most helpful insights into the rules of self-governance trace back to the city-states of ancient Greece. But even in fifth-century B.C. Athens, self-governance was confined to men of a certain standing, with women, servants, and slaves excluded. It is sobering to realize how little has been learned about self-governance in the several millennia that followed that shining moment in history. Countries such as Britain, France, Scandinavia, and the United States have learned some important truths about self-governance, but these have been practiced mainly within their own borders. In the emerging global economy with transnational threats to the environment and in the age of nuclear warfare and the population explosion, it is becoming increasingly clear that humanity must learn much more about applying democratic principles of self-governance across national borders.

How fragile the efforts to do so are against the long heritage of tribalism, ethnocentrism, racism, authoritarianism, and fear of the stranger. Even in places like the United States where democracy is well advanced, the evidence is that we are retrogressing in self-governance. (I have written this book as a protest against this trend.)

The main precondition to self-governance (and perhaps to global survival) is the simple, fundamental ability to communicate with each other across the barriers of individual differences in interests, nationalities, cultures, and frameworks for the purpose of setting common goals and the strategies for achieving them. It is this ability that Habermas equates, correctly in my judgment, with the essence of human rationality. Although it is difficult to practice this form of rationality, it is far from impossible.

My most vivid personal experience with communicating across barriers was in relation to the Soviet Union. In the early 1980s, I became part of an ongoing nongovernmental series of conferences between the United States and the Soviet Union. At first, the meetings were stiff and formal. Each side presented its position, which always contained a heavy dose of faultfinding and criticism of the other. The "conversation" started as a dialogue of the deaf, as each side, in imitation of official diplomacy, sought to score points at the expense of the other. But, under the combined influence of glasnost and the personal relationships that had developed among many of the participants, the process gradually shifted from one of scoring points without listening, to one of listening cautiously and tentatively, and then to listening purposefully and sympathetically to seek a basis for consensual understanding.

What impressed me most was how difficult the task was, *even when there was goodwill instead of mistrust and good faith instead of tactical maneuvering for partisan advantage.* We were separated from our Soviet counterparts by geography, language, culture, history, interests, different institutions, and above all, different presuppositions. Because I was present as an expert in public opinion, I was constantly asked why the American public did not approve of this or that Gorbachev initiative when it was so clearly in the American interest to embrace it? The Soviets were skeptical of my explanation that, far from either approving or disapproving, the American public did not have the foggiest idea of what the Gorbachev initiative in question might be. As the years passed, the Gorbachev design became clearer to Americans. But in the first three Gorbachev years (1985–1988) the Soviets had a hard time understanding that something very familiar to them might not have penetrated the consciousness of the American public in a fashion that enabled the public to reach a judgment.

What the experience demonstrated for me was that, despite all the obstacles and barriers, if one has enough time and patience and just enough trust to want the dialogue to continue, it is possible — with great effort — to reach mutual understanding. No serious effort at self-governance can proceed without it.

The process of self-governance is utterly dependent on the capability Habermas identifies as the essence of human reason — the ability of people of good will to communicate with each other across barriers. In the example above, the barrier is language and culture. In everyday American life, the most difficult barriers are formed by the expert-public gap, by the compartmentalization of knowledge reflecting the Culture of Technical Control, and by the divergent interests of America's heterogeneous population. The goal of creating agreement — even consensus — among the American people despite these barriers about which communal actions will most faithfully realize America's core values is the high purpose to which public judgment as a form of knowing is dedicated.

TRUTH

The biggest stumbling block to considering public judgment as a form of knowledge is the claim that it represents truth. Yet, the claim here is surprisingly strong, provided we understand that it applies to a category of truths different from those empirical science pursues. Let us call the truths of public judgment "value truths," by which I mean truths related to questions about which goals and values and beliefs are best suited to help us live together in organized society. If the word *politics* did not carry so much baggage, we might call these insights "political truths," but such a formulation would almost certainly be misunderstood.

The strength of the claim that public judgment knows an important category of truth is made difficult by history and tradition. Historically, truth has always been defined in *opposition* to opinion, and judgment is unmistakably a form of opinion. The opposition between truth and opinion, a legacy now 2,500 years old, is not easy to challenge. But the insights of twentieth-century philosophers prepare the way for this challenge.

In recent centuries, philosophers have held what is known as the "correspondence" theory of truth. This is the view that the picture of reality one holds in one's mind is true if it somehow corresponds with the reality "out there," and not true if it does not. This theory has gradually lost credibility as the Cartesian dichotomy on which it is based has been questioned. As the distinction between "in one's mind" and "out there" (the notorious mind-body problem) became more problematic, the correspondence theory of truth gradually went out of fashion. The distinction illustrates Whitehead's fallacy of misplaced concreteness. The dichotomy between *mind* and *body* and that between *subjective* and *objective* is a high-level abstraction, not a concrete reality. We present ourselves with insoluble puzzles when we subdivide truth along its lines.

To find a more viable non-Cartesian concept of truth, philosophers like Martin Heidegger and the existentialists reverted to the ancient Greek definition of truth as *aletheia* — that which lies open before us and reveals itself. Truth is here allied to revelation.[2]

The principal difficulty with truth as *aletheia* is that it opens the door to many conflicting claims to know the truth. If truth is that which lies open before us, everyone can and does claim to have access to it. And because people's points of view are invariably diverse, a babel of conflicting "revelations" about the truth ensues.

Plato dealt with this problem by vouchsafing such revelation only to a select few — the philosophers who understood the nature of reason. For Plato, reason brings revelation of a special sort: revelation of those eternal and unchanging forms of being seen by the mind's eye. Rational truth is the truth acquired though the process of reasoning, a gift possessed only by a handful of elites, to be contrasted with *doxa*, the ignorant, unreasoned opinions of the mass.

Note that in his concept of truth and rationality, Plato was struggling with two quite different questions: the ontological question of the true nature of being and the methodological question of the best way to approach it. How do you acquire knowledge of the truth?

On the methodological question Plato was bothered by a pesky fact that has perplexed humankind throughout history. Whatever the truth may be, no two people seem to perceive it in quite the same way. Indeed, individuals perceive reality in an amazing variety of ways. People's points of view are even more diverse than their personalities and experiences. The people closest to us in every other way may nonetheless react to a shared experience with a radically different interpretation and even a different perception of what the experience was (the Rashomon effect).

Sometimes this pluralism of points of view is merely annoying, as when we are irritated that someone close to us dislikes a movie or friend or piece of furniture that we like. But the pluralism can have dangerous consequences in situations where health or safety or even survival may depend on securing agreement on a common course of action. (Is the bridge safe enough to permit traffic? Should the nations of the world spend billions to counter the greenhouse effect?) For action, we need to make a decision one way or the other. For certain kinds of communal decisions we *must* reduce the cacophony of opinions. If we are to control our lives and destiny, we *must* agree on how to act on the threats of global warming, or nuclear weapons, or runaway inflation and so on.

The cacophony of opinion in ancient Greece annoyed the aristocratic Plato as much as public opinion annoys our autocratic experts today. Plato's solution of appointing the faculty of formal reasoning to be the guardian of truth, raising it hierarchically high above the opinion of the masses, eliminated the problem of pluralistic points of view. The opinions of the masses were simply excluded as a form of truth seeking.

It took many centuries to dislodge the hegemony of formal reasoning as Plato and Aristotle conceived it. (St. Thomas Aquinas was still devoted to it as late as the end of the Middle Ages, almost two millennia after Plato.) The history of the modern era is the story of empirical science gradually replacing formal reasoning as the approved method for addressing truth.

It is noteworthy that the success of science has degraded the standards of how we judge knowledge, as defined by historical criteria. For centuries, knowledge acquired by the senses was deemed inferior to knowledge acquired by reasoning because it lacks certainty; it is probabilistic rather than absolute; it is provisional rather than enduring; it deals with hypotheses rather than with proven truths; and it has never succeeded in ridding itself of the subjective standpoint of the observer.

Only rarely does the general public catch glimpses of science in practice, with all of its messy disagreements and differences in experimental results and interpretations of what they signify. Does this mean that science as a method of acquiring truth and knowledge is actually inferior to the neat and elegant methods of formal logical reasoning? Such judgments were once commonplace. Today we know that what is at fault is not the methodology of science but the very standards by which we once determined what knowledge is. The certain, absolute, unvarying knowledge that formal reasoning is presumed to yield has shown itself to be trivial. Formal reasoning — logic — is merely a tool, powerless by itself to reveal truth about the world. Empirical science, for all its messiness and uncertainty and shifting paradigms, has proven incomparably more reliable.

In the present era, the opinions of the masses are once again shoved to the bottom of the hierarchy of knowledge, not this time in deference to logic but in comparison with science and technology. And, on certain types of questions, this is where they belong. For purposes of exercising technical control, the ancient distinctions between truth and opinion, knowledge and *doxa*, remain valid.

But what about purposes other than technical control? How well does the distinction between truth and opinion hold up when we seek knowledge for political purposes? The answer depends on one's concept of politics. If the purpose of politics is to dominate others, to manipulate them, to engineer their consent and control them, then the distinction is valid. Because, in this sense of politics, one is seeking technical control.

At the very outset of the era of modern science and technology, Roger Bacon understood that its address to truth was "putting nature to the rack." Through technology, we exercise control by domination, manipulation, and coercion. We do not seek to live in harmony with nature but to bend it to our purposes. We get at its truth by testing it and poking it and taking it apart and trying to put it back together again. Our methods are intrusive. We approach nature by putting on a white coat and shoving a thermometer up its ass. The crudity of the metaphor is apt. Western technology may be the envy of the world for its successes, but its approach to nature seeks domination and control. One can certainly take this approach to politics in the sense of spin control, brainwashing, manipulating people, and exercising power. This century has witnessed plenty of that.

But if one's political purpose is not control, then the truth/opinion distinction becomes problematic. The essence of democracy, as Habermas rightly observes, is to find ways to live together in freedom and without domination. Democracy depends on discovering modes of communication free from domination and distortion. Here the diversity of people's points of view, far from being an obstacle to truth seeking, becomes an asset. Habermas's philosophy of communicative action presupposes a core of human rationality that finds its expression in dialogue where people can with sincerity and good faith express their diverse views about the life-world they share with others, across all boundaries of nationality, ethnicity, language, and framework, in confidence that so doing is a valid form of truth seeking. Habermas yearns for politics where, in Gadamer's phrase, the "exaggerated authority" of the experts, deriving from their high status in the Culture of Technical Control, yields to the diverse judgments of ordinary citizens.[3]

In exploring this point, we come to the very heart of the search that has animated so many outstanding philosophical thinkers of this century. In addition to Habermas, Richard Bernstein lists Hannah Arendt, Hans-Georg Gadamer, Paul Ricoeur, Charles Taylor, Alasdair MacIntyre, Sheldon Wolin, and Hannah Pitkin among those contemporary thinkers who have "sought to show us the centrality of judgment in politics and the need to resist the temptation to replace judgment with . . . some form of strategic or instrumental thinking [i.e., objectivism]."[4] (To this list of distinguished thinkers I would certainly add Bernstein.)

Representative Thinking. What these philosophers mean by judgment is not wholly identical with public judgment as defined in this book. But its essential meaning is similar, as we can see with a side glance at the work of Hannah Arendt. Hannah Arendt, whom I knew as a colleague on the graduate faculty at the New School for Social Research in the 1970s, was a political thinker of rare gifts. In her thought she walked alone — bold, original, and fearless. She sometimes compared her search for truth and understanding with pearl diving. Some pearls are small, misshapen, and dull, others wonderfully large and luminous. Her reflections on judgment were, I have come to believe, among the most spectacular of her "pearls."

For Arendt, the *polis* is the central metaphor of political life. It contains all its essential elements. It is a public space where citizens gather on an equal footing for the purpose of debating the issues that concern them as a community. The equality of the citizens who gather in the polis is not something they are born with. Such equality is created by the polis. In this public space, citizens form judgments about issues. Through free and open debate they seek to persuade each other. Arendt quotes Kant as describing this process as a form of wooing rather than domination or coercion.[5] *Wooing* implies freedom of choice for one wooed: he or she is free to accept or reject the point of view offered.

Arendt's vision of democracy is strikingly like Habermas's, except that Arendt more explicitly develops the concept of judging. To Arendt, the multiplicity of people's points of view — their diversity, their cacophony, even their perversity — all play a critical role in judging. Each person examines the issue being debated from his or her own perspective, holding it up to the light and seeing it from a different angle. Each participant says, in effect, "I see it my way, somewhat differently from the way you see it."

This process Arendt calls "representative thinking."[6] Representative thinking, she has concluded, is the indispensable element in forming judgments. In debate I present my unique way of looking at an issue, but—this is the key point—before forming a judgment I also take *your* way of looking at it into account. My point of view is enriched by my ability to incorporate your perspective. Together we seek to persuade each other and to arrive at a communal outlook which we call a judgment.

Arendt derives her concept of judging from Kant, whose insights are indispensable to her theory of representative thinking. After Kant, never again would it be possible to conceive of objective reality apart from the imprint of those who perceive it. What Kant realized was that we, as perceivers, are constitutive of the truths we see. All of our truths are in this sense profoundly *human* truths, interpreted within the structures of the perceiving mind. Arendt goes beyond Kant, who was referring to inherent mental structures all humans share in common. As in critical theory and cognitive psychology, Arendt takes the position that our differences as well as communalities shape our perceptions and points of view. When many people sharing a common purpose examine an object, each one begins to see that object from his or her own point of view with a richness of perspective not possible when the object is seen from only one angle. Perhaps that is why knowledge of certain kinds of truths can only be gained by, as it were, comparing notes, that is, by seeing reality from a variety of perspectives.

Especially with the fundamental questions of the meaning of life and the goals and values that make life worth living (or dying for), in the search for truth each of us brings his or her entire life experience to bear. If the truths we seek are those of communal living together, the process of truth seeking must be a joint endeavor as we actively pool our collective wisdom.

According to Arendt, the representative thinking that leads to judging always requires that others be present—either in person, as in the polis, or in surrogate form. The various points of view of all participants weigh alongside each other on a basis of genuine equality, an equality that will disappear once we leave the polis (and its substitutes) and return to our separate roles and responsibilities. This dialogue among equals Arendt believes to be the essence of political life and true political freedom.

Arendt once proposed a form of government called the "council system." Because the country is too big to create a giant polis for mass debate and because the ballot box is too small to include others, why not consider, she suggested, a form of graduated debates starting with ten people sitting around a table. "If only ten of us are sitting around a table, each expressing his opinion, each hearing the opinions of others, then a rational formation of opinion can take place through the exchange of opinions."[7]

Arendt's suggestion was never adopted into our political life, but it is approximated in boards of directors (in corporations), and trustees (in nonprofit organizations) as discussed in chapter 15. Even the number ten is close to the mark: much larger groups have difficulty in realizing the process of representative thinking that Arendt sees, rightly in my view, as indispensable to forming sound judgments. On boards, everyone is supposed to be equal, but rarely is. One or two are usually far more "equal" than all the others. And here, too, Arendt and Habermas reveal the acuteness of their observations. To the extent that inequality prevails and hidden forms of domination distort the board's deliberations, the collective judgment that is the final product of representative thinking is flawed. The council or board of director system is probably a dreadful method for operating and managing the day-to-day affairs of any institution or society; but it has proven its excellence for governance.

Of course, corporate governance and democratic governance are quite different (see chap. 15). But they share in common their search for what I have called "value truths." These are the truths that reveal what goals, values, and meanings to pursue, as distinct from the knowledge that reveals the most efficient means to realize them.

PROOF

To be widely accepted as a form of knowledge, it is not enough for public judgment to fulfill an important human purpose and to assert a strong claim to truth. It must also pass the third test; it must "prove" the truth of its judgments. The claims to possess truth are legion. The practical demands of life require, however, that society possess a method for sorting the valid claims from the invalid ones. It is not enough to say you "know" something; you must know that you know it. You must be able to prove it.

Failure to pass the test of proof has caused many once proud claimants of knowledge to lost credibility. People have always claimed "I know it is true because. . . ." Throughout history that sentence has had a wide variety of endings: "because this is what tradition says"; "because my father told me so"; "because the chief rabbi said so"; "because Aristotle discovered it"; "because it is logically provable"; "because it is documented through scholarship"; "because that's what experience teaches us"; "because it's in the Bible"; "because it is written in the *Times*"; "because that is what we have always believed"; "because the astrologer said so." In contemporary Western culture all of these methods of sorting through competing points of view are less persuasive than the statement, "I know it is true because there is scientific proof for it."

The spectacular success of science is owing mainly to its reliance on a highly formalized method for ascertaining proof. Indeed, when we refer to the "scientific method," we are not referring to how science *discovers* truth. (We know little about the creative process of generating hypotheses.) By scientific method we mean the rules of experimental design and other techniques for testing hypotheses. With respect to its testing methods science is way ahead of all other modes of knowing. The entire scientific enterprise is organized around this method. If science gets a score of 100 on having formalized, institutionalized and well-accepted tests of proof, the best of the other methods hovers around 50 or lower.

The scientific tradition insists that the status of *knowledge* be assigned provisionally and only under certain conditions. The chief condition holds that not only must a hypothesis be put to the test (directly or indirectly) but that others must be able to replicate the results. In 1989, two University of Utah scientists claimed to have discovered cold fusion—the fusing of atoms under conditions not requiring extremely high temperatures. If their experiments could successfully be replicated by others, the discovery would rank among the great practical contributions of all times. The world would have available endless supplies of cheap energy.

Unfortunately, other scientists were not able to replicate the Utah experiments. The two scientists have continued their work, because they are sure they are on the right track. But the scientific community at large has, at least momentarily, refused to recognize their work as a contribution to knowledge because it has failed to meet the scientific test for proof.

Each branch of science has developed its own styles of gaining proof. If we shift from physics to medicine, for example, we find heavy emphasis on experimental methods to ensure that extraneous influences such as wishful thinking and experimenter bias are reduced or eliminated. Medical science favors the double-blind method of testing new interventions; that is, patients do not know whether they are getting the *placebo* and neither do the physicians administering the test because experience has shown that when physicians know they unconsciously influence the results.

So successful are its methods of proof that science has been able to impose on the larger society a unique social contract. What science says to society is this: "We want public support and funding to broaden our theoretical understanding of nature. We don't know where it will lead. We don't know when there will be a practical payoff, if ever. We do know that it will require a great deal of money and other resources." No other claimant for public support could hope to win it by acknowledging in advance that it does not know where, when, or even if there will ever be a bottom line payoff.

Despite these peculiarities, science's case is persuasive. In the public's view, science has proven itself pragmatically through its technology. The society supports certain branches of science because the technology they have generated has proven so astonishingly successful — whether it be satellite transmission of TV images or C-T scanners or nuclear-tipped guided missiles. Those branches of science that have not produced successful technology do not, in fact, receive generous public support — botany, for example, or paleontology, or any of the social sciences except economics.

It annoys scientists when the public fails to distinguish between science and technology. And rightly so, because the two disciplines are very different in their values and results. Many gifted technologists have little patience with basic science. And many scientists, especially in the high-prestige fields like theoretical physics, look down on their technology-minded colleagues. But from the public's perspective, science and technology are inseparable parts of the social contract.

From the public's side, the social contract is: "We are not sure we understand or can justify your priorities. Frankly, we would prefer speedier applications of science to technology, like the Japanese do, but as long as you eventually deliver the goods, we will support you." From the public's pragmatic point of view, the proof of the pudding is always in the eating. The proof of science's success lies in the success of the technology it spawns.

Turning from proof in science to proof in public judgment, we should realize that *proof* has two different meanings: putting what you think you know to a formal test and the pragmatic meaning — producing practical results the society values.

On pragmatic grounds, the potential value of public judgment easily passes the test. On almost every important issue the nation faces, successful action depends on developing a stable national consensus, one that reflects the fundamental values of the American people. If the key to self-governance lies in creating the right balance between public and elites — and I believe it does — our societies have to know how to generate a working consensus on vital issues. Under the principle of majority rule, a working consensus does not mean that 100 percent of elites and 100 percent of the public must concur on a strategy. In practice, a working consensus is one in which those parts of the leadership in positions of power and influence find themselves in rough agreement with a sizable majority of the public (i.e., between 66 percent and 80 percent). In our society — and in the other advanced industrial democracies — this type of consensus is enough for concerted action.

The only sound way to develop this type of consensus is to ground it on public judgment. Public judgment, in turn, depends on creating the circumstances under which representative thinking can thrive: a public space, genuine debate, freedom from manipulation and coercion, the articulation of choices and their consequences, opportunities for working through, the coordination of consciousness raising and "choice work," responsive political leadership offering incentives for the public to do the choice work, and so on.

It is characteristic of our Culture of Technical Control that as a society we know a great deal about how to create technical solutions, but comparatively little about how to create consensus through institutionalizing representative thinking in expert-public dialogue.

One can, however, acknowledge the pragmatic value of consensus building without conceding that a consensus proves the "truth" of anything. History is replete with examples of agreements between leadership and public that, in retrospect, represent bad judgment and untruth. In a world dominated by nationalism, it is all too easy to get momentary consensual support in almost any nation by whipping up nationalist passions. The truthfulness of public judgment cannot be proven merely because a consensus exists at one moment in time.

We are, therefore, still left with the question, "How can we prove whether or not public judgment has truth value?" It is understood that truth here has a different meaning than scientific truth. We are referring to "value truths" — normative judgments regarding what values societies and individuals should pursue. Some people believe that only religious faith can reveal the answer to this question. Others believe that the answer is wholly relative — ultimately a matter of arbitrary individual or cultural preference. But there is another answer implicit in the Habermas theory of human rationality and also in the theory of public judgment offered here.

The concepts of representative thinking and communicative action imply that value truths can be revealed through dialogue developed from a variety of human perspectives under conditions free from domination and coercion. In practice, unfortunately, judgments reached at any moment can almost never be free from some element of domination and coercion. The coercion may be subtle and invisible; it may stem from the passions of the moment and from internal pressures as well as external constraints. We are all bundles of prejudices, emotions, irrationalities, quirkiness. It is likely that value truths for humanity must always be judged (1) in retrospect, when the working-through processes of history reveal the full consequences of our actions, and (2) from a cross-cultural point of view that is cleansed of the ethnocentricity of any one culture. Time must pass to permit people to see their views in the light of its consequences and free from the constraints of power, passion, and ethnocentricity.

This search for truth has inspired the study of the humanities: the human quest in all of its folly and wisdom seen in the light of history. It also inspired the concept of critique that Habermas and others have developed: communicative action free from all forms of domination. Realistically, however, we should recognize that judgment freed from the passions of the moment and from all forms of domination requires the passage of time and also freedom from cultural bias. To prove the truths of public judgment both time and distance are needed.

The "proof" of value truths may not, therefore, be as readily accessible as the kinds of proofs science can provide in its own domain of instrumental reason. But there is at least one aspect of proof that *is* readily accessible. It is in relation to the question, "How can we prove whether opinion that parades as public judgment is the genuine article?" Here, proof is relatively easy to develop. At the beginning of the book I defined public judgment as public opinion that meets three standards of quality: stability, coherence, and, most important of all, evidence that those who hold the opinion recognize its implications and take responsibility for them.

Testing for these characteristics of quality is neither difficult nor costly. Relatively modest investments and efforts are required to apply a test like the volatility index described in chapter 2. Nor is it difficult to learn how consistent persons' views on an issue may be, or to ascertain whether they are aware of the consequences of these views and accept responsibility for them.

In defining the concept of public judgment, I deliberately made it narrower than the traditional description of judgment represented by the quote in this book's introduction from historian Paul Gagnon. I did so in the interests of being able to test and prove it in a practical, affordable, and scientifically acceptable fashion. Admittedly, such narrowing strips away some of the richness and subtlety of judgment at its best. But it preserves the essential distinction of being able to contrast serious, thoughtful, and responsible public views with mindless and impulsive mass opinion.

SUMMARY

The Habermas insight that human purpose governs knowledge can serve as an important corrective for our culture's lopsided attachment to objectivist knowledge. Surprisingly, if we look at practice rather than theory, we see that our society is organized for knowledge in a manner that conforms fairly well to the Habermas prescription.

In their day-to-day practice, all professions attempt to distinguish between false and valid claims of truth. As we have seen in science, immense labors are required to test scientific hypotheses. To "prove" anything in any field of endeavor requires large-scale organization. The organization of big science for securing proof has grown into a major social institution. The organization of scholarship to secure documentation in university departments of the humanities is also large-scale social institutions based on different models of knowing. The "discovery" processes of lawyers and the jury system represent still another social institution; the auditing methods of accountants still another. In each instance the need for some sort of "proof" gives rise to the invention of a method for securing it and a social institution for standardizing and ensuring its implementation.

Each of these arenas possesses its own set of rules regarding purpose, truth, and proof. When it comes to proof, objectivist science has the clearest and best codified — though most expensive — organization and procedures. On the other hand, science has made certain sacrifices in the interests of pursuing rigorous standards of proof. It has, for example, excluded vast areas from scientific inquiry that do not lend themselves easily to computation or experimental testing. The social sciences have been accused — not without justification — of sacrificing the very heart and substance of their subject in the interest of making them more "scientific," that is, more susceptible to scientific methods of proof.

Those disciplines that concern themselves with value truths can never hope to compete with science in developing methods of proof that signify in advance of an action that a consensus based on public judgment is "true" in the sense that its values are sound as well as the strategies for realizing them. (The same constraints apply, of course, to all aspects of nature where scientific knowledge is incomplete.) The "proof" of the validity of public judgment must come after the fact, in historical retrospect.

The practical implication here is to elevate the status of the humanities — the study of history, art, religion, literature, language, and philosophy. These are the disciplines that search for human values after the fact and across cultures. In addition, the potential value of the social sciences is seen to be immense if these disciplines ever succeed in freeing themselves from the artificial constraints of instrumental reason. Social sciences such as political science, economics, psychology, sociology, anthropology, policy studies, communications, and human resources should all be contributing more than they presently do to the art of self-governance. And self-governance *is* an art more than a science. It concerns itself with ends more than with means, with style as well as substance, with wisdom as well as information. All the measurement, number-crunching, poll taking and computer models in the world cannot substitute for a touch of wisdom — the kind of wisdom that comes with the pursuit of public judgment and is necessary for democratic self-governance.

The tests of purpose, truth, and proof for public judgment show a different pattern of results than those same tests applied to science. Because they are less familiar, they will require more time to assimilate and to institutionalize. As a mode of knowing, public judgment performs better than science on some criteria and worse on others. It does worse on proof, and it is, therefore, not as susceptible to developing an accumulative body of knowlege about public judgment. It enjoys parity with science on purpose: both serve fundamental, though different, human interests. And it does better than science on truth. Compared to the truths of science, the truths of public judgment are broader and come closer to the ideals of human wisdom that underlie the bold presumption that we are capable of governing ourselves.

19

A SKETCH FOR ACTION

We turn, finally, to the question of action: What can we as a society do to curb the excesses of the Culture of Technical Control? To narrow the expert-public gap? To reduce resistance to public judgment and enhance the quality of public opinion?

At first glance, the prospects look bleak. Our society tends to ignore the kinds of problems described in this book. They are abstract. They are complex. They lack emotional appeal. They seem to lack urgency. They have zero appeal to the myriad of special interest groups that advance most of America's causes. And, although there are few warriors to fight on the side of public judgment, those who resist it are, as we have seen, legion. Worst of all, even if an active constituency had the will to do so, they might not know how to go about fixing these problems. The two requisites for solving a tough problem are *will* and *means*; when both are absent, the chances for effective action are close to nil.

And yet, a closer look shows grounds for hope. Of these requirements for success — the political will to find a solution and a strategy for carrying it out — the lack of political will is the more serious obstacle. If the will exists, the means will readily be found. Later in this chapter I sketch the elements of a possible program of action based on the experience of the two nonprofit organizations that I have worked with over the past few decades — the Public Agenda and the Charles F. Kettering foundations. Their experience gives confidence that public judgment could be vastly strengthened were the country to give this objective even a moderately high priority. At the moment, it has about as low a priority as the national will to make New York City a quieter, cleaner, safer city in which to live. And that is scraping the bottom of the priority barrel.

What are the chances of mobilizing the nation's political will? Can an abstract-sounding objective such as raising the level of public judgment come close to priorities as urgent as preserving the environment and curbing drug abuse? The answer to these questions is "yes, if. . . ." The *if* is whether the public comes to see how much the American Dream depends on replacing the present state of mass opinion with public judgment. The public needs to grasp the connection between improving the quality of public opinion and making our democracy work better in a practical way.

Once the public does see the connection, pride in democracy may help to generate political will. There is no greater source of pride for Americans than our democratic tradition. When citizens state, "We are Americans," they are proudly asserting membership in the world's oldest democracy—still the source of hope and dreams for people all over the world.

Historians refer to the tradition of "American exceptionalism"—the quasi-religious belief that Americans have held since the Pilgrims landed on Plymouth rock that America has a special destiny and a gift to offer the world.[1] In its contemporary form that gift is a more-than-two-hundred-year history of successful democratic practice.

In our era, American pride in country is humbled almost daily. A mere generation ago, Americans were able to boast about enjoying the world's highest standard of living, most dynamic economy, best system of public education, best athletes, best record of health, lowest level of infant mortality, and countless other bests and firsts. Today, the bests and firsts have dwindled, and many Americans have grown self-critical. But recent events have also reinforced pride in our democracy. Americans take satisfaction in the fact that Eastern Europe and Latin America and even the Soviet Union look to the United States as the exemplar of democracy. My surveys show that 81 percent of the public continue to have faith that America has a special mission in the world.[2]

How does this faith express itself? Let me remind the reader of just one of the examples sprinkled throughout the book. Earlier, I mentioned the inner conflict Americans experience when immigration is discussed. In focus groups, most people start out with a negative attitude. "Why do we need those foreigners? Let's slam the door behind us." That is the sentiment. People fear that immigrants will take away jobs and place a strain on limited resources. Initially, the public's attitudes are ungenerous, protective, and territorial. But as the discussion evolves, invariably someone will say something like this: "Wait a minute. What would have happened to our parents (or grandparents or great-great-grandparents) if America had slammed the door shut on them? What does this country stand for anyway? What does the Statue of Liberty stand for?"

Always, this invocation of the Statue of Liberty is a turning point in the discussion. The appeal to the special meaning of America — sometimes stated awkwardly, sometimes with eloquence — touches everyone in the room. To be sure, it does not cause their positions to flip-flop. But they become more thoughtful, more troubled by the complexity of the issue. Gradually, they start to look for compromises that will take their concerns into account but at the same time keep the door open for further immigration.

The belief in the special mission of America is a powerful force that can, potentially, energize the search for public judgment.

A PLAN FOR ACTION

Political will must have a sharp focus. Otherwise energy will be dissipated. There needs to be a plan for action, however tentative.

Such a plan should have four components: (1) a vision of what success would look like if the plan succeeds, (2) specific goals to pursue, (3) a strategy to achieve these goals, and (4) tactics to implement the strategy. I present next a schematic of each component, devoting the most detailed attention to strategy and tactics because the credibility of the plan, from a practical point of view, lies in the details. The tactical details will reveal whether or not an ambitious plan can truly be implemented in the context of present-day institutional life in America.

VISION

If America were to give a high priority to public judgment, and the effort were to succeed, what kind of nation would result? In what ways would our society and culture be different than they are today? What vision of the future would we seek to realize?

Some of the elements of a desired vision of the future are implicit in the concepts discussed in the last few chapters. One of these is the concept of "democratic dialogue." The essence of democratic dialogue is conveyed in Martin Buber's concept of the "I-thou" relationship. When I and thou engage each other, something deeper than a mere exchange of views is going on. The I-thou interaction implies a genuine receptivity to the other: I do not listen passively to what you are saying; I respond to it with my whole being. I may argue and dispute the correctness of your views, but

I "take them in," in the deepest sense of the word. And you do likewise. From the encounter, both I and thou emerge changed. Each of us has internalized the point of view of the other.[3]

Another concept supporting the vision is Habermas's insight that it is disastrous to divorce human reason from the world of ordinary life — the struggle to make a living, raise families, and live peacefully as a community. When experts, influenced by the Culture of Technical Control, conceive reason as something separate and apart from everyday life — the property of a trained class of specialists, scientists, and other elites — then the deepest ideals of the founding fathers of the nation are betrayed. Reason is *not* the exclusive property of a class of experts whose training and credentials certify the possession of a special endowment. Reason is a more humble, more universal, more democratic gift.

To my mind, these are stunning insights. They shape a vision of a democracy that encourages people to listen to each other and to weigh each other's views seriously. It is a vision of a democracy that involves those who wish to be involved and that recognizes that the highest expression of human rationality is not nuclear physics or econometric models but ordinary people speaking and reasoning together on issues of common concern.

It is a vision of what David Mathews calls a *deliberative* democracy, as distinct from a representative or participatory democracy. It is a democracy that revives the notion of thoughtful and active citizenship. Now citizenship is treated like a passive form of consumer behavior. People fail at citizenship not because they are apathetic but because they do not think their actions or views make any real difference. We need to expand the notion of citizen choice now confined to elections to include making choices on the vital issues that confront us every day.

In the 1988 presidential campaign, candidate George Bush promised a "kinder, gentler nation." This appeal struck a responsive chord in the electorate. But after the election, the phrase "kinder and gentler" became a stock laugh line for TV comedians who used it satirically. Why did this happen? It was not because George Bush was hypocritical. There is no reason to question his sincerity. But it did not take long for observers to realize that his invocation of a kinder, gentler America was a mere slogan, empty words devoid of implementation. This well-meant bit of rhetoric added one more stimulus to the growing cynicism of the American public.[4]

The vision I have is of an America where average citizens engage in serious dialogue about what would truly make America a "kinder, gentler nation." This is what the public wants for America. But with limited resources and conflicting needs, it is difficult to achieve. Slogans and top-down leadership cannot achieve it. It requires serious democratic dialogue to shape a political debate in which the public — the whole public — participates.

As our society is presently organized, few institutions are responsible for the common interest. The theory is that the general interest emerges out of the interplay of special interests. This theory, straight from the textbooks of liberal political philosophy, is today the dominant practice in Washington and the state capitals. It is one of the principal causes of the nation's political gridlock: competing special interests exercise a veto over projects to serve the general interest. The concept of the general interest is, however, an urgent concern for average Americans. As individuals, senior citizens, for example, will give far greater weight to the general interest than will the lobby that represents their special interests.

The vision, then, is of a society in which the general interest is as well represented as special interests and in which average citizens play a decisive role in defining it.

Finally, I see this vision as "actively conservative." It is conservative in the sense of staying true to long-standing American traditions. We need, for example, to recover the public traditions of our political culture, particularly those that understand politics as more than the clash of special interest groups mediated by government. The modern concept of a professional government has no place in it for the public or its citizens. And that concept is at the heart of the resistance to programs for strengthening the public. The public really is not necessary for the prevailing vision of how we govern ourselves. People feel pushed out of this kind of system; they feel incompetent, and so they reject politics.

The vision is active in the sense that staying true to tradition requires a change of direction. The root meaning of conservative is to save, to conserve. Sometimes this translates into protecting the status quo. But sometimes it means transformation. If the tradition is losing its way, then keeping faith with it means finding one's way back to the true path.

A key element of the tradition is captured in the Enlightenment's metaphor of light. Its informing idea was "let in the light." Its faith was that the light of scientific knowledge would banish ignorance and superstition and inequality, conquer poverty and disease, and create freedom with dignity.

As a vision for America we should conserve this heritage — to let in the light of knowledge to elevate the freedom and dignity of people. But in doing so we must also recognize that this means changing our culture and institutions to accommodate a more democratic concept of the light of human reason, one that is not the exclusive property of learned experts but, potentially, of everyone.

For this concept, one does not need a graduate degree to develop sound public judgment. One educates oneself for it but not in the manner the Culture of Technical Control dictates. Eventually, we must reintroduce a broader concept of politics into the educational system. We now teach young people to know about "things"; we teach them forms of scientific knowledge. We do not teach them how to make choices with others. We do not develop the kind of intelligence needed to make public judgments. Not only is our concept of knowledge limited to expert knowledge, so is our pedagogy. Our version of civic education is based on how many students know their state capitals. But the movements that are now changing the political history of the world are not led by people who knew their state capitals better than other people.

GOALS

What specific goals would translate this vision from rhetoric into reality? At least three suggest themselves. If American society were to achieve them, much of the vision could be realized.

Correcting the Expert-Public Imbalance

If our democracy is to remain vital, no goal is more important than bringing the expert-public relationship into better balance. For decades now, a vicious cycle has been unfolding: as the experts usurp more and more of the nation's decision making, the public slumps ever more into mass opinion.

There are several logical alternatives for stopping the vicious cycle. We can weaken the experts. We can try to strengthen the public. Or we can combine the two approaches.

In practice, however, it makes no sense to weaken the experts. A populist, antiexpert, anti-intellectual rampage might give some activists emotional satisfaction. But it would be short-lived. The conservative nature of the vision demands that we accept our identity as heirs of the Enlightenment. To be true to that tradition, we must also accept its conviction that scientific knowledge gives our civilization vast powers of control over the material conditions of life. A concomitant of such acceptance is a willingness to give a place of honor to experts and to scientific/technological knowledge. Given the nature of modern industrial society, to discourage the experts from making their optimum contribution would be mindlessly self-destructive. The great task of our era is to tame the Culture of Technical Control, not destroy it. The strategy of choice, then, is to seek to strengthen the public.

Changing the Culture

A second goal is to broaden several cultural shared meanings, namely, what it means to be a leader in our society, what it means to be a citizen, and what it means to pursue knowledge.

The Meaning of Leadership. Literature on leadership is vast, but seldom does it focus on the leader as a person who helps to shape public judgment. Strong leaders usually are regarded as individuals who arrive at decisions through individual gifts of character, intelligence, and insight. They then exercise leadership through persuasion, calling upon additional gifts of communication, sincerity, and charisma. It is fashionable among elites to regard as craven and despicable the tendency of political leaders to "follow the opinion polls" rather than their own convictions. One recent observer even suggested that people lie to pollers, as Nicaraguans did in their 1989 election, so that leaders would be obliged to act on their own convictions.[5]

It should be clear that the two alternatives of slavishly following the opinion polls or standing on one's own convictions irrespective of public opinion are false choices for a democracy. In a democracy, one of the major qualifications of leaders is that they develop the skill to move the public toward consensus by playing a constructive role at every stage of the public judgment process — consciousness raising, working through, and resolution. For this to happen, the culture has to broaden its definition of leadership to incorporate this ability.

We need to develop programs of leadership training that reflect these requirements. Our present concepts of leadership are based largely on techniques for managing people. There are hundreds of leadership development programs, such as the National Association for Community Leadership. They need to be encouraged to take up this new challenge.

The Meaning of Being a Citizen. What it means to be a citizen must also evolve culturally. In today's America, citizenship is largely a matter of rights and of voting. People are far more mindful of the rights of citizenship than of its obligations. The general view is "This is a free country. I have the right to say what's on my mind, move wherever and whenever I want, and do whatever I want as long as it doesn't interfere with the rights of others."

On the obligation side of the equation, people acknowledge that they ought to vote and to pay some taxes (though not as much as they are now paying). Almost no one feels a personal obligation *as a citizen* to struggle with the issues that confront the country and contribute to their solution. Most Americans do not think they *can* contribute ("I don't know enough about the issue"); and even if they could, they do not think that their contributions are wanted.

They are, of course, correct in this latter assumption: policy makers do not really seek public input. But the task of coming to public judgment requires that people grow convinced that their views count. Making an intelligent contribution is hard work. Americans will not do it unless they have an incentive. It does not have to be a big incentive. But Americans must, at the very least, know that leadership is listening and is responsive. There is no way to change the meaning of leadership without simultaneously changing the meaning of citizenship.

The Meaning of Knowledge. It is also mandatory to modify the meaning of knowledge held by the Culture of Technical Control. Here, again, the task is to broaden a concept that has grown overly narrow. The understanding of what knowledge is must extend beyond expert knowledge and also beyond scholarship and traditional learning. Room in the house of knowledge must be made for representative thinking and working through as the outcomes of democratic dialogue. There is no need to elaborate this point further: it has been developed at length in chapters 15–18.

If these cultural meanings evolve in the right direction, it will reduce the mistrust that now separates the experts from the public. Whatever lip service elites may give to the "common sense" of the public, in practice they shape their views through interaction with other elites. By and large, they are oblivious to the views of the public, except by reading opinion polls or soliciting the views of cabdrivers and secretaries. For its part, the public reacts by growing more cynical, more resentful, and ever more removed from participation in decision making.

To improve public judgment, the adversarial relationship between experts and public must be transformed into a cooperative, mutually supportive one. There is no need for conflict. Experts and public have different roles to perform. The public should not try to play amateur expert. The expert should not permit personal values to preempt the rights of citizens to make their own value judgments.

Parts of the education and training system must be redesigned to pay more attention to the *unfamiliar* methods of representative thinking, public choice formulation, working through, and democratic dialogue. This part of the system is almost totally neglected. If more institutions were devoted to improving the methods needed to advance public judgment, the chances of creating a better expert-public balance would be greatly enhanced.

Replacing the Goal of Creating an Informed Public

This third goal has been implicit throughout this book and needs little further elaboration. When Thomas Jefferson enunciated the goal to base American democracy on an informed public, he used the term "informed" as the Enlightenment understood it—to include thoughtfulness, ethical soundness, and good judgment as well as factual information. When today's experts or journalists use the term, they are more likely to equate being well informed with having a lot of information—an asset that I have labored to show is only marginally relevant to the tasks citizens must perform. To keep faith with the Jeffersonian ideal, we must cultivate public judgment as our goal, not an informed public in the contemporary meaning of the term.

STRATEGIES AND TACTICS

What strategies and tactics have the best chance to accomplish these goals? How much confidence can one have that they will do the job?

It would be naïve to minimize the scope of the task. Success requires not only changes in existing institutions, such as the media and the nation's elite professional training systems, but also the creation of new institutions and the stimulation of cultural change. Moreover, changes need to occur on both sides of the expert-public gap: the public has to change as well as the experts. And, perhaps most difficult of all, these changes must occur despite formidable resistance to the concept of public judgment.

On the other hand, the practical experience gained by the Public Agenda and Kettering foundations over the past several decades gives reason for optimism. They show that the task is doable. Through a variety of programs these two organizations have been chipping away at the many obstacles to public judgment. Their experience suggests that given enough time, some mass opinion can be converted into public judgment. In absolute terms, the amount may be small. But its effects may be far-reaching— enough to change American history.

Ultimately, all practical strategies boil down to questions of money (and other resources) and organization. Strategies for space exploration, for example, or caring for the homeless or business expansion revolve around questions of how much they will cost and how to organize the effort.

Eventually, this will also be true for strategies to enhance public judgment. But at the present time, it is premature to focus on money and organization. Prior strategic needs must be addressed first. At the present stage of development, the main levers of action are *cultural change* and *technique.* If the culture can be stimulated to change in the desired direction and if techniques exist to do what needs to be done, the money and organization will follow. Strategically, technique comes first, for once technique is available, cultural change can be more productive.

CHOICEWORK TECHNIQUES

Techniques for advancing the first of the three-stage public judgment process (e.g., consciousness raising) are already familiar, and there is no need to elaborate them further. Less well understood are techniques for advancing the other two stages of working through and resolution. For both, the key to success is finding techniques to make it easier for people to come to grips with hard choices. In general, people realize that hard choices may cause some agony, avoidance, and procrastination. But there is little understanding that techniques exist for accelerating working through, and for countering the obstacles that beset it.

There is even less understanding that new techniques exist for preparing issues for working through. At present, when experts formulate choices, they highlight an issue's technical components and push its implicit values into the background. For the public to wrestle effectively with choices, it is necessary to reverse the emphasis: the values implicit in choices must be made explicit, and the technical considerations must be shoved into the background. After consciousness raising is well advanced, working through proceeds most expeditiously when alternative choices for the public are translated out of the expert's framework into the public's framework, with their value conflicts set forth and the consequences of each choice clearly and carefully spelled out.

David Mathews, president of the Kettering Foundation, has coined the term "choicework" to refer to the various techniques to help the public expedite working through.[6] Several forms of work are involved in choicework. One is the work of transposing choices from the expert's to the public's framework. Another is the work of overcoming obstacles, and a third is the work involved in making the choices. The neologism "choice-work" helps to convey that the processes are unfamiliar and require new techniques.

Each of the various forms of choicework engage different participants. Transposing choices from an expert to a public framework is a special technical skill based on research. It requires doing research to learn what the expert and public perceptions of an issue are and then comparing them and finding a method to bridge the differences between them. This aspect of choicework is best done by professionals specially trained for the task.[7]

Experts and the public see the various facets of issues from such different perspectives that there is usually a huge gap to bridge. Take education, for example. When the experts look at America's educational system, they see a skill deficit: the failure of the system to train young Americans in the skills needed for the emerging global economy. When the public looks at the education system, they see a moral deficit: the failure of teachers to impose discipline and drive out drugs, and the failure of students to learn because they lack motivation.

As a result, the experts and the public talk past each other. Each laments the decline of the education system, but when it comes to discussing solutions, the two groups systematically misunderstand each other's point of view. The experts think the public does not really understand the problem — and to some extent they are correct. The public, for its part, brushes aside the experts' diagnosis because they (the experts) seem unresponsive to the public's preoccupations. And in this conclusion, the public, too, is correct. In chapter 13, I cited as a principle for overcoming obstacles that when people have a bee in their bonnets they will not pay attention until it is heeded, and this the experts fail to do.

One objective of choicework is to bridge this gap, which is often easy to do once you know what is bothering people. Clearly, a concern with skill training and a concern with discipline and motivation are not mutually exclusive. But it takes sympathetic knowledge of the concerns of both sides to formulate choices that will do justice to the preoccupations of each.

Who is to do this choicework? What institutions are willing and able to do it? This is a key strategic question on which success depends. And the answer is, perhaps surprisingly, encouraging. Carrying it out requires a cooperative effort between leaders concerned with the problem and professionals who have developed techniques for researching and bridging the public-expert gap.

One such cooperative effort is the joint program being undertaken by the Business–Higher Education Forum and the Public Agenda Foundation. The Business–Higher Education Forum is an organization of national business leaders and university presidents who meet regularly to discuss problems common to business and education. In recent years, the forum has focused a great deal of attention on the competitiveness issue, particularly as it affects education. In 1990, the forum and the Public Agenda launched an ambitious three-year program to address several aspects of the choicework needed to reach national consensus. The program studies the different perspectives of experts and the public; it formulates choices that do justice to both perspectives; and it conducts media campaigns in a number of cities to bring these choices to the public's attention and to give the communities involved the opportunity to work through the relevant choices. (I discuss these "public choice" campaigns in the section describing the role of the media.)

The most advanced programs to implement choicework are those stimulated by the Charles F. Kettering Foundation of Dayton, Ohio, under David Mathews's leadership. Kettering has nurtured a network of more than thirteen hundred community organizations using the National Issues Forum issue books.

Each year throughout the 1980s, these civic and educational organizations have mobilized hundreds of thousands of citizens to discuss and work through issues of national concern in National Issues Forums. Each year the forums tackle three issues. For their discussions, the Public Agenda prepares special issue books that set forth the choices for the public to consider. The list of issue books prepared to date includes:

- "The Day Care Dilemma: Who Should Be Responsible for the Children?"
- "The Drug Crisis: Public Strategies for Breaking the Habit"
- "The Environment at Risk: Responding to Growing Dangers"
- "Crime: What We Fear, What Can Be Done"
- "Immigration: What We Promised, Where to Draw the Line"
- "The Public Debt: Breaking the Habit of Deficit Spending"
- "Coping with AIDS: The Public Response to the Epidemic"
- "Health Care for the Elderly: Moral Dilemmas, Mortal Choices"
- "The Farm Crisis: Who's in Trouble, How to Respond"
- "Freedom of Speech: Where to Draw the Line"
- "The Superpowers: Nuclear Weapons and National Security"
- "The Trade Gap: Regaining the Competitive Edge"
- "The Soaring Cost of Health Care"
- "Jobs and the Jobless in a Changing Workplace"
- "Priorities for the Nation's Schools"[8]

The Kettering Foundation has succeeded in taking the concept of choicework out of the realm of theory and putting it into everyday practice. It has also succeeded in reconstructing a concept of public education in which experts and public educate each other through the kind of discussion that comes closer to the American tradition of the past than to the contemporary model of experts lecturing at the public. David Mathews believes that we are making progress in revitalizing the American public forum so that it can serve as a place to do choicework. As Mathews notes:

> The public forums or town meetings are our oldest and perhaps our most distinctive political institution. They date back to 1633. The town meetings did not survive as governing bodies, but they did spawn thousands of public forums across the country. The new and most advanced forums quickly get down to real public dialogue in which citizens deliberate with other citizens over which choices are the best choices, instead of devoting their time to listening to expert speakers or debating the merits of opposing technical solutions. The public forum is the natural home for choicework. To serve their intended purposes, forums need issues framed in terms of choices for the public. That is precisely what the issue books prepared for the National Issues Forums are intended to do.[9]

The Kettering experience has demonstrated both to national and community leaders that they have available to them an alternative to the standard "PR approach" which, as a direct expression of the Culture of Technical Control, offers leaders the temptation to seek to "engineer consent," that is, to manipulate public opinion in order to sell the leaders' point of view to the public. Some legitimate purposes can be served through this approach. But leaders ought to know that they have an alternative method for engaging public opinion. This alternative does not seek to sell the public anything. It does not manipulate. It does not propagandize or seduce. It advances two-way communication and dialogue rather than unidirectional informing. It is a resource to assist the public to make its own choices and to reach public judgment.

Kettering and the Public Agenda foundations are helping to institutionalize this approach so that when leaders in the civil society think about public education and the need to reach consensus on important issues, they can choose between the PR approach that seeks to persuade the public that the leader's choice is the only right one and the choicework approach that seeks only to ensure that the choices and their consequences are presented fairly so that people can make up their own minds.

The experience of various organizations — the Business–Higher Education Forum, Kettering, the National Issues Forums, Public Agenda, Brown University's Center for Foreign Policy Development, and so forth — demonstrates persuasively that there are practical means to engage citizens in choicework, that techniques exist for doing so, that these techniques work in practice, and that select leadership organizations are prepared to move ahead with the task of developing public judgment.

ENGAGING THE MEDIA

The media are among America's most dynamic institutions. But they are difficult to work with. For one thing, they are always busy. Producing TV news or a daily newspaper in today's world is an extraordinarily complex task, requiring relentless attention and hard work. In addition, the media are dominated by a powerful subculture that repels outsiders and powerfully conditions insiders to its rules and values. In recent years, the media have grown increasingly conscious of their vast influence; they take pride in it, but do not quite know what to do with it. They are more comfortable when criticizing others than when being criticized, and they tend to be thin-skinned, prickly, and defensive.

Despite these oddities, it is worthwhile — indeed, indispensable — to find a way to work with them, for they hold the key to strengthening the public. To advance public judgment, it will be necessary to support those in the media who see the standard for measuring journalism to be its effect on the quality of public deliberations. Consciousness raising and presenting expert facts do not by themselves do the job the communications media should be doing. Media that tell the public everything about an issue except what its choices are have not done their job.

Those journalists who are raising a new standard for journalistic excellence by looking at the quality of public debate do us all a service. They need to go further and to break out of their "election" mindset. Journalists tend to treat all politics as if everything were some kind of election. In doing that, they miss the heart and soul of everyday political discourse.

The media must also play a central role in modifying the dominant culture's concept of knowledge. But to interest the media in raising the nation's consciousness about the broader reaches of knowledge requires that the media raise their own consciousness. There is no American institution whose concept of an informed public is narrower than that of the media — especially television. Like so many institutions, the media have a grand concept of their mission (as guarantors of free speech) but a narrow interpretation of how to implement it. The media accept — indeed, they welcome — the challenge of informing and influencing public opinion. (That, and entertaining the public, is their business.) But, as we have seen, they equate this task largely with conveying information.

As we have seen, the media-held model of public opinion is a two-step process: from consciousness raising directly to resolution. One of the main points of this book, however, is that the evolution of public opinion is a *three*-step process: from consciousness raising to working through to resolution. In blocking out the working-through stage, the media inadvertently make the task of forming public judgment almost impossible. If the media were to involve themselves in the working-through stage of public opinion as skillfully as they now carry out the consciousness-raising stage, the quality of public opinion in America would improve immediately.

How likely is this to happen, given the media's well-entrenched habits and traditions? Here, too, we have a surprising — and heartening — answer. Since the mid-1970s, the Public Agenda, with the support of the Markle Foundation, has been working with the media on precisely this question. To be sure, progress has not come with lightning speed. But hardly a month passes without some indication of media interest and willingness to cooperate with efforts to advance working through to public judgment.

In recent years, the Public Agenda has formed alliances with various media for what it calls "public choice campaigns" on issues such as rising health care costs, reform of the public schools, the future of U.S.–Soviet relations, drugs, the environment, and reaching consensus on how to enhance America's global competitiveness. The Public Agenda has found some people in the media willing to acknowledge that expert debate takes one only so far in a democracy like ours. It has found a frustration with mass opinion. It has found a belief that a more constructive and thoughtful form of public opinion is desirable and can be achieved.

The first public choice campaign was conducted in Des Moines, Iowa, in 1982. Called *HealthVote 82*, the campaign aimed to help citizens understand the issue of rising health care costs and to think through alternative means for addressing it. The project was distinctive in several respects:

1. It was visibly supported by leadership groups holding opposing points of view. (The groups included local and state government officials, doctors, hospital administrators, and business and labor leaders.)
2. It specifically attempted to move the public beyond mass opinion by addressing important misperceptions identified in preliminary research (e.g., the belief that doctors' fees were a main cause of rising health costs and that employers' insurance costs were negligible, amounting to perhaps one or two hundred dollars a year).
3. It invited the public to consider a range of choices with the pros *and* the cons clearly spelled out. The project presented choices rang-

ing from closing local hospitals, encouraging more outpatient care, making greater use of paraprofessionals, asking patients to pay more of their own costs directly, and changing malpractice laws.

4. It featured intensive and *repetitive* presentations of public choices on television, radio, in the daily newspaper, and in more than two hundred community meetings organized by the project.

5. It culminated with a HealthVote "ballot" distributed through the *Des Moines Register* that reiterated the pros and cons of the choices and emphasized leadership's desire to know the public's considered views.

Surveys conducted before and after the campaign indicated that it attracted widespread public attention. Over 76 percent of the residents said they were familiar with the campaign and almost half (47 percent) said they had looked at a special supplement appearing in the *Des Moines Register*. Over thirty thousand residents completed and returned ballots, a response rate of over 24 percent, higher than the percentage of residents participating in the Iowa Caucuses in 1980. Comparison of "before and after" surveys showed significant increases in public understanding of the issue and more willingness to consider change, with the greatest increase among those with the greatest exposure to the campaign. Community leaders heartily endorsed the project, and the media committed enormous time and energy to carrying it out.

HealthVote 82 was a significant step forward in making the concept of choicework concrete and practical. Equally important, it suggested that local media could be allies in putting choices before the public if a good case could be made for it. Since *HealthVote 82*, Public Agenda has worked with more than thirty-five television stations and twenty daily newspapers in more than twenty communities to conduct public choice campaigns.[10] With support from the Markle Foundation, the Public Agenda has formed a "network" of media, the Network for Public Debate, whose sole purpose is to conduct public choice campaigns on an annual or biannual basis.

Public choice campaigns demand a serious commitment from broadcasters and newspapers. TV stations are asked to broadcast spots and documentaries intensively for a period of six to ten weeks. They are asked to devote their own public affairs programs to the issue at hand and to cover the issue in the newscasts. They are asked to promote and publicize community meetings and the distribution and results of the balloting. The Public Agenda has deliberately sought the participation of commercial broadcasters — rather than public television and radio — and has been successful in enlisting them.

What is asked of newspapers may well be unprecedented. In addition to devoting news, editorial, and promotional resources to the issue, newspapers are asked to print and distribute a special supplement featuring a choice "ballot" as a public service without charge.

The participation of TV stations and newspapers in public choice campaigns has several advantages. Their reach is almost universal. Most people turn to news on television and in newspapers to learn about important policy questions. And, media are generally perceived to be balanced and disinterested in their coverage of issues.

Moreover, growing numbers of media professionals are showing an unexpected receptivity to the concept of working through. This group sees the public choice campaign as a reasonable extension of their current work. They are already covering the key issues. They aim to present different points of view so that citizens understand them and can grapple with them seriously. For the more thoughtful media professionals who acknowledge the complexity of the issues the country faces and who take pride in promoting honest debate, there is considerable discomfort with "business as usual." The Public Agenda's stress on the need to go beyond consciousness raising strikes a responsive chord.

COMBATING RESISTANCES

Finally, in executing this two-prong strategy — institutionalizing techniques for doing choicework and interesting the media in stimulating public judgment — it is important to take into account the need to combat the resistances documented in earlier chapters. To remind the reader: one is the press's assumption that their mission of informing the public is largely confined to consciousness raising so that when they are asked to take on tasks other than consciousness raising (i.e., working through) they experience these as unwelcome intrusions. ("Don't bother us. We have our own work to do.")

A second resistance relates to the status threat that experts experience when their expertise seems to be devalued. If you put the relatively uneducated and untrained public on the same level as the well-educated and exquisitely trained expert, you seem to be saying, "Your specialized knowledge and training do not count for much."

The third — and most fundamental — resistance is deeply rooted in the Culture of Technical Control. It is the tinge of epistemological anxiety experts feel when anyone suggests that their habitual cognitive style — the information-driven modes of knowing on which they rely day in and day out—are less authoritative, narrower, and more inadequate than they have assumed. Taken together, these three resistances form a formidable obstacle to accepting the concept of public judgment and all that it implies.

So strong are these resistances that it is difficult to attack them head on. But they can be blunted, finessed, eroded, or bypassed. The first source of resistance—"Don't bother me. I'm busy with my own work."—is the most widespread but the easiest to get around. How to do so is implicit in the strategy described above for cooperating with the press. If the press's own definition of its job can be broadened—and the evidence suggests that it can—the cultivation of public judgment becomes an inherent and important part of its mission.

The second resistance—the status threat to the experts—is more difficult. But, on the other hand, it is not universal. Many self-confident experts are not threatened by engaging the public in dialogue. They may not see the point of doing so, or understand how to do it skillfully, but they would be receptive if they came to understand its value and purpose. Once experts come to understand that a populist attack on their credentials is not being mounted, they need not be defensive about protecting their turf.

In fact, the task of creating the conditions for successful expert-public dialogue will entice many experts. Accomplishing it requires a high level of expertise. (The reader will recall the considerable effort needed to translate choices in U.S.–Soviet relations from the framework of the foreign policy expert into a framework susceptible to public debate.) Engaging the public in dialogue adds to the expert's role rather than diminishing it. Such dialogue may give experts and leaders an opportunity to break a stalemate and to advance issues of concern to them.

The third source of resistance—epistemological anxiety—is the most difficult to counter. But, as with all forms of outmoded anxiety, identifying it and making it conscious helps. Once thoughtful people understand that they are being unnecessarily self-protective of their habitual modes of dealing with reality, and that they are thereby blocking their own personal growth, the anxiety begins to lose its force.

In addition, people do not generally realize how destructive the modes of knowing associated with the Culture of Technical Control can be. Americans caught a glimpse of it during the Vietnam War with its body counts, village pacification programs ("to win the minds and hearts of the Vietnamese people"), and its policies of destroying villages "in order to save them." But these odd forms of the logic of technical control were associated in people's minds with the aberrations of the war not with the mind-set of the culture at large.

At present, people do not link some of the society's most troubling problems with the Culture of Technical Control. Most people would be surprised to learn that problems as disparate as pollution, being manipulated in political elections, exclusion from decision making, and the failure to agree on policies for correcting the nation's educational deficiencies all arise out of the distortions that objectivism's modes of knowing create.

A 1990 television show depicted how the Soviet Union's second largest lake, Lake Aral, had been destroyed. In the late 1960s, the Brezhnev regime decided that the waters of the lake should be used to irrigate the desert in order to raise cotton and rice. This agricultural scheme proved a spectacular bust, destroying the lake without succeeding in raising either cotton or rice.

Some will argue that this was simply a bad technical decision and that it was made by the Russians, not by us. But it was, in fact, a political decision. It was reached without regard to the needs and wishes of the region's inhabitants, out of a technocratic mind-set that is all too characteristic of the Culture of Technical Control, the culture shared by all modern industrialized nations.[11] (We have our own inventory of "Lake Aral" horror stories in the United States.)

In short, to preserve America's preeminence in democracy, there is something for everyone to do — average citizens, the institutions that conduct public forums, people in positions of leadership, experts, government officials, the media — all of us. That is the way things get done in a democracy.

NOTES
BIBLIOGRAPHY
INDEX

NOTES

INTRODUCTION

1. Election Research Center, *America Votes* (Washington, D.C.), and Committee for the Study of the American Electorate, *Nonvoter Study '88–89* (Washington, D.C.). Reported in U.S. Department of Commerce and the Bureau of the Census, *Statistical Abstracts of the U.S. 1989*, 109th ed. (Washington, D.C.: GPO, 1989), 258–59.

2. See the Charles F. Kettering Foundation, "On Second Thought: A Report on the 1989–1990 National Issue Forum" (Dayton, Ohio: Charles F. Kettering Foundation, 1990), 18–21.

3. Keith Melville, "On Second Thought: A Report on the 1986–1987 Forum" (Dayton, Ohio: Domestic Policy Association, 1987), 9–11.

4. Paul Gagnon, "Why Study History?," *Atlantic Monthly*, Nov. 1988, 44.

5. Ibid.

6. V. O. Key, Jr., *Public Opinion and American Democracy* (New York: Knopf, 1961), 536.

7. Ibid.

1. A MISSING CONCEPT

1. Daniel J. Boorstin, "Gresham's Law: Knowledge or Information?" remarks at the White House Conference on Library and Information Services, Nov. 19, 1979 (Washington, D.C.: Library of Congress, 1979), 6.

2. Angus Campbell et al., *The American Voter* (New York: Wiley, 1960).

3. Philip E. Converse, "The Nature of Belief Systems in Mass Publics," in *Ideology and Discontent*, ed. David Apter (New York: Free Press, 1964), 242.

4. Campbell et al., 543.

5. Norman H. Nie, Sidney Verba, and John R. Petrocik, *The Changing American Voter* (Cambridge, Mass.: Harvard Univ. Press, 1976), 18.

6. Ibid., 116.

7. Ibid.

8. For an example of this type of research, see the National Opinion Research Center/Institute for Survey Research at Temple University for the National Science Foundation, Oct. 1979.

9. Everett Carl Ladd, *The American Polity: The People and Their Government* (New York: Norton, 1985), 315–16.

10. Ibid., 317–18.

11. Ibid., 318–19.

12. Ibid., 350.

13. George Gallup, "The Quintamensional Plan of Question Design," *Public Opinion Quarterly* 11, no. 3 (Fall 1947): 386.

14. Eleanor Singer, "Presidential Address: Pushing Back the Limits to Surveys," *Public Opinion Quarterly* 52 (1988): 416–26.

15. Ibid., 424.

2. WHAT IS QUALITY IN PUBLIC OPINION?

1. CBS News/*New York Times* survey, Sept. 1987.

2. NBC News/Associated Press survey, Aug. 1983.

3. See surveys conducted by the Roper Organization 1973–1983. Surveys conducted by CBS News/*New York Times* in May 1985 and Jan. 1987 show a similar pattern.

4. See NBC News/*Wall Street Journal* survey, Oct. 1985.

5. Yankelovich Clancy Shulman survey for *Time* and Cable News Network, June 1989.

6. CBS News/*New York Times* survey, Apr. 1989.

7. See the surveys conducted by the National Opinion Research Center from 1972 to 1988.

8. Ibid.

9. The percentages reported are for 1988 data (National Opinion Research Center survey, Feb. 1988). Data going back to 1972 show a similar pattern.

10. National Opinion Research Center surveys, 1972–1988.

11. The Gallup Organization survey for *Newsweek*, Dec. 1988 and Jan. 1985.

12. See the following surveys: National Opinion Research Center, Feb. 1982 and Feb. 1984; and Yankelovich, Skelly & White, Inc., for *Time*, May and Sept. 1981.

13. See the surveys conducted by the National Opinion Research Center from 1974 through 1988.

14. See Yankelovich Clancy Shulman for *Time*, Nov. 1986, for survey questions that probe some of the possible consequences of sex education in the schools.

15. See the following surveys: the Gallup Organization for Phi Del Kappa, Apr. 1987; Yankelovich Clancy Shulman for *Time*, Nov. 1986; and Associated Press/Media General, Sept. 1986.

16. For a comprehensive summary of current American attitudes toward U.S. foreign policy in Central America, see Market Opinion Research for Americans Talk Security, survey no. 5, registered voters, Apr.–May 1988. Americans Talk Security (ATS), a nonprofit organization, was founded by Boston philanthropist, Allan Kay. During the 1988 presidential election year, ATS sponsored a series of twelve national surveys, eleven conducted before the election and one after it. The surveys were conducted in rotation by three organizations: Market Opinion Research (MOR), which also conducted President Bush's pre-election polls, Marttila and Kiley, a democratic polling organization that conducted polls for Governor Dukakis, and the Daniel Yankelovich Group, Inc., a nonpolitical and neutral attitude research company. The purpose was to ensure bipartisanship by having the three firms review each

other's questionnaires and interpretations. In 1990, two additional surveys were undertaken (nos. 13 and 14) to test improved methodology in policy issue research and to further understand the values, opinions, and judgments of the public on critical issues. Throughout this book, I will be drawing extensively on this body of work.

17. For a detailed discussion of this and other similar patterns regarding popularity ratings, see Charles W. Roll, Jr., and Albert H. Cantril, *Polls: Their Use and Misuse in Politics* (New York: Basic, 1972), 128-29.

18. Jean Johnson of the Public Agenda Foundation is given credit for coining this term. The New York based Public Agenda Foundation is a nonprofit organization, founded in 1975 by Cyrus Vance and myself. Its research is designed to test and elaborate many of the ideas presented in this book.

19. The Daniel Yankelovich Group, Inc., for Americans Talk Security, survey no. 7, registered voters, July 1988.

20. See Marttila and Kiley, Inc., survey no. 1, Oct. 1987, and the Daniel Yankelovich Group, Inc., Sept.-Oct. 1988, survey no. 10, for Americans Talk Security. Both surveys were conducted with registered voters.

21. *Los Angeles Times* survey, Apr. 1985, reported in "Ten Years of Public Opinion. An Ambivalent Public," *Public Opinion* 11 (Sept.-Oct. 1988), 21.

22. Ibid., 21.

23. Stephen Immerwahr, "U.S.-Soviet Relations in the Year 2010; Americans Look to the Future, Technical Appendix" (New York: Public Agenda Foundation and the Center for Foreign Policy Development at Brown University, 1988), posttest table 19.

24. Ibid., posttest table 21.

25. Ibid., pretest table 9.

26. Ibid., posttest table 23.

27. Ibid., pretest table 6.

28. Ibid., posttest table 20.

29. Yankelovich, Skelly & White, Inc., and *Time*, "The Mushiness Index: A Refinement in Public Policy Polling Techniques," report, Mar. 1981.

30. To my knowledge, the only media reporting of the results highlighted in the press conference was the single page article by Dom Bonafede, "'Mushy' on the Issues," *National Journal*, June 6, 1981, 1029.

3. MASS OPINION VS. PUBLIC JUDGMENT

1. Major research findings are highlighted in the report, Daniel Yankelovich, Inc., "Generations Apart," (New York: CBS News, 1969).

2. Kurt W. Back, "Metaphors for Public Opinion in Literature," *Public Opinion Quarterly* 52 (1988): 278.

3. Key, 4.

4. Leo Bogart, *Polls and the Awareness of Public Opinion*, 2d ed. (New Brunswick, N.J.: Transaction, 1985), 14.

5. See R. A. Fisher, *Statistical Methods for Research Workers*. 13th ed. (Edinburgh: Oliver and Boyd, 1958).

6. Singer, 416-26.

7. See the survey conducted by the Gallup Organization, Apr. 1975.

8. For example, majorities believed that the United States "did the right thing by

deciding to help form and become a member of NATO" (55 percent) and favored the United States "strengthening military security arrangements with our allies" (63 percent) (the Roper Organization, June 1975, and Louis Harris and Associates, Aug. 1976, respectively). In line with this position, a Nov. 1978 Gallup survey for the Chicago Council on Foreign Relations found majority support (54 percent) for sending U.S. troops if Soviet troops invaded Western Europe. Yet during that same period, another survey found a divided public (43 percent vs. 43 percent) in response to an almost identical question (Roper Organization survey, July 1978).

4. KNOWLEDGE VS. OPINION

1. Adam Clymer, "Polls Show Contrast in How Public and E.P.A. View Environment," *New York Times,* May 22, 1989, sec. B7.

2. Ibid. Quote by Frederick W. Allen.

3. Ibid.

4. Michael R. Kagay, "Public Knowledge of Civics Rises Only a Bit," *New York Times,* May 28, 1989, sec. L31.

5. Ibid. Quote by Michael X. Delli Carpini.

6. Ibid.

7. Quoted in Philip Wheelwright, ed., *The Presocratics* (Indianapolis: Bobbs-Merrill, 1966), 91.

8. Ibid., 96.

9. Ibid., 97.

10. *Plato's Republic,* trans. G. M. A. Grube (Indianapolis: Hackett, 1974), 136-40.

11. Henry Steele Commager, *The Empire of Reason,* (New York: Anchor Press/Doubleday, 1977), xii.

12. Ibid., 1.

13. Ibid., 41.

14. Quoted in Back, 285.

15. Barry Sussman, *What Americans Really Think and Why Our Politicians Pay No Attention,* (New York: Pantheon, 1988), 7.

16. See Paul F. Lazarsfeld, "Public Opinion and the Classical Tradition." in *Communications and Public Opinion: A Public Opinion Quarterly Reader,* ed. Robert O. Carlson (New York: Praeger, 1975), 615-29.

5. THE BUMPY ROAD FROM MASS OPINION TO PUBLIC JUDGMENT

1. Sussman, 8.

6. CONSCIOUSNESS RAISING

1. Quoted in the National Issues Forum briefing book on AIDS, Keith Melville, ed., "Anatomy of an Epidemic: Coping with the Crisis", (Dubuque, Iowa: Kendall/Hunt, 1988), 4.

2. These numbers were obtained by an item count of survey questions containing the word *AIDS* (but not the word *beauty*) in the specified years through the use of POLL,

a data base archive housed and maintained by the Roper Center for Public Opinion Research, Storrs, Conn.

3. Survey conducted by the Roper Organization, Aug. 1985.

4. See surveys conducted by ABC News/*Washington Post*, Sept. 1985, Sept. 1986, Mar. 1987; and ABC News, June 1987.

5. Survey conducted by the Gallup Organization, Aug. 1985.

6. Survey conducted by the Roper Organization, Oct. 1987.

7. See John Doble and Jean Johnson, "The Nation Reacts to AIDS. A Report from Six Cities." (New York: Public Agenda Foundation, 1988).

8. See the following surveys: Associated Press/Media General, May 1989; CBS News/*New York Times*, Sept. 1988; Louis Harris and Associates for Metropolitan Life/Paul Loewenwarter Productions, July–Aug. 1987; and CBS News/*New York Times*, Sept. 1988.

9. See the following surveys: Gordon S. Black Corporation for *USA Today*, Aug. 1988; *Los Angeles Times*, July 1986 and July 1987; the Gallup Organization, Nov. 1986 and Oct. 1987; and ABC News June 1987.

10. See the following surveys: ABC News, June 1987; ABC News/*Washington Post*, Mar. 1987; and the Roper Organization for *U.S. News & World Report*/Cable News Network, Mar.–Apr. 1987.

11. One survey found that 7 in 10 (70 percent) have made no change in their lifestyles because of the AIDS epidemic (*Los Angeles Times*, July 1989); only 4 percent say they use condoms to reduce their chances of getting AIDS (CBS News survey, Jan. 1989).

12. See the following surveys: the Gallup Organization, June and Oct., 1987; Louis Harris and Associates for Metropolitan Life, July 1987, ABC News/*Washington Post*, Mar. 1987; and ABC News, June 1987.

13. See the survey conducted by Associated Press/Media General, May 1989.

14. For a commentary on the insurance debate of AIDS victims, see Bruce Lambert, "Insurance Limits Growing to Curb AIDS Coverage," *New York Times*, Aug. 7, 1989, sec. A1. See also the following surveys: the Roper Organization for *U.S. News & World Report*/Cable News Network, Mar.–Apr. 1987; and the Roper Organization, Dec. 1985.

15. *Los Angeles Times* survey, July 1987.

16. Survey conducted by the Gallup Organization for *Newsweek*, Aug. 1985.

17. Survey conducted by Mark Clements Research for *Family Circle*, June 1987.

18. Survey conducted by Mark Clements Research for *Glamour Magazine*, women aged eighteen–sixty-five, Aug.–Sept. 1987.

19. *Los Angeles Times* survey, July 1987.

20. Survey conducted by the Center for Work Performance Problems/Georgia Institute of Technology, Feb. 1988. See Melville, ed., "Anatomy," 34.

21. Louis Harris and Associates survey for Metropolitan Life/Paul Loewenwarter Productions, July 1987.

22. Survey conducted by the Gallup Organization, Oct. 1987.

23. Ibid.

24. Survey conducted by the Roper Organization for *U.S. News & World Report*/Cable News Network, Mar.–Apr. 1987.

25. See Doble and Johnson, 36.

26. ABC News survey, June 1987.

27. Survey conducted by the Roper Organization for *U.S. News & World Report*/Cable News Network, Mar.–Apr. 1987.

28. Survey conducted by the Gallup Organization, Oct. 1987.

29. A recent poll reported that two out of five (39 percent) people have made some

change in their life-styles because of AIDS (*Los Angeles Times* survey, July 1989). A much smaller number (19 percent) said they had changed some aspect of their sexual behavior (CBS News survey, Jan. 1989).

30. For a more detailed description of these problems, see Thomas E. Graedel and Paul J. Crutzen, "The Changing Atmosphere," *Scientific American,* no. 261 (Sept. 1989): 58–68; and Stephen H. Schneider, "The Changing Climate," *Scientific American,* no. 261 (Sept. 1989): 70–79. For a concise, nontechnical presentation of this issue, see Keith Melville, ed., "Environment at Risk: Responding to Growing Dangers" (Dubuque, Iowa: Kendall/Hunt, 1989).

31. Resources for the Future, survey conducted for the Council for Environmental Quality, Jan.–Apr. 1980.

32. Louis Harris and Associates survey for the Office of Technology Assessment, Oct.–Nov. 1986.

33. Associated Press/Media General survey, May 1989.

34. Survey conducted by the Roper Organization, Dec. 1974.

35. Ibid., Dec. 1980.

36. John Carey and Larry Armstrong, "The Next Giant Leap for Mankind May Be Saving Planet Earth." *Business Week* (July 31, 1989) 90.

37. Survey conducted by the Roper Organization, Mar. 1982.

38. Opinion Research Corporation survey, Mar. 1981.

39. Kane, Parsons and Associates survey for *Parents Magazine,* Sept.–Oct. 1988.

40. Ibid.

41. Quoted in John Noble Wilford, "His Bold Statement Transforms the Debate on Greenhouse Effect," *New York Times,* Aug. 23, 1988, sec. C4.

42. Survey conducted by the Gallup Organization for *Times Mirror,* registered voters, Aug. 1988.

43. See Marttila & Kiley, Inc., for the Americans Talk Security Project, survey no. 8, registered voters, July 1988.

44. Market Opinion Research for the Americans Talk Security Project, survey no. 9, registered voters, Sept. 1988.

45. An Apr. 1990 Gallup survey revealed that less than one-third of Americans (30 percent) worry about the "greenhouse effect or global warming" "a great deal." Almost an equal number (27 percent) worry about this problem "a fair amount."

46. Michael Oreskes, "H.U.D., Wright, Meese. To the Public, It's All the Same Network," *New York Times,* July 30, 1989 sec. E1.

47. One survey shows that 19 percent of the public personally has known someone who was infected with or died from AIDS (Associated Press/Media General, May 1989). Although still relatively small, this percentage is up sharply from 1985 (5 percent) (*Los Angeles Times* survey, Dec. 1985).

48. AIDS' rapid spread into the teen population is one of the latest concerns. See Gina Kolata, "AIDS Is Spreading in Teen-Agers, A New Trend Alarming to Experts," *New York Times,* Oct. 8, 1989, sec. A1.

49. See Alan Weisman, "L.A. Fights for Breath," *New York Times Magazine,* July 30, 1989, 33.

50. See Shearon Lowery and Melvin DeFleur, *Milestones in Mass Communication Research: Media Effects* (New York: Longman, 1983), 22–29.

51. For an overview of the diversity of scientific emphasis, see William C. Clark, "Managing Planet Earth," *Scientific American,* no. 261 (Sept. 1989): 47–54.

52. Survey conducted by the Gallup Organization, Apr. 1990. Interestingly, Gallup

asked a similar list the year prior. In May 1989, the public was most worried about "air, ocean and beach pollution" (51 percent), "followed by damage to the earth's ozone layer" (51 percent); "the loss of tropical rain forests" (42 percent), and "acid rain" (34 percent). Again, at the bottom of the list was "the greenhouse effect or global warming" (30 percent), five percentage points *higher* than the Apr. 1990 level!

53. In Jan. 1974, a solid majority of the public (62 percent) believed that "a very important reason for the energy crisis" was that "oil companies have deliberately held back supplies in order to raise prices" (Opinion Research Corporation survey) and that "there really isn't a shortage but that big companies are holding it back for their own advantage" (73 percent) (the Roper Organization). Five years later, this level of mistrust remained equally high (Opinion Research Corporation and ABC News/Louis Harris and Associates surveys, May 1979).

54. William K. Stevens, "Skeptics Are Challenging Dire 'Greenhouse' Views," *New York Times*, Dec. 13, 1989, sec. A1.

55. William K. Stevens, "Study Supports Global Warming Prediction," *New York Times*, Dec. 14, 1989, sec. A36.

56. Graedel and Crutzen, 62.

57. Gina Kolata, "How Much Is Too Much to Pay to Meet Standards for Smog?" *New York Times*, Apr. 3, 1989, sec. A1.

58. Ibid. See also Weisman, 15–17.

59. See "U.S. Will Mail AIDS Advisory to All Households," *New York Times*, May 5, 1988, sec. B10.

60. Survey conducted by the Gallup Organization, Inc., July 1988.

7. TRANSITION OBSTACLES

1. Conversation with Robert Teeter, former president of Market Opinion Research, Detroit, Mar. 1988.

2. Lowery and DeFleur, 23.

3. Ibid., 366–67.

4. Ibid.

5. Ibid., 24–27.

6. Ibid., 369.

7. Maxwell E. McCombs and Donald L. Shaw, "Structuring the 'Unseen Environment,'" *Journal of Communication* 26, no. 2 (Spring 1976) 13.

8. Survey conducted by the Gallup Organization, Dec. 1938. The crisis in Czechoslovakia ranked first as the news event that interested the public the most.

9. See the following surveys: Gallup Organization, 1937, 1939; the Office of Public Opinion Research, Princeton Univ., 1942 and 1943; and the Roper Organization, July 1939.

10. Survey conducted by the Gallup Organization, 1938.

11. Ibid., 1939.

12. Ibid., Feb. 1943.

13. Ibid., Apr. 1943.

14. Ibid., May 1945.

15. Ibid.

16. The conference, sponsored by the Harvard Divinity School, the Neiman Foundation, WCVB TV, and the Anti-Defamation League, was entitled "The Holocaust and the Media" and was held at the Harvard Divinity School, Cambridge, Mass., May 19, 1988.

17. Polls show that as late as Jan. 1943, more than half the public (52 percent) did not believe or did not know that "2 million Jews have been killed since before the war began" (the Gallup Organization) and that months before the war ended in Europe, almost the entire public (more than 95 percent) greatly underestimated the numbers murdered in the German concentration camps (the Gallup Organization, Nov. 1944.)

8. THE EXPERT-PUBLIC GAP

1. Key, 557.
2. See Kolata, "How Much," sec. A1; and Weisman, 15-17.
3. See John Doble and Josh Klein, "Punishing Criminals: The Public's View" (New York: Edna McConnell Clark Foundation, 1989); and Stephen Immerwahr, "Prison Overcrowding and Alternative Sentencing: The Views of the People of Alabama, Technical Appendix" (New York: Public Agenda Foundation, Feb. 1989).
4. Stephen Immerwahr, "Prison," 93.
5. Ibid.
6. Doble and Klein, 43.
7. See John Immerwahr, Jean Johnson, and John Doble, "The Speaker and the Listener: A Public Perspective on Freedom of Expression" (New York: Public Agenda Foundation, 1980).
8. See Public Agenda Foundation, "Water Efficiency in the West: The Public's View" (New York: Public Agenda Foundation, 1986).

9. THE COMPETITIVENESS ISSUE

1. Survey conducted by the Roper Organization, Sept.–Oct. 1977.
2. Opinion Research Corporation survey, Aug. 1987.
3. *The Los Angeles Times* survey, 1985.
4. Survey conducted by the Gallup Organization for *Times Mirror*, Jan.–Feb. 1989.
5. See the survey conducted by Louis Harris and Associates for *Business Week*, July 1989.
6. See Martin Feldstein, "Retreat from Keynesian Economics," *Public Interest* 64 (Summer 1981): 92-105.
7. See John Immerwahr, "Saving: Good or Bad? A Pilot Study on Public Attitudes Toward Saving, Investment, and Competitiveness." (New York: Public Agenda Foundation, 1989).
8. From 1973 to 1985, the Roper Organization repeatedly has asked the survey question: "Here is a list of possible causes of some of our problems in this country. Would you call off the ones you think are the major causes of our problems today?" In Sept.–Oct. 1973, "A letdown in moral values" ranked second (50 percent) in a list of twelve items. Consistently from 1975, the public ranked this item as their top cause. By Feb. 1985, this view was held by three out of five Americans (59 percent). More recently, 64 percent of the public said "the nation is undergoing a period of moral decline" (*Los Angeles Times* survey, Mar. 1989).
9. An Apr. 1988 Gallup Organization survey conducted for Phi Delta Kappa found people ranked "use of drugs" and "lack of discipline" to be the "biggest problems" with the public schools in their communities.
10. John Immerwahr, "Report to the Business Higher Education Forum" Working paper (New York: Public Agenda Foundation, Fall 1989), 7.

11. Survey conducted by the Gallup Organization for *Times Mirror,* Jan.–Feb. 1989.

12. Ibid.

13. The Daniel Yankelovich Group, Inc., for Americans Talk Security, survey no. 3, registered voters, Feb. 1988.

14. Marttila and Kiley, Inc., for Americans Talk Security, survey no. 6, registered voters, May 1988.

15. John Immerwahr, "Saving," 5.

16. Ibid., 4–6.

17. See the following surveys: *Los Angeles Times,* May 1984, Oct. 1984, Sept. 1985, Feb. 1986; and CBS News/*New York Times,* Jan. 1987.

18. John Immerwahr, "Saving," 5.

19. Yankelovich, Skelly & White, Inc., "Meeting Japan's Challenge: The Need for Leadership" (Schaumburg, Ill.: Motorola,, Inc. 1982), 4.

20. Akio Morita, personal conversation, Oct. 19, 1989.

21. John E. Reilly, ed., "American Public Opinion and U.S. Foreign Policy 1987" (Chicago: The Chicago Council on Foreign Relations, 1987), 37.

22. Personal confidential conversation, May 1989.

23. See Nathaniel C. Nash, "Persuading Americans to Save: Congress and the Administration Prepare New Incentives." *New York Times,* Dec. 17, 1989, sec. F1.

24. Ruben F. Mettler, "America's Competitive Challenge," paper presented to the Conference Board, New York Marriot Marquis, Apr. 23, 1986, 6.

25. Daniel Yankelovich and Sidney Harman, *Starting with the People* (Boston: Houghton Mifflin, 1988), 156–57.

26. See the William T. Grant Foundation Commission on Work, Family, and Citizenship, "The Forgotten Half: Non-College Youth in American" (Washington, D.C.: Youth and America's Future/William T. Grant Foundation, 1988), 21.

27. Ibid., 1.

10. FROM MINUTES TO CENTURIES

1. For evidence of this drop in public support, see surveys conducted by CBS News/ *New York Times,* Apr. 15, 1986, through Jan. 21, 1987.

2. "President and Mrs. Bush Talking with David Frost: Interview in Kennebunkport, Maine," taped Aug. 29, 1989. Aired on WNET, channel 13, Newark, N.J., Sept. 5, 1989.

3. See Melville, "On Second Thought, 1987–1988."

4. Leon Festinger, *A Theory of Cognitive Dissonance* (Stanford: Stanford Univ. Press, 1957).

5. Ladd, 310–11.

6. A. N. Oppenheim in *A Dictionary of the Social Sciences,* ed. Julius Gould and William L. Kolb (Glencoe, Ill.: Free Press of Glencoe, 1964), 477.

7. Joseph B. Cooper and James L. McGaugh, "Attitude and Related Concepts," in *Attitudes,* ed. Maria Jahoda and Neil Warren (Baltimore: Penguin, 1966), 29–30.

8. Alfred North Whitehead, *Adventures of Ideas* (Harmondsworth, England: Pelican, 1927), 7.

9. Survey conducted by the Gallup Organization, Jan. 1937.

10. Ibid., Oct. 1938.

11. Mark Clements Research survey for *Glamour,* Aug.–Sept. 1987.

12. See Daniel Yankelovich, *New Rules: Searching for Self-Fulfillment in a World Turned Upside Down* (New York: Random House, 1981).

13. See the survey conducted by the Gallup Organization for *Newsweek*, Dec. 1987.

14. See the survey conducted by the Roper Organization for Virginia Slims, 1974.

15. Ibid., Mar. 1985.

16. A June 1989 *New York Times* survey reported that 68 percent of the wives in marriages in which both partners worked outside the home said they "do not get enough time for themselves." A dramatic 84 percent of full-time working mothers expressed this view. In addition, 83 percent of working mothers said they were "torn between the conflicting demands of their jobs and the desire to see more of their families."

17. See the survey conducted by the *New York Times*, June 1989. Results are summarized in Alison Leigh Cowan, "Women's Gains on the Job: Not Without a Heavy Toll," *New York Times*, Aug. 21, 1989, sec. A1.

18. See Susan Diesenhouse, "Many Smokers Hope to Quit, but Few Get Proper Help," *New York Times*, July 20, 1989, sec. B6.

19. Ibid.

20. Survey conducted by the Gallup Organization, June 1954.

21. Ibid., June 1987.

22. See the Gallup Organization surveys, June 1954 and Mar. 1987.

23. Survey conducted by the Gallup Organization, June–July 1957.

24. Ibid.

11. THE END OF THE COLD WAR

1. The Daniel Yankelovich Group, Inc., for Americans Talk Security, survey no. 3, registered voters, Feb. 1988.

2. Survey conducted by the Gallup Organization, 1949.

3. In May 1982, researchers found from a CBS News/*New York Times* survey that less than one-quarter of the public (24 percent) viewed "nuclear development as a good thing."

4. See Yankelovich and Harman, 46–54.

5. In 1955, fewer than one out of three believed that "all mankind would be destroyed" if a nuclear war broke out between the Soviet Union and the United States. By 1987, 83 percent agreed "There can be no winner in an all-out nuclear war; both the U.S. and the Soviet Union would be completely destroyed." (Both surveys were conducted by the Gallup Organization.)

6. See Yankelovich, Skelly & White, Inc., for *Time*, Dec. 1983.

7. For a description of the ATS project, see chap. 2, n. 16.

8. ABC News/*Washington Post* survey, May 1988.

9. The 1945 and 1947 polls were conducted by the Roper Organization for *Fortune*, the 1985 poll by the *New York Times*, and the Nov. 1989 poll by CBS News/*New York Times*. These results are summarized in Robin Toner, "The Malta Summit: New Friends in Old Places — Americans Much Warmer Toward Soviets, Poll Finds," *New York Times*, Dec. 3, 1989, sec. A29.

10. See the survey conducted by the Gallup Organization, Dec. 1989.

11. See Louis Harris and Associates survey for *Business Week*, Nov. 13, 1989.

12. See the Gallup Organization survey, Dec. 7, 1989.

13. See NBC News/*Wall Street Journal* survey, registered voters, Dec. 4, 1989.

14. The Daniel Yankelovich Group, Inc., for Americans Talk Security, survey no. 11, registered voters, Nov. 1988.

15. From a Feb.–Mar. 1990 survey conducted by Market Strategies, Inc., for Ameri-

cans Talk Security, survey no. 13, researchers found that more than four in five registered voters (81 percent) have a favorable impression of Gorbachev.

16. See the survey conducted by Louis Harris and Associates, Aug. 1989.

17. See the survey conducted by Yankelovich Clancy Shulman for *Time*/Cable News Network, Oct. 1989.

18. See Market Opinion Research for Americans Talk Security, survey no. 2, registered voters, Jan. 1988.

19. See the survey conducted by Louis Harris and Associates, Aug. 1989.

20. See CBS News/*New York Times* survey, May 1989.

21. See the following surveys: Louis Harris and Associates, Aug. 1989; and the Gallup Organization, Dec. 1989.

22. Ninety percent of the public held this view in early 1990. See the survey conducted by Louis Harris and Associates, Feb. 1990.

23. See the survey conducted by Louis Harris and Associates, Aug. 1989.

24. In Dec. 1988, Market Opinion Research analysts for Americans Talk Security, survey no. 12, found that about two in three (64 percent) believe that nuclear weapons are likely to be used by "a terrorist or a madman." About equal numbers (60 percent) believe they will be used by "a country other than the U.S. or the Soviet Union in a regional conflict." See also Marttila & Kiley, Inc., for Americans Talk Security, survey no. 4, registered voters, Mar. 1988. More recently (Feb.–Mar. 1990), Market Strategies, Inc., analysts for Americans Talk Security, survey no. 13, found that three out of four registered voters (74 percent) view "the possession of nuclear weapons by Third World countries and terrorists" to be a "serious threat to national security." (Only 46 percent felt this way about "Soviet nuclear weapons.") Almost all (90 percent) chose "keeping nuclear weapons from Third World countries and terrorists" as a leading national goal.

25. See the following surveys conducted with registered voters for Americans Talk Security: Market Strategies, Inc., survey no. 13, Feb.–Mar. 1990; and Marttila & Kiley, Inc., survey no. 5, Apr. 1988.

26. See the following surveys conducted with registered voters for Americans Talk Security: Daniel Yankelovich Group, Inc., survey no. 10, Sept. Oct. 1988, and survey no. 3, Feb. 1988; and Marttila & Kiley, Inc., survey no. 1, Oct. 1987.

27. See the following surveys conducted with registered voters for Americans Talk Security: Market Strategies, Inc., survey no. 13, Feb.–Mar. 1990; Marttila & Kiley, Inc., survey no. 8, Aug. 1988 and survey no. 4, Mar. 1988.

28. From a survey conducted with registered voters by the Daniel Yankelovich Group for Americans Talk Security, survey no. 3, analysts found large majorities agreeing that "spending on the arms race causes us to neglect domestic problems" (79 percent) and that "the arms race with the Soviets is too expensive" (71 percent).

29. See Marttila & Kiley, Inc., for Americans Talk Security, survey no. 8, registered voters, Aug. 1988.

30. Public Agenda Foundation, May 1984. See the Public Agenda Foundation and the Center for Foreign Policy Development at Brown University, "Voter Options on Nuclear Arms Policy: A Briefing Book for the 1984 Elections (New York: Public Agenda Foundation, 1984).

31. See Market Opinion Research for Americans Talk Security, survey no. 12, registered voters, Dec. 1988.

32. Public Agenda Foundation, May 1984, and Market Opinion Research for Americans Talk Security, survey no. 12, registered voters, Dec. 1988.

33. *Los Angeles Times* survey, Mar. 1982.

34. Market Opinion Research for Americans Talk Security, survey no. 12, registered voters, Dec. 1988.

35. Yankelovich, Skelly & White, Inc., survey for *Time*, registered voters, Nov. 1985.

36. Market Opinion Research for Americans Talk Security, survey no. 12, registered voters, Dec. 1988.

37. The Daniel Yankelovich Group, Inc., for Americans Talk Security, survey no. 10, Oct. 1988.

38. Market Opinion Research for Americans Talk Security, survey no. 12, registered voters, Dec. 1988.

39. Ibid.

40. Ibid.

41. Ibid.

42. Daniel Yankelovich and John Immerwahr, "The Public, the Soviets, and Nuclear Arms: An Experiment in Public Judgment" (New York: Public Agenda Foundation, 1989), 33. See also Public Agenda Foundation and the Center for Foreign Policy Development at Brown University, "U.S.–Soviet Relations in the Year 2010: Americans Look to the Future" (New York: The Public Agenda Foundation, 1988).

43. Ibid., 37.

44. See the following surveys: CBS News/*New York Times*, Jan. 13, 1990, and Nov. 26, 1989; Yankelovich Clancy Shulman for *Time*/Cable News Network, Nov. 15, 1989; *Los Angeles Times*, Nov. 17, 1989; Louis Harris and Associates for *Business Week*, Nov. 13, 1989; and NBC News/*Wall Street Journal*, registered voters, Dec. 4, 1989.

45. Remarkably, just weeks after the collapse of the Berlin Wall, more than three out of five Americans (62 percent) said, "The Soviet Union is becoming a more trustworthy nation (Louis Harris and Associates survey, Dec. 1989). In addition, from a mid-Nov. 1989 survey conducted by Associated Press/Media General, analysts found a majority (52 percent) who believed, "Communism in Eastern Europe is becoming less of a threat to the security of the United States than it has been in the past."

46. From a Feb. 1990 poll conducted by ABC News/*Washington Post*, analysts found a majority (52 percent) who believed there was "not much" or "almost no danger" that the Soviet Union would return to the "hard-line communism it practiced before."

47. See Market Strategies, Inc., for Americans Talk Security, survey no. 13, registered voters, Feb.–Mar. 1990.

48. See Associated Press/Media General survey, Nov. 1989.

49. See NBC News/*Wall Street Journal* survey, Dec. 1989.

50. Ibid.

51. Ibid.

12. AN EXPERIMENT IN WORKING THROUGH

1. See Public Agenda Foundation and the Center for Foreign Policy Development, "Voter Options." An accompanying technical appendix is also available from the Public Agenda Foundation, 6 East 39th Street, New York, N.Y. 10016.

2. Ibid., 24–27.

3. The Bohen Foundation, the Carnegie Corporation, the Joyce Mertz-Gilmore Foundation, the George Gund Foundation, the William and Flora Hewlett Foundation, the Charles F. Kettering Foundation, the John D. and Catherine T. MacArthur Foundation, the James C. Penney Foundation, Inc., and the Veatch Program.

4. Yankelovich and Immerwahr, 30.

5. Ibid., 37–38.

6. Ibid., 45.

7. For a more detailed discussion of these findings, see Public Agenda Foundation and the Center for Foreign Policy Development, "U.S.–Soviet Relations," chaps. 2, 3. A more concise summary appears in Yankelovich and Immerwahr, 29–52.

13. TEN RULES FOR RESOLUTION

1. See Jean Johnson, John Doble, and Jeffrey Tuchman, "Curbing Health Care Costs. The Public's Prescription," (New York: Public Agenda Foundation, 1983).

2. See the Domestic Policy Association, "The Domestic Policy Association's National Issues Forums: A Report on Its First Year" (Dayton, Ohio: Domestic Policy Association/ Charles F. Kettering Foundation, 1983), 18–26.

3. John Immerwahr, "Report."

4. See John Doble, "Infant Mortality in the Third World: The Public's Reactions to Child Survival" (New York: Public Agenda Foundation, 1986.)

5. See Keith Melville and Mary Komarnicki, "Campaign Finance: Defining the Problem, Proposing a Remedy" (New York: Public Agenda Foundation, 1985), 7.

6. Jean Johnson, "Introduction" in Doble and Klein, 9. See also, John Doble, "Crime and Punishment: The Public's View" (New York: Edna McConnell Clark Foundation, 1987).

7. Yankelovich and Harman, 189–90.

8. CBS News/*New York Times* survey, Feb. 1986.

9. Ibid., Feb. 1985.

10. Survey conducted by the Roper Organization, Mar. 1985.

11. CBS News/*New York Times* survey, Feb. 1986.

12. Louis Harris and Associates survey for the U.S. Department of Agriculture, Oct.– Nov. 1979.

13. CBS News/*New York Times* survey, Feb. 1986.

14. See Melville, "On Second Thought, 1986–1987."

15. Ibid., 4.

16. Ibid., 5.

17. Ibid., 4–5.

18. Ibid., 5.

19. Survey conducted by the Roper Organization, Feb. 1984.

20. Ibid., Mar. 1985.

14. EPISTEMOLOGICAL ANXIETY

1. Quoted in Daniel Yankelovich et al., *The World at Work: An International Report on Jobs, Productivity, and Human Values* (New York: Octagon, 1985), 40–43.

2. Ibid.

3. John Dewey, *The Quest for Certainty* (New York: Putnam, 1960).

15. DEFINING OBJECTIVISM

1. See Thomas Kuhn, *The Structure of Scientific Revolutions* (Chicago: Univ. of Chicago Press, 1970).

2. Among other occasions, Kissinger stated this observation during a meeting of executives in the travel industry ("World Travel Roundtable") sponsored by the American Express Related Service Company, Inc., Paris, Apr. 1989.

3. David Halberstam, *The Best and the Brightest* (New York: Random House, 1972).

4. Thomas L. Whisler, "Rules of the Game: Inside the Corporate Boardroom," Selected Paper no. 66 (Graduate School of Business, University of Chicago, 1987), 8.

5. Richard Bernstein, *The Restructuring of Social and Political Theory* (Philadelphia: Univ. of Pennsylvania Press, 1978), 111.

6. Ibid.

7. Ibid., 119.

8. Ibid., 157.

9. Ibid., 112.

16. DECONSTRUCTING OBJECTIVISM

1. Alfred North Whitehead, *Science and the Modern World* (Harmmondsworth, England: Penguin, 1938), 12.

2. Ibid.

3. Whitehead, *Adventures.*

4. William James, *The Principles of Psychology*, 2 vols. (New York: Dover, 1950).

5. Quoted in Whitehead, *Science*, 13.

6. Ibid., 29.

7. Ibid., 66.

8. Ibid., 64.

9. Ibid., 29.

10. Ibid., 29-30.

11. See Alfred North Whitehead and Bertrand Russell. *Principia Mathematica* (Cambridge: Cambridge Univ. Press, 1925).

12. William Barrett, *The Illusion of Technique: A Search for Meaning in a Technological Civilization* (Garden City, N.Y.: Anchor Press/Doubleday, 1979), 30.

13. See Ludwig Wittgenstein, *Tractatus Logico-Philosophicus.* trans. D. F. Pears and B. F. McGuinness (London: Routledge and Kegan Paul, 1961).

14. Barrett, 44.

15. Quoted in T. Z. Lavine, *From Socrates to Sartre: The Philosophic Quest* (New York: Bantam, 1984), 404.

17. SEARCHING FOR PUBLIC JUDGMENT

1. Quote cited in Richard J. Bernstein, "Pragmatism, Pluralism and the Healing of Wounds," inaugural lecture at the New School for Social Research, New York, Feb. 8, 1989.

2. Richard J. Bernstein, "Introduction," in *Habermas and Modernity*, ed. Richard J. Bernstein (Cambridge, Mass.: MIT Press, 1985), 2.

3. See Jürgen Habermas, *Knowledge and Human Interests* (1968), trans. Jeremy J. Shapiro (Boston: Beacon, 1971).

4. For an excellent preliminary discussion of these three forms of knowledge, see "Appendix" in Habermas, *Knowledge*, 301-17; and Bernstein, "Introduction," 1-32.

5. Karl-Otto Apel, "The A Priori of Communication and the Foundation of the

Humanities," in *Understanding and Social Inquiry,* ed. Fred R. Dallmayr and Thomas A. McCarthy (Notre Dame, Ind.: Univ. of Notre Dame Press, 1977), 308.

6. For an excellent description and analysis of critical theory, see Paul Connerton, ed., *Critical Sociology* (Harmondsworth, England: Penguin, 1976) 11–39; and Norman Birnbaum, *Toward a Critical Sociology* (New York: Oxford Univ. Press, 1971).

7. Quoted in Bernstein, *Restructuring,* 181.

8. See Anthony Gidden, "Reason Without Revolution? Habermas' Theories des Kommunikativen Handelns" in *Habermas and Modernity,* ed. Richard J. Bernstein, (Cambridge, MA: MIT Press, 1985), 96.

9. Jürgen Habermas, *The Theory of Communicative Action,* trans. Thomas McCarthy, vol. 1, *Reason and the Rationalization of Society;* vol. 2, *Lifeworld and System: A Critique of Functionalist Reason* (Boston: Beacon, 1981/1987).

10. Quoted in Bernstein, "Introduction," 20.

18. YOU *CAN* ARGUE WITH EINSTEIN

1. See Anthony Gottlieb, "Heidegger for Fun and Profit," *New York Times Book Review,* Jan. 7, 1990, 1.

2. For an enlightening discussion of Heidegger's interpretation of *aletheia,* see Barrett, 144–45.

3. Hans-Georg Gadamer, "Hermeneutics and Social Science," *Cultural Hermeneutics* (1975), 312.

4. Richard L. Bernstein, "Judging — the Actor and the Spectator," paper prepared for the conference "Hannah Arendt: History, Ethics, Politics," at the New School for Social Research, New York, Oct. 1981, 21.

5. Hannah Arendt, *Between Past and Future: Eight Exercises in Political Thought* (New York: Viking, 1968), 222.

6. Ibid., 241.

7. Hannah Arendt, *Crises of the Republic* (New York: Harcourt, 1972), 232 33.

19. A SKETCH FOR ACTION

1. Henry Steele Commager, *The American Mind, An Interpretation of American Thought and Character since the 1880's* (New Haven: Yale Univ. Press, 1950), 10–11.

2. See the following surveys: the Daniel Yankelovich Group, Inc., for Americans Talk Security, survey no. 7, registered voters, July 1988, and the Roper Organization for American Enterprise Institute, Nov. 1981.

3. See Martin Buber, *I und Thou.* 2d ed., trans. Ronald Gregor Smith (New York: Scribner's, 1958).

4. See Donald L. Kanter and Philip H. Mirvis, *The Cynical Americans: Living and Working in an Age of Discontent and Disillusion* (San Francisco: Jossey-Bass, 1989).

5. Jacob Weisberg, "Poles Lied to Pollsters, Why Not You?" *Philadelphia Inquirer,* Apr. 11, 1990, sec. A23.

6. See David Mathews, *The Promise of Democracy, A Source Book for Use with National Issues Forum* (Dayton, Ohio: Charles F. Kettering Foundation, 1988), 62–116.

7. Since 1975, the Public Agenda has been developing special skills to carry out this task. These skills involve conducting research with the public and experts to uncover each

one's "starting position" and cooperative efforts with specialists and interest groups to for-mulate choices that do justice to the major political and substantive positions various groups of Americans have taken.

8. These issue books can be ordered from Kendall/Hunt Publishing Company, 2460 Kerper Boulevard, Dubuque, Iowa, 52004-0539, (phone: 800-338-5578).

9. Personal communication with David Mathews, president of the Charles F. Kettering Foundation, Jan. 17, 1990.

10. The television stations included network affiliates in Baltimore, Denver, Milwaukee, Minneapolis, Philadelphia, Raleigh, and Seattle. The newspapers included the *Des Moines Register, Kansas City Star*, the *Philadelphia Inquirer*, the *National Tennessean*, and the *Wilmington News Journal*.

11. News report on the "MacNeil/Lehrer News Hour," Apr. 19, 1990 (viewed on WNET, channel 13, Newark, N.J.).

BIBLIOGRAPHY

The following surveys were obtained from the archives of the Roper Center for Public Opinion Research at the University of Connecticut at Storrs using the database, POLL. POLL is a question level index of over six decades of public opinion research. It can be accessed directly by contacting the Roper Center (203-486-4440) or through DIALOG Information Service (800-334-2564).

ABC News, 1981–1987
ABC News/*Washington Post*, 1981–1988.
Associated Press/Media General, 1986–1990.
CBS News/*New York Times*, 1977–1990.
CBS News, 1989.
The Daniel Yankelovich Group, Inc., for Americans Talk Security, surveys no. 3, 7, 10, and 11, 1988.
Kane, Parsons and Associates for *Parents Magazine*, 1988.
Los Angeles Times, 1980–1989.
Louis Harris and Associates, 1965–1990.
Louis Harris and Associates for *Business Week*, 1989.
Louis Harris and Associates for the Office of Technology Assessment, 1986.
Louis Harris and Associates for Metropolitan Life/Paul Loewenwarter Productions, 1987.
Louis Harris and Associates for the U.S. Department of Agriculture, 1979.
Louis Harris and Associates for Virginia Slims, 1971.
The Gallup Organization, 1937–1990.
The Gallup Organization for the Chicago Council on Foreign Relations, 1978.
The Gallup Organization for *Newsweek*, 1985–1988.
The Gallup Organization for Phi Delta Kappa, 1987–1988.
The Gallup Organization for *Times Mirror*, 1988–1989.
Gordon S. Black Corporation for *USA Today*, 1988.
Mark Clements Research for *Family Circle*, 1987.
Mark Clements Research for *Glamour Magazine*, 1987.

Market Opinion Research for Americans Talk Security surveys no. 2, 5, 9, and 12, 1988.

Market Opinion Research, 1985.

Market Strategies, Inc., for Americans Talk Security, survey no. 13, 1990.

Marttila & Kiley, Inc., for Americans Talk Security, surveys no. 1, 4, 5, 6, and 8, 1987–1988.

National Opinion Research Center, 1972–1988.

National Opinion Research Center/Institute for Survey Research at Temple University for the National Science Foundation, 1979.

NBC News/Associated Press, 1983.

NBC News/*Wall Street Journal*, 1985–1989.

New York Times, 1989.

The Office of Public Opinion Research, Princeton Univ., 1942–1943.

Opinion Research Corporation, 1974–1987.

Opinion Research Corporation and ABC News/Louis Harris and Associates, May 1979.

Public Agenda Foundation, 1984.

Resources for the Future for the Council for Environmental Quality, 1980.

The Roper Organization, 1939–1985.

The Roper Organization for the American Enterprise Institute, 1981.

The Roper Organization for *U.S. News & World Report*/Cable News Network, 1987.

The Roper Organization for Virginia Slims, 1974–1985.

Yankelovich Clancy Shulman for *Time*, 1986.

Yankelovich Clancy Shulman for *Time* and Cable News Network, 1989.

Yankelovich, Skelly & White, Inc., for *Time*, 1981–1985.

Apel, Karl-Otto. "The A Priori of Communication and the Foundation of the Humanities." In *Understanding and Social Inquiry*, edited by Fred R. Dallmayr and Thomas A. McCarthy, 292–315. Notre Dame, Ind.: Univ. of Notre Dame Press, 1977.

Arendt, Hannah. *Between Past and Future: Eight Exercises in Political Thought.* New York: Viking, 1968.

———. *Crises of the Republic.* New York: Harcourt, 1972.

Back, Kurt W. "Metaphors for Public Opinion in Literature." *Public Opinion Quarterly* 52 (1988).

Barrett, William. *The Illusion of Technique: A Search for Meaning in a Technological Civilization.* Garden City, N.Y.: Anchor Press/Doubleday, 1979.

Bernstein, Richard J. "Introduction." In *Habermas and Modernity*, edited by Richard Bernstein, 1–32. Cambridge, Mass.: MIT Press, 1985.

———. "Judging — the Actor and the Spectator." Paper prepared for the conference Hannah Arendt: History, Ethics, Politics at the New School for Social Research, New York, Oct. 1981.

———. "Pragmatism, Pluralism, and the Healing of Wounds." Inaugural lecture at the New School for Social Research, New York, Feb. 8, 1989.

————. *The Restructuring of Social and Political Theory.* Philadelphia: Univ. of Pennsylvania Press, 1978.

Birnbaum, Norman. *Toward a Critical Sociology.* New York: Oxford Univ. Press, 1971.

Bogart, Leo. *Polls and the Awareness of Public Opinion.* 2d ed. New Brunswick, N.J.: Transaction, 1985.

Bonafede, Dom. "'Mushy' on the Issues." *National Journal,* June 6, 1981, 1029.

Boorstin, Daniel. "Gresham's Law: Knowledge or Information?" Remarks at the White House Conference on Library and Information Services, Nov. 19, 1979. Washington, D.C.: Library of Congress, 1979.

Buber, Martin. *I and Thou.* 2d ed. Translated by Ronald Gregor Smith. New York: Scribner, 1958.

Campbell, Angus, Philip Converse, Warren E. Miller, and Donald Stokes. *The American Voter.* New York: Wiley, 1960.

Carey, John, and Larry Armstrong. "The Next Giant Leap for Mankind May Be Saving Planet Earth." *Business Week* (July 31, 1989): 90–92.

Charles F. Kettering Foundation. "On Second Thought: A Report of the 1989–1990 National Issues Forums." Dayton, Ohio: Charles F. Kettering Foundation, 1990.

Clark, William C. "Managing Planet Earth." *Scientific American* 261 (Sept. 1989): 47–54.

Clymer, Adam. "Polls Show Contrast in How Public and E.P.A. View Environment." *New York Times,* May 22, 1989, sec. B7.

Commager, Henry Steele. *The American Mind: An Interpretation of American Thought and Character since the 1880's.* New Haven: Yale Univ. Press, 1950.

————. *The Empire of Reason.* New York: Anchor Press/Doubleday, 1977.

Connerton, Paul, ed. *Critical Sociology.* Harmondsworth, England: Penguin, 1976.

Converse, Philip E. "The Nature of Belief Systems in Mass Publics." In *Ideology and Discontent,* edited by David Apter, 206–61. New York: Free Press, 1964.

Cooper, Joseph B., and James L. McGaugh. "Attitude and Related Concepts." In *Attitudes,* edited by Maria Jahoda and Neil Warren, 26–32. Baltimore: Penguin, 1966.

Cowan, Alison Leigh. "Women's Gains on the Job: Not Without a Heavy Toll." *New York Times,* Aug. 21, 1989, sec. A1.

Daniel Yankelovich, Inc. "Generations Apart." New York: CBS News, 1969.

Dewey, John. *The Quest for Certainty.* New York: Putnam, 1960.

Diesenhouse, Susan. "Many Smokers Hope to Quit, but Few Get Proper Help." *New York Times,* July 20, 1989, sec. B6.

Doble, John. "Crime and Punishment: The Public's View." New York: Edna McConnell Clark Foundation, 1987.

————. "Infant Mortality in the Third World: The Public's Reactions to Child Survival." New York: Public Agenda Foundation, 1986.

————, and Jean Johnson. "The Nation Reacts to AIDS: A Report from Six Cities." New York: Public Agenda Foundation, 1988.

————, and Josh Klein. "Punishing Criminals: The Public's View." New York: Edna McConnell Clark Foundation, 1989.

Domestic Policy Association. "The Domestic Policy Association's National Issues Forums: A Report on Its First Year." Dayton, Ohio: Domestic Policy Association/Charles F. Kettering Foundation, 1983.

Feldstein, Martin. "The Retreat from Keynesian Economics." *Public Interest* 64 (Summer 1981): 92–105.

Festinger, Leon. *A Theory of Cognitive Dissonance.* Stanford: Stanford Univ. Press, 1957.

Fisher, R. A. *Statistical Methods for Research Workers.* 13th ed. Edinburgh: Oliver and Boyd, 1958.

Gadamer, Hans-Georg. "Hermeneutics and Social Science," *Cultural Hermeneutics* (1975): 307–16.

Gagnon, Paul. "Why Study History?" *Atlantic Monthly* (Nov. 1988): 43–66.

Gallup, George. "The Quintamensional Plan of Question Design." *Public Opinion Quarterly* 11, no. 3 (Fall 1947): 385–93.

Gidden, Anthony. "Reason Without Revolution? Habermas' Theories des Kommunikativen Handelns." In *Habermas and Modernity,* edited by Richard J. Bernstein, 95–121. Cambridge, Mass.: MIT Press, 1985.

Gottlieb, Anthony. "Heidegger for Fun and Profit." *New York Times Book Review,* Jan. 7, 1990, 1.

Graedel, Thomas E., and Paul J. Crutzen. "The Changing Atmosphere." *Scientific American,* no. 261 (Sept. 1989): 58–68.

Habermas, Jürgen. *Knowledge and Human Interests.* Translated by Jeremy J. Shapiro. Boston: Beacon, 1971.

————. *The Theory of Communicative Action.* Translated by Thomas McCarthy. Vol. 1, *Reason and the Rationalization of Society;* vol. 2, *Lifeworld and Systems: A Critique of Functionalist Reason.* Boston: Beacon, 1981, 1987.

Halberstam, David. *The Best and the Brightest.* New York: Random House, 1972.

Immerwahr, John. "Report to the Business Higher Education Forum." Working paper. New York: Public Agenda Foundation, 1989.

————. "Saving: Good or Bad? A Pilot Study on Public Attitudes Toward Saving, Investment, and Competitiveness." New York: Public Agenda Foundation, 1989.

————, Jean Johnson, and John Doble. "The Speaker and the Listener: A Public Perspective on Freedom of Expression." New York: Public Agenda Foundation, 1980.

Immerwahr, Stephen. "Prison Overcrowding and Alternative Sentencing: The Views of the People of Alabama, Technical Appendix." New York: Public Agenda Foundation, 1989.

————. "U.S.–Soviet Relations in the Year 2010: Americans Look to the Future, Technical Appendix." New York: Public Agenda Foundation and the Center for Foreign Policy Development at Brown University, 1988.

James, William. *The Principles of Psychology.* 2 vols. New York: Dover, 1950.

Johnson, Jean, John Doble, and Jeffrey Tuchman. "Curbing Health Care Costs: The Public's Prescription." New York: Public Agenda Foundation, 1983.

Kagay, Michael R. "Public Knowledge of Civics Rises Only a Bit." *New York Times*, May 28, 1989, sec. L31.

Kanter, Donald L., and Philip H. Mirvis. *The Cynical Americans: Living and Working in an Age of Discontent and Disillusion*. San Francisco: Jossey-Bass, 1989.

Key, V. O., Jr. *Public Opinion and American Democracy*. New York: Knopf, 1961.

Kolata, Gina. "AIDS Is Spreading in Teen-Agers, A New Trend Alarming to Experts." *New York Times*, Oct. 8, 1989, sec. A1.

———. "How Much Is Too Much to Pay to Meet Standards for Smog?" *New York Times*, Apr. 3, 1989, sec. A1.

Kuhn, Thomas. *The Structure of Scientific Revolutions*. Chicago: Univ. of Chicago Press, 1970.

Ladd, Everett Carll. *The American Polity: The People and Their Government*. New York: Norton, 1985.

Lambert, Bruce. "Insurance Limits Growing to Curb AIDS Coverage." *New York Times*, Aug. 7, 1989, sec. A1.

Lavine, T. Z. *From Socrates to Sartre: The Philosophic Quest*. New York: Bantam, 1984.

Lazarsfeld, Paul F. "Public Opinion and the Classical Tradition." In *Communications and Public Opinion: A Public Opinion Quarterly Reader*, edited by Robert O. Carlson, 615–29. New York: Praeger, 1975.

Lowery, Shearon, and Melvin L. DeFleur. *Milestones in Mass Communication Research: Media Effects*. New York: Longman, 1983.

McCombs, Maxwell E., and Donald L. Shaw. "Structuring the 'Unseen Environment.'" *Journal of Communication* 26, no. 2 (Spring 1976), 11–17.

Mathews, David. *The Promise of Democracy: A Source Book for Use with National Issues Forums*. Dayton, Ohio: Charles F. Kettering Foundation, 1988.

Melville, Keith, ed. "Anatomy of an Epidemic: Coping with the Crisis." Dubuque, Iowa: Kendall/Hunt, 1988.

———, ed. "The Environment at Risk: Responding to Growing Dangers." Dubuque, Iowa: Kendall/Hunt Publishing, 1989.

———. "On Second Thought: A Report on the 1987–1988 Forums." Dayton, Ohio: Domestic Policy Association, 1988.

———. "On Second Thought: A Report on the 1986–1987 Forums." Dayton, Ohio: Domestic Policy Association, 1987.

Melville, Keith, and Mary Komarnicki. "Campaign Finance: Defining the Problem, Proposing a Remedy." New York: Public Agenda Foundation, 1985.

Mettler, Ruben F. "America's Competitive Challenge." Paper presented to the Conference Board, New York Marriott Marquis, Apr. 23, 1986.

Nash, Nathaniel C. "Persuading Americans to Save: Congress and the Administration Prepare New Incentive." *New York Times*, Dec. 17, 1989, sec. F1.

Nie, Norman H., Sidney Verba, and John R. Petrocik. *The Changing American Voter*. Cambridge, Mass.: Harvard Univ. Press, 1976.

Oppenheim, A. N. In *A Dictionary of the Social Sciences*, edited by Julius Gould and William L. Kolb. Glencoe, Ill.: Free Press of Glencoe, 1964.

Oreskes, Michael. "H.U.D., Wright, Meese: To the Public, It's All the Same Network." *New York Times*, July 30, 1989, sec. E1.

Plato's Republic. Translated by G. N. A. Grube. Indianapolis: Hackett, 1974.

Public Agenda Foundation and the Center for Foreign Policy Development at Brown University. "U.S.–Soviet Relations in the Year 2010: Americans Look to the Future." New York: Public Agenda Foundation, 1988.

Public Agenda Foundation and the Center for Foreign Policy Development at Brown University. "Voter Options on Nuclear Arms Policy: A Briefing Book for the 1984 Elections." New York: Public Agenda Foundation, 1984.

Public Agenda Foundation. "Water Efficiency in the West: The Public's View." New York: Public Agenda Foundation, 1986.

Reilly, John E., ed. "American Public Opinion and U.S. Foreign Policy 1987." Chicago: Chicago Council on Foreign Relations, 1987.

Roll, Charles W., Jr., and Albert H. Cantril. *Polls: Their Use and Misuse in Politics*. New York: Basic, 1972.

Schneider, Stephen H. "The Changing Climate." *Scientific American*, no. 261 (Sept. 1989): 70–79.

Singer, Eleanor. "Presidential Address: Pushing Back the Limits to Surveys." *Public Opinion Quarterly* 52 (1988): 416–26.

Stevens, William K. "Skeptics are Challenging Dire 'Greenhouse' Views." *New York Times*, Dec. 13, 1989, sec. A1.

———. "Study Supports Global Warming Prediction." *New York Times*, 14 December 1989, sec. A36.

Sussman, Barry. *What Americans Really Think and Why Our Politicians Pay No Attention*. New York: Pantheon, 1988.

"Ten Years of Public Opinion: An Ambivalent Public." *Public Opinion* 11 (Sept.–Oct. 1988), 21.

Toner, Robin. "The Malta Summit: New Friends in Old Places—Americans Much Warmer Toward Soviets, Poll Finds." *New York Times*, Dec. 3, 1989, sec. A29.

U.S. Department of Commerce, and the Bureau of the Census, *Statistical Abstracts of the U.S. 1989*, 109th ed. Washington, D.C.: GPO, 1989.

"U.S. Will Mail AIDS Advisory to All Households." *New York Times*, May 5, 1988, sec. B10.

Weisberg, Jacob. "Poles Lied to Pollsters, Why Not You?" *Philadelphia Inquirer*, Apr. 11, 1990, sec. A23.

Weisman, Alan. "L.A. Fights for Breath." *New York Times Magazine*, July 30, 1989, 15–49.

Wheelwright, Philip, ed. *The Presocratics*. Indianapolis: Bobbs-Merrill, 1966.

Whisler, Thomas L. "Rules of the Game: Inside the Corporate Boardroom." Selected Paper no. 66. Graduate School of Business, University of Chicago, 1987.

Whitehead, Alfred North. *Adventures of Ideas*. Harmondsworth, England: Pelican, 1927.

————. *Science and the Modern World.* Harmondsworth, England: Penguin, 1938.

————, and Bertrand Russell. *Principia Mathematica.* Cambridge: Cambridge Univ. Press, 1925.

Wilford, John Noble. "His Bold Statement Transforms the Debate on Greenhouse Effect." *New York Times,* Aug. 23, 1988, sec. C4.

William T. Grant Foundation Commission on Work, Family, and Citizenship. "The Forgotten Half: Non-College Youth in America." Washington, D.C.: Youth and America's Future/William T. Grant Foundation, 1988.

Wittgenstein, Ludwig. *Tractatus Logico-Philophicus.* Translated by D. F. Pears and B. F. McGuinness. London: Routledge and Kegan Paul, 1961.

Yankelovich, Daniel. *New Rules: Searching for Self-Fulfillment in a World Turned Upside Down.* New York: Random House, 1981.

————, and John Immerwahr. "The Public, the Soviets, and Nuclear Arms: An Experiment in Public Judgment." New York: Public Agenda Foundation, 1989.

————, and Sidney Harman. *Starting with the People.* Boston: Houghton Mifflin, 1988.

————, Hans Zetterberg, Burkhard Strumpel, and Michael Shanks. *The World at Work: An International Report on Jobs, Productivity, and Human Values.* New York: Octagon, 1985.

Yankelovich, Skelly & White, Inc. "Meeting Japan's Challenge: The Need for Leadership." Schaumburg, Ill.: Motorola, Inc., 1982.

————, and *Time.* "The Mushiness Index: A Refinement in Public Policy Polling Techniques." Report, Mar. 1981.

INDEX

COMING TO PUBLIC JUDGMENT

was composed in 10 on 12 Palatino on Digital Compugraphic equipment
by Metricomp;
designed by Sara. L. Eddy;
printed by sheet-fed offset on 50-pound, acid-free Glatfelter Natural Hi Bulk,
Smyth-sewn and bound over binder's boards in Holliston Roxite B,
and notch bound with paper covers
by Braun-Brumfield, Inc.;
with dust jackets and paper covers designed by Victoria M. Lane,
and printed in 4 colors
by Frank A. West Co., Inc.;
and published by

SYRACUSE UNIVERSITY PRESS
Syracuse, New York 13244-5160